SPINSTRESS craft

MAGICK FOR THE INDEPENDENT WITCH

LESLIE J. LINDER

LLEWELLYN PUBLICATIONS
WOODBURY, MINNESOTA

FIRST EDITION
First Printing, 2021

Book design by Samantha Peterson
Cover design by Shira Atakpu

Llewellyn Publications is a registered trademark of Llewellyn Worldwide Ltd.

Library of Congress Cataloging-in-Publication Data
Names: Linder, Leslie J. (Leslie Joan), author.
Title: Spinstress craft : magick for the independent witch / by Leslie J.
   Linder.
Description: First edition. | Woodbury, MN : Llewellyn Publications, 2021.
   | Includes bibliographical references. | Summary: "This guide to
   becoming a spinstress is a rally cry to find your true, unbridled voice
   through magickal practices and modern spirituality"—Provided by
   publisher.
Identifiers: LCCN 2021011582 (print) | LCCN 2021011583 (ebook) | ISBN
   9780738765198 (paperback) | ISBN 9780738765464 (ebook)
Subjects: LCSH: Magic. | Witchcraft.
Classification: LCC BF1611 .L476 2021 (print) | LCC BF1611 (ebook) | DDC
   133.4/3—dc23
LC record available at https://lccn.loc.gov/2021011582
LC ebook record available at https://lccn.loc.gov/2021011583

Llewellyn Publications
A Division of Llewellyn Worldwide Ltd.
2143 Wooddale Drive
Woodbury, MN 55125-2989
www.llewellyn.com

Printed in the United States of America

SPINSTRESS
craft

© carolmillerphotots.com

About the Author

Leslie J. Linder (Downeast Maine) is an author, priestess, and vegan who has written for *Sage Woman*, *Circle Magazine*, and *Witches & Pagans*. She has published several short stories, poems, and a horror novel, and she is ordained by the Temple of the Feminine Divine. Leslie also speaks locally about veganism and volunteers at local animal sanctuaries.

To Write to the Author

If you wish to contact the author or would like more information about this book, please write to the author in care of Llewellyn Worldwide Ltd. and we will forward your request. Both the author and publisher appreciate hearing from you and learning of your enjoyment of this book and how it has helped you. Llewellyn Worldwide Ltd. cannot guarantee that every letter written to the author can be answered, but all will be forwarded. Please write to:

Leslie J. Linder
℅ Llewellyn Worldwide
2143 Wooddale Drive
Woodbury, MN 55125-2989

Please enclose a self-addressed stamped envelope for reply,
or $1.00 to cover costs. If outside the U.S.A., enclose
an international postal reply coupon.

Many of Llewellyn's authors have websites with additional
information and resources. For more information,
please visit our website at http://www.llewellyn.com.

Other Books by Leslie J. Linder

Catherine Hill

Revenant

Featured In

Ghost Stories

Northern Frights

The Shadow Over Deathlehem

DEDICATION

Great thanks and love go out to the womxyn in my own life and line with a spinstress vibe. To my mother, Mary Jane Hammill Carter. To my grandmothers, Hester Calderwood Hammill and Ethel Nelson Linder. Definitely to my badass, spiritualist, table-tipping great grannie, Frances (Frankie) King Calderwood. She was doing spinstress craft way before it was cool. To Willa Cather and Charlotte Perkins Gilman for writing through the pain. To Mary Godwin Shelley, mad (scientist) respect. To my splendiferous besties Boots Garrett, Gwen Clark Goodrich, and Christina Perkins for inspiring me and helping me hold myself together. My dad, Rev. Dr. Lyle Dean Linder, gets a shoutout for raising me as a proud feminist man. To all of them and to all my readers, I conclude with, "Ars longa, vita brevis." Google it.

CONTENTS

RITUALS, SPELLS, EXERCISES, AND BLESSINGS

DISCLAIMER

This book is presented solely for educational and entertainment purposes. The author and publisher are not offering it as medical advice. For diagnosis or treatment of any medical condition, readers are advised to consult or seek the services of a competent medical professional.

While best efforts have been used in preparing this book, the author and publisher make no representations or warranties of any kind. Neither the author nor the publisher shall be held liable or responsible to any person or entity with respect to any loss or damages caused, or alleged to have been caused, directly or indirectly, by the information contained herein. Every situation is different, and the advice and strategies contained herein may not be suitable for your situation.

References are provided for informational purposes only and do not constitute endorsement of any websites or other sources. Readers should be aware that the websites listed in this book may change.

In the following pages you will find recommendations for the use of certain herbs, essential oils, incense blends, and ritual items. If you are allergic to any of these items, please refrain from use. Each body reacts differently to herbs, essential oils, and other items, so results may vary person to person. Essential oils are potent; use care when handling them. Always dilute essential oils before placing them on your skin, and make sure to do a patch test on your skin before use. Perform your own research before using an essential oil. Some herbal remedies can react with prescription or over-the-counter medications in adverse ways. Please do not ingest any herbs if you aren't sure you have identified them correctly. If you are on medication or have health issues, please do not ingest any herbs without first consulting a qualified practitioner.

Err on the side of caution, especially when trying something for the first time, including sex toys or yoni eggs. If you experience any discomfort, discontinue use immediately.

PREFACE

Inside the pages of this magickal book, you might have expected a table of contents, an introduction, and a bunch of author advisements. Sure, all that stuff is here. But first, you encounter a beautiful clearing amid magickal woods. Who knew?!

Tall autumn grass caresses the stems of a purple forest of valerian flowers. A nest of brown baby bunnies explodes into chaos near your feet. Your heart pounds as you watch them zigzag into the safety of the nearby woods.

Where the bunnies ran, you see a winding path. It is trampled grass with a few worn-through patches of mud. You can only see a short distance into the tangled wood. It seems peaceful but dark. The gnarled branches of apple trees, heavy with late fruit, bend down near this opening. It looks inviting. You think for a split second, then walk in.

Take some time to walk a meandering path and take in the sights, sounds, and smells. You hear rainwater running off the trees. Or is it a small stream? The earth smells moist. The trees sigh in the wind.

A little creature blasts past you, its wings buzzing. Not so little. Was it a dragonfly? Maybe you're going crazy, but it almost looked like Tinkerbell. You aren't sure what kind of place you just wandered into. One thing is for certain: you can sense the electric snap of magick in the air.

Sure enough, the whole place gets even cooler. There is a nearby cave opening hidden by grasses and rocks. As you approach the opening, it widens for you, almost as if it is beckoning. It moved by itself! You aren't sure whether you should be jazzed or terrified. The cave opening widens even more. "Come on, already!" it seems to say.

You find yourself on a stone staircase that descends into the blackness of the underworld. You take a deep breath, reaffirm that you are safe, and start heading down. You still smell damp earth and rain. The scents are more pungent than ever. The soft sound of worms churning the soil behind the walls is like a whisper of encouragement. The earth, the insects, and the water bid you to enter. "Climb down, sister, and meet your fate. It is a good thing. Celebrate your destiny."

The staircase ends and you begin down a winding spiral of hallways. There are openings to one side and the other. You cannot get lost. Whichever pathway you choose is the correct one.

The way time moves in the underworld is different. You can walk miles and miles in mere seconds. There is no telling now how far you have gone. Only know that you are safe.

Finally, the path widens. The labyrinthine hallways you have been negotiating open into a vast, wide space. Other womxyn are exiting hallways around you. There are womxyn of every race, shape, age, and identity. If they felt the call, they are womxyn. They are welcome in this sacred space.

Though you all took different pathways, you have arrived at the same space. All of you are meant to be here at this precise moment in time. You smile to one another in welcome. This place is great!

All the womxyn around you are filing into a single line. They are waiting to enter a smaller cave chamber just beyond this open space. Join in the line. You are all here to partake of the same initiation. You are all waiting to be received and welcomed by your fates.

In the timeless realm of the underworld, your wait in this line is quick. You barely have time to enjoy the presence of your sisters before it is your turn to pass into the chamber of initiation.

Inside the chamber, the thick smell of herbs engulfs you. The energy in this place is different. It is a sanctified space filled with holiness and power. You realize now that all of this was meant to happen. You didn't know when you started your walk, but you've been called to come here.

The chamber forms an oval. Beyond that detail, it is hard to see. The smoke of the burning incense clouds the air like a heavy fog. Just as you are wondering which way to move, something soft and light thumps into your toes: a soft ball of yarn. Its thread trails off into the cave.

Notice the color and the texture of the yarn. You might recognize your thread by the quality of its energy. Is it thick and woolly or more like a beam of pure light? It can be one of these or anywhere in between. Just take note of the thread and what it tells you about your soul's journey.

You pick up the ball and begin following the trailing thread, rolling it up as you go. The smoke clears as you walk, and you realize that your own focus clears the path before you. This is part of the path you are discovering, called spinstress magick.

In the center of the oval cave, near where you now stand, you see a tall, ancient loom. It towers above you in what remains of the mysterious smoke. The tapestry hanging from it is like nothing you have ever seen. It blinks with lights and swirls with changing colors. Images appear and then dissolve.

The threads that hang from the loom are of different fabrics. Some seem to be made of pure light. Some hum, making the loom reverberate like a harp. The tones of it vibrate. You can feel it in your crown, your throat, your belly, and your heart. You can feel it in your feet, and it guides you closer. Your heart pounds even harder than it did when those baby bunnies startled you. But you've come this far. You're seeing this through.

Shadows pass in front of you and you see that three womxyn are busy working at the loom. Their bobbins click as they wave them like magick wands, passing them to and fro through the warp of the loom.

These womxyn are the three fates. They are past, present, and future. They are maiden, mother, and crone. You've heard about them in stories. As the smoke clears you squint and stare, eager to see what they look like in person.

The three fates turn to meet you. You feel a jolt of surprise as you realize that they all look like you! Even if you have not yet achieved all these phases in your life, you can see them reflected back to you.

The maiden looks like you when you were a girl. When in your childhood were you the most brave and optimistic? This is what the maiden mirrors.

The mother looks like you at your most nurturing and productive prime. She births not only children but activism and art. She is a badass caregiver of others as well as herself.

The crone, also known as the wise one, is you at your wisest peak of both lived and learned experience. She is a leader in her chosen realms of expertise. She is ready to mentor other womxyn, ensuring her legacy.

As you face yourself in the fates, know that they welcome you with joy and love. Thank them for the gift of this initiation. Let them know that you are ready to receive their wisdom about how you should proceed. While the tapestry of your life story has not yet been completed, the fates give you advice on making it resonate with your authentic self.

The maiden fate steps forward and squeezes your hand. She looks up and says to you, in your own childhood voice, "Remember playfulness."

Then she gently pulls the ball of thread from you and carries it to the mother. The mother winks at you with your own set of eyes and squeezes the thread, saying, "Remember passion."

She passes the thread to the crone, who quickly fixes it to a bobbin. This wise woman, bearing your own face, smiles at you and says, "Remember purpose."

The crone's hands flash almost too fast to be seen as she works your thread into the weave. The other fates join her, passing the threads of many others across the warp along with yours. You realize, as you watch the journey of your own soul take shape, how interdependent you are on those around you.

Look into the tapestry the fates are weaving. You see images reflected from your past. They appear and then disappear in the fabric, echoing some of your best memories. There are images of you at your happiest and strongest. You see yourself doing the things that you love most. Take note of these images. Let them teach you about your own aptitudes and joys.

If you have any questions for the fates, ask them now. The answers may come in their words or in images that appear on the tapestry.

In the timelessness of the underworld, you might stand and watch this weaving for dozens of lifetimes. Yet, the fates slow their hands. They let the bobbins hang loose from the loom as they turn to offer you their benediction.

"Be brave," says the maiden, "and don't forget to have fun."

"Be passionate," adds the mother. "Never cease to create."

"Return to life now, spinstress," the crone says to you. "Be a leader. The weaving shall be done by you and your sisters now."

Smoke rises from a crack in the stone floor, like a stage curtain dropping over a wonderful play. You know it is time to leave the cave of initiation. Intuitively, you also know which way to go.

You pass through a doorway and are back in the darkness of the winding hallways. The line of your sisters is nowhere to be seen. Have no fear, though. You will find them again on your life's journey.

The walls of this passageway are so narrow that you can reach out and touch each side. Feel the moist stone and soft dirt beneath your fingers. Trace the words and images that you find there.

You have stepped out of the underworld into the peaceful outdoor setting where you first began. You see the light of that peaceful clearing shining from not far away. Hurrying along the tangle of a path, you quickly enter the meadow. The sun on your skin makes you feel grounded.

Did that really just happen? *you think to yourself.*

As if in answer, a double rainbow appears. Amazing! The voices of the three fates, in perfect unison, whisper clearly in your mind. You hear them saying, "All promise is inside you. All presence is before you. Call upon the inner strength that is us, but ultimately, you. Weave your own fate. Weave it with us. Be your own spinstress."

Spinstress? *you think to yourself.* What the heck is that?

INTRODUCTION

It's a great time to be independent womxyn. We are standing on the shoulders of so many generations of brave womxyn who came before us. Few had the legal protections and diverse opportunities that we have in the twenty-first century. But that doesn't mean it's always easy: fair pay remains elusive. Womxyn are underrepresented in high levels of government, business, and religion. Sexual and physical abuse and harassment remain pervasive. At the same time, womxyn are running more households, doing more of the care for kids and elders, and earning more of the cost of living on their own.[1]

Don't get me wrong; I love the men and boys in my life. Even if you don't date men, there are dads and brothers and sons and friends. What I don't love is the patriarchy, a system of government in which certain men find the top, keep the top, and teach their sons, interns, or apprentices how to stay at the top.

These "one percenter" types towering over cultural power pyramids are still looking like extras from *Mad Men*. In other words, with #MeToo, rollbacks on reproductive rights, and hate crimes against trans and gender-diverse folks soaring, the patriarchy is far from being smashed.[2] It's looking like titanium, sisters.

---

1. Glynn, "Breadwinning Mothers."
2. Elks, "Factbox."

Womxyn of the World, Unite!

Some of us bear the burden of this inequality more than others, yet it's a sure thing that independent girls and womxyn need a huge range of skills. Yes, sometimes we get some help. But you might easily find yourself teaching sixth-grade math, retiling your shower, doing basic car repairs, balancing a budget (after earning the money in the first place), providing care to family members with special needs, negotiating complex boundaries in your relationships, and everything in between.

How do we ease our burdens? When we are lonely or sad, where do we go for comfort? I can't solve every problem, but I have one really good suggestion: magick, baby. And it's even better if we work to innovate, communicate, and make the craft fresh and relevant. That's what the spinstress path is here for. It's for womxyn who do it all.

Meet the Spinster, Be the Spinstress

The term *spinster* comes from a time when working womxyn tended to find opportunity in the textile industries. This was often how the unmarried found a way to survive and carve a niche into the community. Though you might think a spinster's productivity and self-sufficiency would be appreciated, you'd be wrong.

In patriarchal cultures, womxyn who take care of their own business are a threat. Therefore, the spinster has a long history of being dumped upon. She was portrayed as ugly, humorless, unpleasant, or sometimes comical. Defined as a failed female, she was made even more pathetic by the self-delusion that she was successful.

A modern version of the spinster is the old maid. Maid, like maiden, means unmarried. Patriarchal culture says a woman who is unmarried when she is old (a variable term) is a failure, somehow inferior to those who married.

In Victorian times, the spinster or old maid was harshly ridiculed. Comics would portray an ugly single auntie, often rude and churlish to men, to make sure everyone casually consuming that media would know that single womxyn were bad womxyn. (You can search for these images online if you want a history lesson that will really piss you off.)

You might think these old images villainizing single womxyn would be laughably out of date. Nope! Earlier this year, I found the card game Old Maid at work. It had been left with UNO and Go Fish! in case any parents brought their kids to the office. The card deck was new, but it was filled with those old-fashioned images of womxyn with warty noses, bad clothes, mean expressions, and so on. All drawn in "funny" cartoon caricatures. It was especially ironic because I work at a domestic violence prevention agency, where we advocate feminism and educate about womxyn's rights as part of our mission!

The old maid is a bulwark of the patriarchy—an image for womxyn and girls of what *not* to be. Like the spinster, the warty old maid serves as a joke for men and as a cautionary tale for womxyn. Both female tropes have been used over the decades as a societal cudgel through which men and boys learn they can claim power over womxyn and girls.

Independent womxyn have often been stigmatized as "wicked witches" due to their status. Those of us who have already done work to reclaim the concept of the witch know that whenever an aspect of femininity is strongly reviled, it is wise to ask why. A lady who is alone (or all-one) carries the power and creativity of the great mother within her. Whether or not she births children, she births creativity and sustenance for all in her orbit.

I have come to prefer the term spinstress in order to keep the image of the weaver (the goddess of fate and her daughters, us), but also to underscore the point that a spinstress is self-identified. She is not living within the etymology or the social structure of the patriarchal spinster.

How does the identity of the spinstress inform a magickal path? In this book, I will work with the premise that the work of the spinstress is that of co-creation. Spinstress womxyn are unafraid to be sovereign and to call all the shots in their own lives.

Who Are Womxyn, Exactly?

Now, on to some other key terminology. In case you were wondering, I do know how womxyn is usually spelled. I took women's studies in college, for goddess' sake! My choice of spelling in this book is meant to welcome cisgender and transgender womxyn as well as nonbinary folks.

While I'm defining terms, I will also write using the shorthand Q+ in these pages. This means "queer, plus." It's a term equality advocates have taken to using so they can quickly acknowledge the huge diversity of terms and identities in the queer community without spending too much time on language.[3]

If this seems silly and unnecessary, think about the many books (including this one) that add a k to the word *magic*. Many magickal folks use this spelling to make it clear they are not talking about old-time ideas of magic, like pulling rabbits out of hats or Harry Houdini's shenanigans. People who wanted to distinguish modern occult and spiritual practices changed the spelling of the word to reclaim it.

This is the same idea behind my spelling of womxyn. I know this book cannot be all things to all people—not even to all womxyn—yet, I wanted to use a nontraditional spelling of that word to make it clear that I am trying to move away from old-fashioned ideas of who or what womxyn may be. Transgender and nonbinary folks are often left out of magickal materials that use rigid ideas about male and female bodies and energies. Changing the spelling won't solve that problem, but I want it to inspire and empower more folks to feel welcome here, and to define the term *womxyn* for themselves.

Womxyn caring about womxyn are not haters. Taking space for ourselves is not an attack on other genders. For instance, it may feel strange or guilt-inducing to not constantly reference men or boys. But remember that healthy womxyn love others better. Try thinking about it this way if you (or someone in your life) feel that this book is too exclusive: there is room for every book. There is room for every womxyn, too.

The Spinstress Path

It's all well and good to parse old-fashioned, sexist words and how we can work around them. But why am I writing a whole book of what I call *spinstress craft*? Here's the scoop. The spinstress path is about connecting to the oppressive past (and its footprint in the oppressive present), smashing it, and weaving (spinning) something new.

There are things that womxyn need and some we only want. For instance, I want all the shades of my fave lipstick. I don't need them (though it's hard to convince me when they release a new color). In this path, we definitely

---

3. One resource for understanding terms like cisgender and transgender is https://uwm.edu /lgbtrc/support/gender-pronouns/.

have some fun thinking about what we want, but we also spend some time making sure we get what we need.

In practical, immediate terms, spinstress magick will empower womxyn and those who love womxyn to identify and access what we need. The pages within offer practical tips for self-esteem, independence, abundance, and personal safety. Financial planning, setting healthy sexual and relationship boundaries, and dealing with abuse are a few examples. Spells, crafts, and guided meditations offer assistance for these issues, and practical information and advice are also included.

This path encourages womxyn to support womxyn. Together, we will:

- Choose when to have sex and discover what kind of sex we like, as well as who we like to have sex with (including ourselves, obviously)
- Define the boundaries of our relationships, both in and out of committed arrangements
- Make our own decisions about when (and whether) to have children
- Choose where to live, how to live, and how to manage our own money
- Call our own shots on what is right and wrong (within the bounds of the law!)
- Own leadership in our spiritual community as a creator, a ritualist, a healer, and more
- Take care of ourselves as well as the men, womxyn, kids, and critters in our lives
- Allow ourselves to exist in our authenticity: emotional, rational, sexual, and magickal beings who are enough exactly as we are, thanks very much

This journey is divided into the somewhat typical sections of maiden, mother, and crone. You met them in the preface. But I don't want to get same old same old about this. These sections aren't about your age. They are about the work that is archetypally within the wheelhouse of that particular goddess (and that particular part of you).

When we talk about the maiden, we are discussing singleness, sex, and self-esteem. The maiden energy is also about new beginnings, so we'll spend some time developing a personal power altar and deciding whether to take a magickal name. Then we'll make our self-esteem rock solid with glamour (beauty) magick, ways to check jealousy, and combat skills (to fight body shame).

The mother section is obviously about parenthood, but there is so much more to mother energy. We all know this. That's why we call the planet Mother Earth. She's the whole thing, baby. In our mother chapters we look not only at parenthood (and grieving kids we have lost), we also dig into the other ways womxyn birth, nurture, and create. We'll talk about art, activism, and sacred sound in the mix.

The crone is the archetypal, black-robed witch. We'll enjoy that energy in a section about badass arts of the occult like divination, automatic writing, and working with graveyard energies. The crone also embodies our lived experience and expertise. We'll work with her energies on showing what we know and stepping into our role as leaders. Since owning our power may also involve setting some limits, we'll deal with magickal self-defense, things like sigils and wards.

Some of the topics in this book are heavy. Others are just a laugh. Most are a bit of each. Use it as a jumping-off point to take the spinstress path and weave a lot more magick of your own.

In this book you will also be reading a bit about my own experiences and opinions. You may, therefore, want to know something about where I came from.

About Me: Unraveling My Spinstress Journey

While attending graduate school at Vanderbilt University for a master of divinity degree, I unexpectedly stumbled upon the goddess. In 1997, I was shelving books at the Divinity Library when I found the section labeled "women's spirituality." I felt like I'd found home.

From that day forward, I was in the rather awkward position of attending a Christian ministry program while I was becoming more and more excited about goddess spirituality books. Some of the material was allowed within the discourse of my college classes, but we had to call it women's spirituality (not Wicca or Paganism and *certainly* not witchcraft). By the time I graduated, I had come to terms with the fact that I was not in my authenticity as a United Methodist parish minister. I returned home to Maine to regroup—and to continue reading.

Books about women's spirituality led me to *Ariadne's Thread: A Workbook of Goddess Magic* by Shekhinah Mountainwater. I didn't know any of the bubble, bubble lingo in the occult cauldron at the time, but it turns out I had stumbled across a queer author of a path grounded mostly in Dianic Wicca. I am happy I found inclusive witchcraft so early in my journey.

I sought teachers and other sources of wisdom for my craft. Over the years, I have gathered knowledge from many places. I took two degrees of learning and initiation from Laurie Cabot on the Cabot Kent tradition of witchcraft, based in Salem, Massachusetts. I joined the Covenant of Unitarian Universalist Pagans along the way and led a few local groups. I joined Kay Gardner's Iseum Musicum in Bangor, Maine, where I took a three-year course and was ordained as a priestess. And along the way, I developed the spinstress craft. Here's the core idea of the spinstress craft for me: Know what you want, be what you want, and have what you want.

The spinstress path is based on my own religious and magickal work. But it is also informed by my work in the "mundane" world. In the twenty years I have worked for a local domestic violence program, I've helped thousands of womxyn identify what isn't working in their lives and relationships. I've also helped them decide what they want: what to believe, who to love, where to live, how to build financial stability, how to parent, and how to stand up for themselves. Remember that your craft is cut into the middle of your mundane spaces with wands and incense and broomsticks. In earth-centered spirituality like Wicca and most types of Paganism, there is no distinction to begin with. The spiritual *is* the physical.

As you can see, I am a very eclectic hodgepodge of spiritual, religious, and intellectual oddments. I know that through all my own hard times, my spiritual beliefs have been my safety net. This path is here for you to blend magick and meditations with the real-life stuff that independent womxyn have to (and get to) do.

I am offering to you the spinstress path as I see it, but I want you to make it your own. Are you ready? Here we go! Let's open the broom closet and go over some magickal housekeeping.

chapter one

STOCKING THE BROOM CLOSET

ere comes the sort of boring part (unless you're a witchcraft wonk like me). What follows are the typical introductory statements about my magickal beliefs, tips for preparing your journey, and some general information that may be helpful. Especially if you are new to the craft, it will be worth reading this through. Feel free to skip ahead, however, if you have been there and done that.

A reminder: You don't have to have the same magickal beliefs as me to use the spells and rituals in the book. If you come with a bunch of your own witchy expertise, that's great. I just want to introduce the way that I'll be working in these pages.

Along those lines, I consider myself a witch and a priestess. I'm comfortable holding those terms interchangeably. You do you when it comes to your own identity. You can use the spinstress path in many flexible ways within other traditions.

What I am not is a doctor. Or a therapist. Or an herbalist. Or a chef. Use common sense when trying out new recipes, techniques, ingredients, and so on. There are practices in this book that you will want to do additional research on before going all in. If you like my ideas, use my experiences as a springboard and go from there. (The use of a yoni egg is a perfect example.) We'll get to all that good stuff later. For now, here's some crafty housekeeping.

Theory of Magick

You know that feeling when everything just clicks into place? Sometimes it's a state of being that we're lucky to experience over a long period of time; sometimes it's just a fleeting gift. You throw the ball knowing it's absolutely going in the basket. You look a friend in the eyes and both say the exact same thing at the same time. You put yourself in for a promotion you'd never dared to consider before, intuitively knowing that you've got it in the bag. In all these cases, you feel like you're "in the zone."

Regularly practicing the craft is one way that spiritually inclined folk can get into that zone more often. Some are blessed enough to exist in their zone for large periods of their lives. This is because a spiritual discipline (when regularly evaluated and allowed to evolve with new information) enhances our correct energetic balance.

The magick I suggest in the spinstress path (as tweaked and built upon by you) will help you get in and stay in your zone. My suggestions are by no means authoritative. I want you to grab the threads from my work that most call to you and then spin your own tapestry!

I take a very eclectic approach to magick and spirituality. I am not going to spend a bunch of time explaining one theory of the craft or one pantheon of deities. This makes room for all the womxyn reading this book (and participating in our adventure) to fill in their own beliefs and preferences. You can always hit up the recommended reading list at the end of the book if you want to learn more about something in particular.

The only real "rule" for me is safety. This means safety of the spirit as well as the body. I will therefore always include a suggestion for creating a sacred space for your practice in which you only allow positive and correct energies. It's just another type of boundary, like the ones you set in all the personal and professional spaces of your life.

If you have never practiced a magickal tradition before this, you will still be able to do the rituals and spells by following my simple instructions. You can work with my path in conjunction with another one if that's easier for you. Keeping my spells very simple and informal makes it easy to adapt them for other types of ritual structure.

For the record, I consider a spell to be a simple act of magick that you could perform just as easily at your desk as you could at an altar. A spell is like what other religions call a prayer. It can be as simple as wishing. A ritual, however, has a more formal structure. The routine of ritual practice helps your mind and spirit slip into crafty mode. Where a spell is like prayer, a ritual might be like a wedding or a communion practiced at a church or temple (or other formal religious space).

Magickal Prep

Before we can dive in to ritual work, there are a few building block bits that are worth mentioning.

Altars

Designing an altar is an important part of the craft. Through it, you may learn things about your subconscious self. Magick is like a prayer with punch. You are using your mind and your heart, but you are adding many ingredients that will amplify the particular goal you have. Building an altar is therefore like building a wish battery.

When people start out with altar design, they often make something pretty elaborate, but altars can be as simple as you'd like. Some people choose to have multiple altars, using a different table for each of the directions and filling an entire room. It's normal to want to play with all the elements of the craft while you learn. There are whole articles and books on designing altars. Though different traditions teach different things, I feel any type of altar can be equally effective. The most important ingredient for your magick is *you*.

I personally use one altar. I don't worry about making sure all the elements are represented on the altar, though I know many folks do. Instead, I tend to focus on whatever element I'm vibing off for the work. When you first get started, you may want to work with all the cardinal elements in your altar. Then, if it's a barrier to doing ritual in your busy life or if you just aren't into it, modify or simplify things.

To get started with your altar, you will want at least one table, windowsill, or other flat surface to work with. Cover it with an altar cloth in a color that corresponds to your magick; the rituals in this book have suggestions. You could also select a color by using your almanac, another system of magick, or your own preference.

Place at least one representative of the elements in roughly the correct direction on your altar. Sometimes the directions are too difficult to manage, but you can at least have the items. Be creative! What represents air for you? A feather you found in the park? Spiraling incense smoke? The sound of a bell? And so on for each direction.

Many folks like to add candles to their altar. This may not work for you if you have house rules, active pets, or other barriers to safely using real fire. It's easy to get LED candles in your fave colors and keep them on hand for magick. Don't let candle restrictions be a barrier to your practice.

In the end, there are folks who never use altars at all. Your body is the ultimate altar. You contain all the elements within you: earth in your flesh, air in your lungs, fire in your passion (or your circulation and pumping heart), water in your blood, and spirit in your mind.

The same idea goes for working in nature. All of Mama Earth is an altar. You have access to all the elements out there. A single flower contains the nutrients of earth, air in its leaves, water in its root and stem, fire (sun) in its petals, and spirit. Many folks believe all living things, including plants, have a certain kind of elemental spirit. So, there you go!

When it comes to designing altars, the most important thing is for you to experiment. Use my rituals and their altar suggestions for help, then go to town on your own. Whatever fires you up about your magick work is what's going to be most powerful for your homemade wish battery.

Guided Meditations

You've already completed the book's first guided meditation—remember in the introduction, when you journeyed to meet the fates? There are guided meditations throughout this book. I think developing a meditation practice is a great way to train your mind for creating magick.

When you come across a meditation, there are a few ways to go about it. Certainly, you could simply read through it and picture the journey as you go. This is like being caught up in a good story. It's up to you to decide if that method will allow you to really experience the meditation, though. Another option is to read through the meditation a couple of times, familiarize your-self with it, and then meditate upon it based on your memory. In that case, the meditation probably wouldn't be the same as the meditation written in the book. Then again, it might be better! Also consider recording yourself or a friend reading the meditation out loud.

You may want to personalize the meditations in order to control the pac-ing. Most of the book's meditations allow for gaps of time where you can wander in the setting that has been created. You may want to give yourself extra time to explore symbolic information that the meditations are set up to deliver.

I will always encourage you to set up a meditation environment that is both safe and comfortable. Though people have different preferences, pri-vacy is often an asset. When preparing for meditation or trance work, always think about your physical safety while you are in the meditative state. This may sound strange, but think it over. If you're stretching out in a public park, leave your wallet and personal items at home or locked in the car; maybe even have a buddy keep an eye on you. In magickal circles, we call these bud-dies guardians.

Also make sure you are dressed appropriately for whatever conditions you are in. Do you need an eye mask to keep out distracting light? Have some drinking water. You get the picture: plan ahead. Most importantly, never try to listen to a guided meditation while you are driving. Wandering even part-way into an alternate universe is a form of distracted driving.

Lastly, set aside the time and the supplies to take notes immediately after you meditate. The details of spiritual work can quickly dissipate once you reenter your normal waking state, much like dreams.

Journaling

The spinstress path is a very self-directed one, so a spiritual journal (oth-erwise known as a grimoire or a Book of Shadows) is important. I will be including journaling prompts throughout the chapters, and I always encour-age you to take notes after doing any dreamwork or meditation.

In any case, you don't have to keep a written journal. If you prefer to draw or keep a collage of clippings/plants/photos, that works too; I love to keep family photos in my magickal tomes. Write online. Write in a fancy grimoire.

Write in the spaces between the lines of your favorite novel. Draw, color, Instagram, paint. You're engaged in co-creation. You're weaving your tapestry.

For a first journaling prompt, consider beginning a list of your favorite womxyn mentors from history. These could be your own ancestors, fictional characters, or heroines from various ages. As you study the womxyn who came before you, you will see a chain of feminine influence you may not have noticed before. One heroine was often influenced by others. This connection stretches spinstress energy across time and place.

Magickal Teas

My philosophy on tea is that mixing your own blends works best. Like with incense, I prefer to use a base ingredient that I know and trust whenever I try a new recipe. Experiment with tea and pick a base brew that you really like. It might be a type of green tea or black tea. Or it might be a common blend, like Earl Grey. When you have a base tea, add just a pinch of dried herbs in order to add a ritual effect.

Each tea recipe I include in this book will suggest herbal add-ins for a magickal purpose and a blessing to be said while your cup or pot steeps.

Magickal Oils

Making your own oil blends can save you a fortune compared to buying a special blend for every type of spell you ever want to do. Making supplies whenever possible also puts more of your personal energy and intention into your working tools.

Making scented oils is kind of like making teas. You want a base that is pretty common and affordable. You then add the crafty ingredients (scents, gem chips, herbs, etc.) that correspond to your purpose.

I have a few oil blends in this book. I don't always go into the types of base oils you could use. Therefore, I'm going to list some base oils here: olive, coconut, sunflower, canola, grapeseed, almond, and jojoba. My preferences are grapeseed or almond oil. If I just want to quickly grab something from the kitchen, I'll go for olive. As you know if you cook with it, olive oil will leave its own distinct odor.

Which oil you choose will have to do with trial and error, preference, and—most importantly—any allergies you have. Use caution! If you're working with a new oil, you may want to test for allergies by rubbing a small amount on your skin prior to preparing a full recipe.

For an oil you plan to bathe in, you may want to give coconut a shot. Even a small amount of coconut oil in your tub is amazing on your skin but will leave a film in your hair if you don't wash it afterward. Coconut oil also becomes solid at room temperature, so bear that in mind when making your choice.

I will often suggest you anoint candles with oil. Some crafty people call this *dressing*. What it means is you apply oil to the candle with a ritual intent. The oil ingredients are thoughtfully planned to correspond to your magick. That's all there is to it, really.

Crystals

Crystals and gemstones can be used in many ways; they aren't just for looking pretty on your finger or your altar. For instance, slipping a charged crystal or gemstone under your pillow can give you an extra boost when you want to harness the subconscious powers of dreamtime and sleep. You can use crystals and gemstones to:

- Stave off nightmares
- Infuse extra energy into oils, incense blends, or even drinking water
- Place on your body or nearby during energetic healing like prayer, polarity, or Reiki
- Contain negative or incorrect energies that you wish to cast away (if you focus on placing them into the stone and then bury or ritually cleanse it)
- Give your aura an extra boost when you have a blind date, job interview, or just a rough day

For all these reasons and more, it's great to have some crystals and gemstones on hand. Whatever crystals or gemstones (or natural stones) you gather to use in your craft, it's handy to know a quick way to cleanse and bless them. You can do blessings on rough stones as well as jewelry. This is basically a process through which you introduce yourself to the stone. Conscious partnering with crystals and gemstones enhances the power of your spells because once they are activated, they will be hard at work for you even when you aren't aware of it.

GENERAL CRYSTAL CLEANSING

Prior to doing this work, it's good to rinse the stone in water. You may prefer to smudge it by fanning it with ritual smoke or incense. Neither of these are crucial, but I like to do one or both when possible. The most important aspect of cleansing and blessing is focused thought.

First, ask that all incorrect energies be cleansed from the stone. If you use the symbol of the pentacle, you may want to visualize one enveloping the stone. I like to blow the outline of a pentacle onto the surface of the stone I am cleansing. This has the added bonus of letting your spiritual life force connect more deeply with that of the stone via your breath.

Replenish the energy of the stone with a blessing. Say, "I affirm that the energy of this stone is charged for my purposes." Again, you could blow the outline of a pentacle over the stone. Or, if you prefer, use your breath to trace another meaningful symbol. Even the first letter of your name would do.

When you are done with your blessing, hold the crystal or stone in your hand and say, "Let this correct and empowered energy be set. With harm to none and for the good of all, so shall it be."

Your crystal or gemstone should now be ready to help you with your goals. While you have set the energy in order to hold it in place, it wouldn't hurt to occasionally recharge the piece. You can do this by rinsing it in water, charging it in the light of the full moon, or repeating this spell.

Cleansed gemstones make a perfect addition to ritual oils. You can buy blends in occult shops, but there's nothing like making your own. Like a recipe, you can tweak the ingredients to suit your needs, allowing you to come up with a blend no one else has.

Other Items for Your Spinstress Journey

- **Sounds:** A killer playlist for every mood you can think of.
- **Almanac:** A magickal almanac for the current year will always come in handy.
- **Outfits:** Ritual garb (clothing) that makes you feel like a spiritual badass.

- **Bling:** At least one awesome piece of jewelry. It should mean a lot to you and make you feel good.

- **Scents:** If you like working with scents, you may want to begin a collection of essential oils and herbs. I will make suggestions for the workings in this book, and an almanac will give you lots of guidance.

- **Candles:** For candle magick, you will want multiple colors of taper or LED candles, a collection of candle holders, and at least one dish of sand or salt that is deep enough to stick a candle in (this comes in handy for odd-sized candles). Passover candles or birthday candles are great meditation tools because they burn so quickly that you can use them to time your meditation or spell work.

- **Miscellaneous:** Other items you may want include multiple colors of twine, a few bells or wind chimes, parchment or nice paper for spells and letters, a quill or fountain pen with colored ink, a Rider-Waite-Smith-inspired tarot deck, and a magickal blade or wicked hatpin for carving symbols into candles and food offerings.

Outdoor Magick

There are several rituals in this book that can or should be practiced out in nature. "Nature" will be defined partly by your location and partly by your comfort level. You can do natural magick on a mountaintop, in a city park, in your backyard, or even in your living room next to a house plant.

If you plan to work outdoors, it's a good idea to pack a crafty bag. If you think you'd like to do a lot of your practice outdoors, make it a literal backpack or something else you can keep near you at all times. Here are a few suggestions for things to include:

Water: A small and sturdy cup or chalice

Earth: A wooden or metal pentacle

Air: A folding fan or a wand (depending on your tradition)

Fire: An athame (ritual knife) or wand (depending on your tradition)

Spirit: A small statue of your fave deity or their image on a medallion

Natural sunscreen and bug repellent

A towel or cushion to sit on

A compass (or phone app to determine cardinal directions)

A flashlight

Optional: Matches (remember to be mindful of fire safety) and mace

You may find other ritual items in nature, like a stone or a feather. With this mix of magickal and practical items, you will always be able to do rituals on the run.

Using This Book to Work in Groups

The diverse yet symbiotic identities of the triple goddess have long encouraged womxyn to team up and work together. It's perfectly fine if you choose to have a solo journey on your spinstress path, but sometimes we crave the bonds of sisterhood. Some of the ways you might grow a community of womxyn include the following:

- Work with social media and/or local womxyn's groups to start a circle of support.
- Attend group events held by other similar groups (like a local Neopagan tribe) in order to learn about group work and perhaps make some great friends.
- Use this book as a group anchor. Host an event centered around one of the group rituals in this book and see who attends.
- Use Zoom, Google Hangouts, or a similar platform to conquer distance and increase the accessibility of your events. Weave in the technological web!

If something appeals to you, give it a try! The best way to learn about group work is to do it.

Tips for Group Work

It all boils down to planning in advance. Whether in person or online, have the organizing participants go over your ritual. Split up the tasks that need doing. Don't focus only on the magick; think about logistics. Who will welcome guests and tell them what to do to get started? Who will announce basic housekeeping, like restroom locations? Who will help with setup, refreshments, cleanup, and opening and closing the venue? The more often you use a certain space, the easier this will become.

If you're hosting at a group member's home, there are other considerations. Are you comfortable with everyone on the invite list having a member's personal address? Even if you host at a home, the work involved in holding an event should still be shared. Hosts shouldn't be left with all the setup, cleanup, snack prep, and sundry costs.

To make all this planning easier—or maybe just a bit more fun—I'm suggesting a few kickass roles you could use to designate and take turns with certain duties. (These aren't directly based on the historical roles of these divas.) You don't need five womxyn to designate group work; one person could fulfill all of these duties if she wanted to. Just figure out who is willing to help with what.

- **Nike:** This messenger goddess deals with flyers, emails, social media posts, and related publicity.
- **Isis:** This goddess of 10,000 names knows how to multitask. She is the overall organizer of the event, keeping track of everyone's roles and requirements and making sure the worker bees get what they need.
- **Hestia:** The hearth goddess oversees setup, cleanup, refreshments, and general hostess tasks.
- **Artemis:** This protective person serves as the circle-keeper, sometimes called the guardian. Tasks include welcoming latecomers and helping people in and out of the ritual space (generally parents with little kids who must come and go during a ritual). Guardians can also be literal protectors at larger events, overseeing event security.
- **Habondia:** Ms. Moneybags keeps track of event budgets and expenses, handles donations, and manages a group bank account, if needed. If capital is needed to cover the cost of rental space or other supplies, Habondia takes the lead on organizing fundraisers. Bake sales, raffles, concerts featuring local talent, movie nights, or silent auctions are some possibilities. While Habondia can hold the purse strings, she shouldn't be left with all the work. It takes a village to raise some cash.

All this logistical talk may seem stressful, but it will save a lot of headache if your spinstress tribe plans to meet often. If organizing roles is too much to tackle at first, go ahead and wing it. You'll learn from experience how to create your own recurring roles.

Ritual Structure

Having the set routine of ritual in your craft can help you slip into your safe boundaries more quickly. This especially true when you are new to the practice. For this book I will stick to a predictable process (except for a few little spells or mantras that you might use while in a social situation or during a time of stress). This structure will include the following:

Ideal Time

This will usually have to do with moon phases or days of the week. You can purchase a magickal almanac and get into the witchy weeds finding all sorts of factors that might increase the power of your spells. We call these *correspondences*. Planetary phase, day of the week, time of year, and other things can always be factored in. For simplicity's sake, I stick with weekdays and phases of the moon.

MOON PHASES

There are certain common ideas about what the phases of the moon correspond to. You can track these phases with your almanac. The basic correspondences are thought to be as follows:

- **Full Moon:** When the moon is full, this as a time of peak energy and culmination. This is when you "seal the deal" on energetic work you have been doing.
- **Waning Moon:** As the moon wanes from full to dark, do magick to recycle or dispose of what is unwanted. Healing old wounds, cutting old ties, or removing financial barriers to your desires are some examples. The keywords for a waning moon are decrease, eliminate, and detoxify.
- **New Moon:** With the new moon, the sky is dark. It is a time of spring-loaded potential before the next cycle of growth. Use this time for rest,

bindings (neutralizing something unwanted), and work related to both beginnings and endings. The new moon (also called a dark moon) is associated with the underworld and with death-related deities.

- **Waxing Moon:** As the new moon waxes back toward full, do spells to create or expand what is desired in life. The keywords for a waxing moon are increase, grow, and begin. Your understanding of your goal should increase throughout this two-week period so that, by the time of the full moon, you are ready to release this work to spirit and allow for its manifestation.

Days of the Week

Another popular magickal correspondence has to do with the seven days of the week. While there are variations, each day of the week has several common associations. (If you want to harness extra weekday correspondences, consult an almanac or snag a copy of a book like *Candle Magic for Beginners* by Richard Webster.) A brief summary of the days of the week as I work with them is as follows:

- **Sunday:** Success, wealth, acclaim, charisma; when in doubt, it's a good catchall day for nearly any spell
- **Monday:** Psychic work including divination, past-life work, and guided meditations
- **Tuesday:** Things requiring bravery and strength, like activism, popping the question, or asking for a promotion at work
- **Wednesday:** Communication of ideas, studying, writing, and making art
- **Thursday:** Professional or contractual issues involving advancement, big business deals, important negotiations, and matters of the law
- **Friday:** Issues around physical and emotional well-being, like love, health, sex, and friendship
- **Saturday:** Setting healthy limits, including doing bindings and banishing or activating wards

Preparation and Items to Gather

This section is simple as it sounds! Here you will learn what you need in order to perform the spells and rituals I suggest. Remember, though, there is always room for customization—and your magick will probably be even stronger the more you personalize it. Just stay focused on your intent when you plan your rituals and spells.

I will suggest some items known to enhance the type of spell being performed. Herbs, scents, colors, gemstones, and other suggestions will be provided. Again, improvisation is always encouraged.

Circle Up

I will suggest several different ways to set a safe spiritual boundary for yourself. This is called casting a sacred circle. Just like in other aspects of your life, you are defining what you will or won't put up with inside your personal space. When casting a circle, many witchy folks work with the elements of the natural world.[4] The idea is to create a whole other little world within (yet outside of) the world where we normally live. There are many different ideas for how to define these elements.

When I cast a sacred circle in this book, I will use the following:

Cardinal Elements and Directions

I practice an eclectic, Pagan sort of craft that makes use of the cardinal directions. The idea is that we are calling in the powers behind all the major elements that create life when we seek to create (manifest) our spells.

The cardinal elements associated with the directions are earth, air, fire, water, and spirit. Here is how they break down into directions, as well as some examples of symbolism associated with each.

- **North:** Earth (stones, plants, an apple cut into a pentacle, nuts, flowers)
- **East:** Air (a wand, feathers, fans, leaves, statues of birds)
- **South:** Fire (a sword/blade, shedding of reptile skins, charred wood from a past ritual, lit candles, incense)

---

4. Webster, *Candle Magic for Beginners*, 65–66.

- **West:** Water (a chalice, a cup or bowl of water, statues of fish or mermaids, seaweed, shells)
- **Center:** Spirit (statues or pictures of deities, angels, faeries, photos of your ancestors or yourself, a mirror)

Bear in mind, this is a brief summary. You will learn as you work with the craft that there are many other associations. You don't have to fully agree with my definitions; I suggest you start with these ideas and then build your own. If you'd prefer, you can skip the elemental parts of magick I use or tweak them to suit yourself.

Spell Work

Within the structure I've laid out here, this is the place where you will work your spell. Sometimes there will be props, other times not. Sometimes the spell will even rhyme! Whether you like to rhyme is an individual choice. Some folks choose to rhyme almost all their spells, feeling that it raises energy and aids with remembering what to say.

Close Up Shop

This is the time to help yourself exit your magickal/spiritual state and reenter daily life. Many refer to this as grounding or centering.

• • • • • • •

So, just like that, you've learned a ritual structure! Not so hard, is it? On to the next piece of housekeeping.

CONE OF POWER RITUAL

The wicked hat that you see on the cover of this book isn't just a badass symbol of powerful and magickal womxyn. It *is* that, don't get me wrong, but the shape of that hat has another meaning that can help you in your craft.

I mentioned that one of my first experiences of the craft was through Shekhinah Mountainwater's book *Ariadne's Thread*. She gave a basic cone of power meditation in the introduction to that book. A cone of power is a gradually elevating level of energy that you build up during your magickal practice.

When you feel it is ready and well imbued with your wish (spell), you release it. This energy then flies to the spiritual source, carrying your wish wherever it needs to go. It's like Dorothy's tornado, whisking her off to Oz.

While the energy isn't always visualized as a cone, it often is. (Shekhinah Mountainwater's cone of power was extra awesome because she suggested visualizing it as a rainbow.[5]) Magickal practitioners raise energy using different techniques. Some dance in a circle to raise the cone of power. They may sing and chat. They may spin, raising their own level of energy along with the spiritual intention. They may raise energy through sex, solo or partnered.

For now, let's practice the cone of power in a fairly placid way. Once you get the hang of it, you can branch out.

IDEAL TIME: As often as possible, especially when you are new to the craft.

PREPARATION AND ITEMS TO GATHER:
- Have a journal and some water nearby.
- Pick a short, simple wish that you can send up in your cone of power. This wish, if you're new to craft, is going to be your first spell. It should be simple and quick to say. Just be careful what you wish for—you just might get it. Record the date and your wish in your journal.

CIRCLE UP: Plan a comfy place to sit. It's best if you are upright rather than reclining. Use cushions or whatever it takes to keep your spine comfortably straight. Play with the lighting and the space so you are nicely relaxed. Make sure your space is silent or pick a playlist with appropriate music; instrumental is usually best so the lyrics don't mess with your magickal thoughts. Once you are comfy in your seat, take a few deep breaths. In through the nose and out through the mouth tends to be the conventional recommendation.

SPELL WORK: Time to practice the cone of power. Have your wish (your spell) at the ready, but don't worry about it yet. Set the intention that the energy raised during this ritual will be beneficial and will cause you no pain or distress.

Begin noticing the rainbow band of energy appearing below you and creeping up, all around your body. It begins to take the shape of a witch

---

5. Mountainwater, *Ariadne's Thread*, 29.

hat, encasing your whole body with energy. Watch it slowly work its way up toward your head. The rainbow energy encases you in your cone of power, the pointy tip a few inches above the top of your head.

How does this energy feel? It's no big deal if you don't notice much. Just spend some time thinking about it. Parts of your body may experience it differently. Do you feel any sensations? Is it hot? Cold? Tingly? Sexy? Does anything feel uncomfortable? Emotional? Remind yourself this energy is positive and that you are safe.

What colors do you see? If you have one color really taking over, you may want to look that one up later. Colors have meaning in magick and in energetic healing.

Play with this energy a bit. Chant something, like "Om," or sing the names of the elements (earth, air, fire, water, spirit). Try thinking of energetic requests, like "Spin around me faster," "Get taller," or "Glow brightly, please!" See how you are able to work with the energy around you.

Next, begin focusing on your wish (spell). Sing it, chant it, or simply think it repetitively until you feel like it is integrated with the rainbow energy. You may see the cone changing its colors or spinning faster, and you may hear it humming. Record any observations in your journal later; this is a learning experience.

When you feel ready to release the cone and your spell, build the energy toward a climax. People do sometimes use sex for this, and it's a similar idea. You want the energy of the cone to get stronger and stronger before you set it free to manifest your goal. Mind you, it isn't necessary to send a spell off like a cannonball; your casting can be gentle and peaceful. For this exercise, though, try building the energy with your various techniques.

When you feel ready to release the cone, send it off with a big exhale. You can also say your spell out loud while raising your arms. You could yell, "Go for it! Blessed be!" However you decide to do it, release your cone of power to the spiritual source. It may shoot up into the sky like a rainbow and then fade away. It may float away like a balloon. It may spin off like a twister. No matter what, send it merrily on its way with your thanks.

CLOSE UP SHOP: When the cone is gone, you may need to ground and center yourself. Touch the floor and take a few deep breaths. Try sipping some water. When you raise energy to a climax like that, you often need to ground like this so that you don't leave feeling spacey. You may want to say a little affirmation like, "I release my spiritual energies back to the spiritual source for manifestation. Blessed be."

· · · · · · ·

That, womxyn, is spinstress craft. If it was your first spell, congrats! I suggest journaling on the experience. For the next few days, note any manifestations of your spell. Are they what you expected? Better? Worse? This is how we learn about the craft. Assume you will get results.

I won't detail this process in all the rituals or spells in the book. Now that you know how to use it, you can integrate the cone of power into some or all of the work. Keep experimenting with different techniques and take notes. Most importantly, have fun!

part one
MAIDEN: PLAYFULNESS

The maiden aspect of the goddess often celebrates traits like boldness, self-discovery, passion, and the positive aspects of vulnerability. These are traits womxyn exhibit at every age. An additional gift of the maiden is what modern self-help refers to as "inner child" energy.

> *The message of the maiden is: "Remember playfulness." Playfulness is more than fun and games. It is the key to bravery, adventurousness, and growth.*

Warrior princesses and fairy tale beauties aren't the only womxyn who can tap into the maiden energies. No matter your age or stage, you embody maiden energy when you're playful, adventurous, and brave. Maiden energy helps you to:

- Start a new life phase like college, marriage, or a year abroad
- Strengthen your self-image and stay grounded in authenticity through playful activities like cosplay, karaoke, or a dance class
- Embrace yourself with pride and use your voice without fear by being grounded in your brave inner child

- Experience the excitement of love and sex as if for the first time by redefining your sexual self, taking new lovers, or deciding to be on your own for a while
- Make time for friends and hobbies without being totally consumed by your responsibilities and roles

The material gathered in this chapter will help you connect with your inner maiden. There is glamour, self-esteem, safe sex, and personal power magick of many kinds. Enjoy, and don't forget to play!

Goddesses with Maiden Energy

- **Artemis:** Goddess of the wilderness, wild animals, and wild womxyn, Artemis didn't buy in to traditional female stereotypes. She spent most of her time out hunting in the woods with her nymph girlfriends and pack of dogs.
- **Athena:** Goddess of wisdom and tough as nails, she sprang fully grown (and fully armored) from Zeus's skull. Talk about blowing the patriarchy's mind!
- **Brigid:** Goddess of the hearth, the forge, the waters, and the flames, Brigid was changed into a saint by the Catholic church. As a saint, she is mythologized as the founder of an enduring convent of maiden womxyn. As a goddess, she was associated with the protection of domestic animals like sheep and cattle. Womxyn sought her blessing as they became wives and mothers. Don't let her domestic rep fool you, though. The origin of her name means "fiery arrow," as well as "the high one," and she fuels all manner of creativity.[6]

---

6. Monaghan, *Encyclopedia of Goddesses and Heroines.*

chapter two

MAGICK FOR SELF-ESTEEM AND AUTHENTICITY

'm not one of those "law of attraction" folks who believes that positive thoughts bring good luck and disaster strikes if you have a few negative thoughts. I *do* believe that people live happier lives if they feel they deserve it. Maybe others have told you what they think you deserve, or perhaps you've picked up on some of society's subliminal messages. But you are much more than others' limitations; you can achieve and do whatever you set your mind to. You just have to believe in your power!

The following rituals, meditations, and crafts are meant to help you connect with your true self. Find that special thing about you that no one else has in quite the same way. There is only one you, and the world needs you!

PERSONAL POWER ALTAR DEDICATION

Remember how I talked about altars as a type of magickal "wish battery"? This altar is for practicing the art of altar-making while you celebrate your awesomeness.

As we discussed in chapter 1, the altar is where you create your sacred space. The items you put there enhance the goals of your spells. The personal power altar does even more; it is strategically designed to celebrate *you*, both the you that you are today *and* the you that you hope to be.

Being powerful, independent womxyn is an active process. It can be tough to find the balance between celebrating yourself and working on yourself. When possible, the celebrating should come first so you don't find yourself in a self-critical funk.

While most altars serve as a one-time project, I suggest you find a place in your space to make your personal power altar a permanent thing. If you can't, no biggie. You could keep the items you like for this altar in a special box and assemble it more quickly in the future.

Over the course of your work with spinstress craft, you may find that the items you want on your altar will shift and change. It may be a totally different altar from one week to the next, and that's great!

IDEAL TIME: The full moon, baby!

PREPARATION AND ITEMS TO GATHER:

- Collect cloth(s) and candle(s) of your favorite color(s)—this ritual is all about you!
- Print photos of yourself at different ages, preferably doing some of your favorite things or hanging out with your favorite people.
- Gather flowers, stones, jewelry, magazine clippings, or whatever else you find that represents your inner spinstress. (Rose quartz or your birthstone are good choices for stones.)

CIRCLE UP: Call the circle by welcoming the cardinal elements in their directions. Some folks like to use a wand or athame to cast a circle around them as they go clockwise from direction to direction. This is a more formal way to cast a sacred space. You may want to invest in a compass (or download a compass app on your phone) so you can easily find the directions.

Using your finger, wand, blade, or simply your mind, move clockwise from direction to direction as you speak this invocation:

"Welcome north, element of earth and the body. I call this circle to name and claim my own sacred space. I give thanks for my body and all that it can do. I also celebrate my home and all who live within it.

"Welcome east, element of air and of thought. I welcome your inspiration as I create and maintain my sacred space. Guide me in the creation of positive and productive thoughts as I create my life.

"Welcome south, element of fire and passion. I welcome the heat of life to enliven me and awaken my authentic, joyous passions.

"Welcome west, element of water and love. I trust in your ever-present sustenance as I follow my bliss and share my love with the world."

Face your altar or the center of the circle and say, "Welcome spirit. I call in my ancestors, deities, and guides." (Name some explicitly, if you'd like.)

Say, "The circle is cast. Blessed be." Set down any casting tool you used.

SPELL WORK: Spend some time gazing at the items you have assembled on your altar. Enjoy the energy that they create. This is grounding energy. It is there for you to connect with whenever you need it.

Pass your hands above your altar, feeling its energy. It may feel a bit like sampling the heated air above a campfire. Imagine the energy being created by your altar is growing. What color is it? Know that this energy is for your own highest good. Affirm that the energy of this altar is fixed with positivity. It is there for you whenever you enter the sacred space and activate it with your conscious presence.

When you feel ready, light your ritual candle (or flip the switch if you are using an LED candle). Say, "I light this candle to symbolize my personal North Star. This is the light of my soul's inspiration. May it always be protected. May it always burn bright. I know that I can return to this altar or to the feelings it evokes whenever I need to ground myself in its strength. I ask my inner spinstress to be present here. I know that I can come to my altar and draw from her wisdom through meditation or divination or requests for dreams. May all the magick that I work in this sacred space be assured of correct and positive results. With harm to none, so shall it be."

If you wish to spend some time in meditation or divination, go for it. You could even settle down and take a nap. Just be mindful of any lit candles, especially around pets.

CLOSE UP SHOP: Put out your ritual lights and thank all the spiritual powers that helped you.

To open the circle, go in reverse order of how you cast it. Start in the center and then move counterclockwise while holding your casting tool. Say:

"Farewell center, element of spirit. All those I have called to me, I thank for coming. As you journey on, go with my love.

"Farewell west, element of water and love. Watch over me and sustain me as I journey on.

"Farewell south, element of fire and passion. I ask for your blessing so that the flames of my authentic passion and joy burn in my heart for all of this lifetime.

"Farewell east, element of air and of thought. As you return to the four winds of the world, I ask that you carry forth and manifest my thoughts.

"Farewell north, element of earth and the body. Though I am opening the circle, I know you are always with me in my flesh and in the earth that gives me life."

When you've finished opening the circle, say, "The circle is open. Blessed be."

• • • • • • •

Your personal power altar can serve as a source of inspiration for you anytime you find it difficult to appreciate the things that make you special and important. You are here for a reason.

To truly connect with your most authentic self, consider taking on a magickal name. Many magickal practitioners take on a special name that they feel embodies their core self. By tapping into what makes you feel special and strong, you bring extra power to everything you seek to achieve. If you'd like to explore the world of craft names, the following material should help.

Magickal Names and the Decision to Take One

It's a persistent and intriguing idea in sacred circles that taking a name for use in sacred space can boost your power. "Naming is claiming" is the basic idea. If you were raised in a Christian household, you may recall a biblical character's name changing in order to teach a lesson. This also conveys the theology that names have great power.

Some reasons that folks might change up their name include:

- Anonymity if one is keeping their craft private
- Fun and creativity
- Questing for one's true spiritual name in hopes of gaining wisdom from one's oversoul and karmic journey
- Expressing a new path, identity, or phase in life

Be clear with yourself about what type of name you are looking for. You may find one and think, *This is awesome, but it's not my powerful, authentic name.* You might use that name in witchy chat rooms or in public circles. Conversely, you may feel that you have had a powerful spiritual experience and that you have found your spiritual name. If this is the case, I recommend taking some time to think about when and why you might share it. When someone uses their true spiritual name, it is not like they are using a pseudonym; rather, they are expressing their true identity. Those who have found this powerful name are often careful about whom they share it with. Oversharing can have spiritual risks, depending on who you ask. Ceremonial practitioners of the past sometimes used an alias so that the supernatural critters they called on wouldn't be able to find them outside their ritual space, for example.

Some witches and wizards like to take a name based on that of their patron(ness) deity. You might also choose your name based on a revered ancestor or historical figure. Favorite colors, power animals, or times of year serve as frequent inspiration. Names may be regal and serious, playful and silly, or some hybrid of the two. Examples include Salem B. Anthony, Azure Ravenfeather, or Bastet Pussyfoot. If you take the name of a deity (for example, Macha Stormcrow), make sure you check in with that entity first. Be prepared to carry the energy of that deity in a strong way.

It's not uncommon to encounter folks who have several different names for different purposes. Sometimes these names are for use only in sacred spaces, like religious classes or public rituals. It may be because they are "in the broom closet" and want to keep their mainstream name private, or a magickal name may simply be for fun. Others use magickal names to help them transition into sacred space, similar to wearing different clothes than you might wear in your daily life.

When a person's circle name is shared with you, take it as a compliment. If you meet this person in a ritual environment, ask them if they use that name outside of the circle. If not, what should you call them? This is good etiquette. Similarly, let people know whether your circle name is for use in other environments. Let them know what they should call you if they see you out and about.

Next, I'm going to give you the opportunity to do a self-dedication. A self-dedication is a great time to inaugurate your new name, if you've chosen one.

BEST WITCHES PATH DEDICATION

A dedication is something you do yourself by defining your goals and pledging yourself to them. Don't feel that this dedication must be done right away in your spinstress journey just because of its placement in the book; you can perform it at any time. Conversely, you might choose to do a self-dedication at the beginning of your journey with this book and again after you have worked your way through the other chapters.

Like dedicating your personal power altar, this dedication will help you define your craft so you can be your best witch.

IDEAL TIME: Depending on your theory of things, a dedication might happen on the new moon (germination) or the full moon (culmination). I think your choice will have to do with where you are in your spiritual journey. Is this a rededication amid a long journey? Does the spinstress path make you feel like you've finally come home (full moon)? Or is everything brand new to you, making you feel like there's a blank canvas in front of you (new moon)? It's dealer's choice.

PREPARATION AND ITEMS TO GATHER:

- For this ritual you'll want to incorporate your fave colors, scents, and sounds. Plan what to wear and what to listen to ahead of time. The bells or smells you use as accessories are powerful. If you've already made your personal power altar, you're well on your way.

- Journal in advance about why you are dedicating yourself to your path. If you feel overwhelmed by this question, it may help to choose your top three reasons. Bring this writing into the circle during your ritual.

- Bring a candle and the tools to inscribe it with your name during the ritual. Or, if you prefer, bring a piece of parchment and a pen.

- If you'd like to incorporate flowers, the lily symbolizes rebirth. Be cautious if you have pets, though, because this plant is extremely toxic to cats. Other plants associated with new beginnings include lady's mantle, apples, roses, and strawberries.

- If you'd like to incorporate gemstones, try rose quartz, emerald, or tourmaline. Your birthstone or your favorite stone are both excellent additions.

CIRCLE UP: I suggest you take a bath or shower and use it as a sort of baptism. While you are in the water, affirm that you are emerging a newer version of yourself. Everything that happened before you got in the water is the past. Everything that happens once you emerge is your future on the new path you have chosen.

After you dry off, put on whatever outfit you've chosen to celebrate your dedication. Proceed to your sacred space and visualize a silver pentacle surrounding you. The pentacle is a geometric form that strengthens energy patterns and therefore can be both powerful and protective. Say to yourself, "My circle is cast by the manifestation of the north, the inspiration of the east, the power of the south, the love of the west, and the sanctification of the spirit. Blessed be."

SPELL WORK: If you haven't yet carved your name (mundane or magickal) into a candle, do so now. Alternatively, write your name on a piece of parchment. Spend some time reviewing what you have written about your goals. If you are dedicated to deities, talk to them about what you want to accomplish and ask for their blessing.

Take some centering breaths and close your eyes. Picture a hot-air balloon in front of you. The balloon is fired up and ready to go. Violet spiritual flames are blowing fuel into the shimmering material of the balloon. Imagine yourself rolling up a parchment scroll that summarizes your writing and your goals. Place it in the balloon and watch as it takes off, drifting into the world of magickal elements in order to help you manifest all that you desire. Thank any deities, ancestors, or guides for their help in guiding this balloon.

Open your eyes and say, "I call upon the fates and my guides to bless me on my path. As I have written upon paper and carved upon wax, let it be. Work with me to bend and shape the energy of my world in order to conform with my goals. Shape the path before me and guide me as I walk upon it. Let my life be a joy for me and a blessing for others. Let all my wishes and goals be manifested in a good and correct way. By the powers, so mote it be."

CLOSE UP SHOP: Visualize the silver pentacle dissolving back into the ether. Say, "May the powerful magick of my circle rejoin the elemental powers to work my will. Blessed be."

• • • • • • •

I developed the next ritual because it pisses me off that womxyn are expected to carry the burden of other people's biases against us. Many of us have experienced varying degrees of shade or even overt discrimination due to our race, size, relationship status, income, religion, and more. It's time to say, "Sorry, world. It's not me. It's *you*." And for that, I offer the following ritual. You can do it whenever the bullshit of others is sticking to your best pair of heels.

ROCK MY WORLD RITUAL

As exhausting as it can be, facing challenges gives your life texture and context. As Buddhist master Thich Nhat Hanh puts it, "No mud, no lotus."[7] How would you understand what joy is if you had never known sadness?

No question that the world can be unfair and unkind. The good news is that the world is also vast. I believe that there is opportunity to co-create the world around you, at least to a certain extent. This doesn't mean you'll never find yourself mired in the mud, but the richness of the mud will make all the difference in the loveliness of your lotus.

---

7. Hanh, *No Mud, No Lotus*.

This ritual will help you build a practice where you co-create your world. This is the type of work that you will want to (and need to) repeat over time. Its energy corresponds to the Neopagan holy day of Imbolc. Imbolc is a spring holiday that features the energies of germination and new beginnings. At the very least, you may want to consider doing this ritual around the time of Imbolc every year.

IDEAL TIME: The full moon, a Sunday, or Imbolc.

PREPARATION AND ITEMS TO GATHER:

- As a focal point on your altar, consider using the World card from a Rider-Waite-Smith-inspired tarot deck. You could also use the Wheel of Fortune card. If you don't own a tarot deck, you can easily find images of these cards online.

- If you'd like to incorporate essential oils or incense, rose, geranium, orange, grapefruit, or sandalwood all bring the correct energies of love, positivity, and healing to this work.

- If you'd like to incorporate gemstones, lepidolite is the perfect stone for this work. Moonstone or labradorite are also appropriate.

- A palo santo smudge stick or incense based in styrax (pine) would also enhance your focus and clarity for the task of world-building.

- Have at least one white candle (birthday candles are fine) that you can anoint with oil and use to cast the sacred space. Birthday candles burn well in a dish of sand or salt. Of course, it's always optional to stick them in an actual cupcake to eat for grounding after your ritual is complete!

CIRCLE UP: Anoint your candles with oil and light them, saying, "As this candle burns, the sacred space is also alight. May only correct energies and forces be present here." If you have a smudge stick, light it and use it to purify the space around your altar.

SPELL WORK: Set the Wheel of Fortune tarot card on your altar. Think about what it will be like to have positive people, opportunities, and experiences around you all the time. Think about what you have that you already treasure.

Imagine that you have spun this wheel of fate and are choosing what to popu-late your world with. When you feel ready, say the following:

"I draw to myself only joy and authenticity. I draw to myself only health and vitality. I draw to myself only love and desire. I draw to myself only truth and respect. I draw to myself only partnership and equality. I draw to myself only abundance and blessing. I draw to myself only justice and good faith. I draw to myself only intimacy and connection. I draw to myself only laughter and joy. I draw to myself only success and correctness."

Next, set the World tarot card on your altar and say, "May all the correct people, materials, and opportunities be drawn into my world and come with my blessing. May all those who do not correspond to my goals go on their way and go with my blessing. I trust the correct and loving forces of the spirit world to guide me and to co-create my world. With harm to none and for the good of all, so shall it be."

CLOSE UP SHOP: As you extinguish your candle, say, "This sacred space is open. May the smoke from my candle carry my intentions back to the spiritual source, where I know it will be made manifest in the perfect way. Blessed be."

• • • • • • •

Along the lines of envisioning a brave new world, you can enhance your per-sonal power by really claiming your time spent being single. Some womxyn even choose this lifestyle for the long haul. No matter what your preferences are, I hope the following information will help.

Magnificent Maiden Voyages
(Enjoying Independent Energy)

We spoke in the early pages of this book about the nasty old stereotypes about who and what a spinstress might be. In historical times, spinsters were self-employed womxyn taking life into their own hands while they provided valuable input for their communities. In terms of girl power and feminism, they were way ahead of the societal curve.

You can see from the preface that this book defines single womxyn and spinstresses much differently. I like the idea that a spinstress is really a "whirling dervish," meaning a powerful spiritual shot-caller.[8] Like the maiden aspect, the spinstress is powerful when she is alone. She is complete within herself. The maiden energy of the goddess is not focused on long-term relationships or nurturing others; she is taking time for herself. Like a young girl, her job is to play and explore. Her job is to name and claim her place in the world.

A spinstress is not always a single woman, but she shares the heritage of the historical spinster. A spinstress, as a female reality weaver, seeks to rock and reclaim the single status. She know that single womxyn are blessed. Independent. Sexy. Self-sufficient. Generous with their time and skills. Singleness can last a month or a lifetime; sometimes it's a chosen state, and sometimes it is most definitely not. Still, shouldn't we find a way to name it and claim it for ourselves?

What are your ideas of what it really means to be single? Write your ideas in your journal, or copy down some of mine. I say single womxyn get to:

- Take space
- Heal
- Reset
- Prepare
- Focus
- Study
- Learn new skills
- Use energy to produce things in life other than a relationship

Great Spinstress Ancestors

The role of the maiden sounds pretty darn important, right? The patriarchy made single womxyn out to be unsociable and selfish. Wrong again, guys. The gifts of one's singleness become gifts to the whole community. Consider some of the great single womxyn of history:

- **Hildegard of Bingen (1098–1179):** A precocious child when her parents "tithed her to God," Hildegard blossomed under the church's

---

8. Daly, *Gyn/Ecology*, 8.

training in history, theology, and Latin. Her spiritual visions and super smarts drew attention over time. So many other girls wanted to study with her that she ended up running her own convent. While managing her mothership for several decades, Hildegard continued to amaze as she created plays, opera, poetry, hymns, and books.[9]

- **Jacobina Felicie, also known as Jacqueline Felice de Almania (fourteenth century):** An Italian socialite who moved to Paris to practice medicine in the fourteenth century, Jacobina caused an uproar by practicing medicine—but perhaps even more so for dressing in breeches. After accruing dozens of fines for medical malpractice (because womxyn weren't supposed to be doctors) and enduring excommunication, Jacobina prevailed. Unable to get rid of her, the old boys of the Paris medical scene saved face by conceding that there may as well be some female doctors so that their wives and daughters could be examined in a way that protected their modesty. Nice save, guys.[10]

- **Joan of Arc (1412–1431):** Otherwise known as "the Maid of Orléans," Joan had spiritual visions in which God asked her to lead an army that would help the French defeat an English invasion. She was a super-heroine until her luck ran out and she lost a major battle over Paris. Left to her fate in the hands of the English, Joan was tried for witchcraft and heresy and was then burned at the stake.[11]

Like the words *witch*, *bitch*, *feminist*, and *hag*, the status and terminology of single womxyn must be re-evaluated and reclaimed. Independent womxyn have lots to regain, but so does the world that counts on us for our wonderful contributions.

Inner Maiden Journaling

Let your inner child's maiden essence spend some time communicating with you. It may have been quite a while since you really listened to what she has

---

9. Leon, *Uppity Women of Medieval Times*, 168–69.

10. Leon, 80.

11. Leon, 136–37.

to say. Have her tell you about her current hopes and dreams. Ask your inner maiden what she is proud of you for doing. Ask what she'd still like to do with your help. If you want to go all-in, give her some construction paper, crayons, and finger paint. Wear a plastic tiara. Try on some ridiculous shoes. Have fun with your inner maiden. It's good for you! You can let your inner maiden write a journal entry, or just play with her and write about the experience later. (Or, bonus—do both!)

Me-Time Rites for Celebrating Singleness

- Take a class to enhance one of your hobbies or interests. Adult education programs run out of many public schools and offer everything from ballroom dancing to beekeeping. You can also teach classes in these settings in order to meet like-minded folks.

- Take yourself on a date. Go to a nice restaurant, see a movie, or take a rickshaw ride in the park. Whatever your "dream date" is, give yourself a night on the town (or spend time indoors and Netflix and chill!).

- Go out with some friends and enjoy the company of others. If your social network needs expanding, taking an aforementioned class should help. You could also join a meet-up group or a club that matches one of your interests, such as a book club.

- Build on your meditation practices. Try to find at least one type of meditation that feeds your soul. Try a phone app that times you in order to help you improve your stillness stamina. Perhaps moving meditation is more your speed; yoga is a physical form of meditation.

• • • • • • •

We all spend a lot of time sleeping on our trusty pillows. The following craft encourages you to make a pillow that will give you the very best loving energies. Boost your self-image every time you get some sleep! This is a great activity to do with girls, whether you are parenting or mentoring them.

PERSONAL DEVOTION SELF-ESTEEM PILLOW

Even the most awesome womxyn feel a bit down on themselves from time to time. A self-esteem pillow is a great boost for your boudoir. Use your favorite pillowcase or pick up a new one. Smooth fabric is best to draw on.

IDEAL TIME: The waxing moon or the full moon.

PREPARATION AND ITEMS TO GATHER:
- A pillowcase.
- Fabric markers or permanent markers in a variety of colors.
- A lead pencil for practice marks.
- Optional: Iron-on designs.

CIRCLE UP: Use your pencil to pre-draw lettering and designs. (That is, unless you are a super-bold goddess who prefers to let the ink fall where it may.)

Ideas for designs might be an embellished version of your name (mundane or magickal) and a list of positive traits that describe you. Make sure you stay positive! This pillow is for boosting your positive emotions. If you feel too modest to gush about yourself, list positive traits you aspire to.

Iron-on design patches are an option, or you can freehand decorations that inspire you: cats, cars, stars, or what have you. These should be images that fill you with happiness and inspiration. Use your favorite colors. You could even write inspirational literary quotes or an entire poem. All that matters is that you love the things you are putting on your pillowcase.

To set the ink on your work of art, put it in the dryer for about fifteen minutes.

SPELL WORK: Bless your pillow by saying, "Goddess of unconditional love and self-esteem, I know that I should value myself as much as you value me. I ask for your blessing on this pillow so that it will strengthen my positive thoughts and energies as I rest on it."

CLOSE UP SHOP: Hug your pillow and take three deep, grounding breaths. When you feel ready, you can end your ritual and go place your pillow in its happy new home. Sweet dreams!

• • • • • • •

If resting on your self-esteem pillow isn't quite doing the trick, here are some more crafty tips for shifting away from negativity and self-doubt.

Banishing Body Negativity

Body negativity is hard to avoid. There are billion-dollar companies working to create insecurities about age, size, race, style, odor, and more in order to sell their products. It's hard to avoid; we are bound to come across negative messages in songs, television shows, commercials, and movies. You might even hear the indoctrinated opinions of folks around you.

It helps to develop your own emotional first aid kit for when body negativity is really beating you down. Come up with a list of ways to combat body shame and allow it to change over time. I've included an example, but I encourage you to make it your own. This technique works best when you base the list on your own style and needs.

Ways to Combat Body Shame

- Listen to a badass playlist of self-affirming tunes.
- Curate a collection of guided meditations for healing and/or body positivity.
- Read or write a body-positive story.
- Do a type of exercise/movement that lets you enjoy moving your body. Do this to feel good, not to change your body.
- Go out and enjoy the arts in a way that moves you. It could be a concert, opera, ballet, play, movie, art exhibit, etc.
- Make a gratitude list for your body. Thank your eyes for seeing beautiful things, your tongue for allowing you to enjoy the taste of food, and more. Don't take anything about your wonderful body for granted.
- Pray, chant, and/or do a ritual that honors your body.
- Get together with a trusted friend and paint each other's toenails. The friendship is as awesome as the pedicure.
- Explore aromatherapy with soothing and loving scents. Some good candidates include rose, lavender, amber, jasmine, grapefruit, and myrrh.

- Snuggle with a loved one (human or nonhuman) and give thanks for the body that gives you life, allowing you to give and receive the blessings of love.
- Do grounding work. Give yourself a massage (arms, legs, shoulders) to feel your own skin. Get outside whenever you can—barefoot is best! Grounding after your other self-esteem activities will help keep that good energy in.

Remember to be patient with yourself. Given the pervasive social messages we receive to be self-critical, this type of radical self-acceptance is always a work in progress.

BAY LEAF BODY SHAME BINDING

Bay leaves can be found in the bulk section of a health food store, in the spice aisle at the corner grocery, or in many metaphysical shops. In magick, they are commonly used for protection and purification. They also have a rather dark origin story in Greek myth, which relates directly to our work on sexual healing.

In Greek myth, Daphne was one of the forest nymphs who hung out with the goddess Artemis. Unfortunately, Artemis's twin brother, Apollo, had a crush on his sister's girl. He chased and harassed Daphne until her own forest-deity dad decided that he'd have to change Daphne's form in order to protect her from Apollo's advances.

Daphne was changed into a bay laurel tree. Apollo backed off at that point, though he continued to wear a commemorative laurel wreath in his hair. For a god of prophecy, he was clueless when it came to the meaning of the word no.

When you do the following spell, take a minute to think about Daphne and ask her to help you say no to all things that do not serve you.

IDEAL TIME: The waning moon, the new moon, or a Tuesday.

PREPARATION AND ITEMS TO GATHER:
- Take some time prior to the ritual (preferably during a waning moon phase) to journal on what ideas, habits, and even relationships you may need to let go of in order to heal your self-esteem. After you journal, boil your ideas down into one-word concepts. For instance,

you may find that you need to let go of things like "body shame," "guilt," "unhealthy relationships," or "judgment." Don't worry if one word doesn't cover a whole concept; it's just a symbol. The words you choose should be firmly connected to whatever energetic pattern or thoughtform you are trying to remove from your life.

- A black permanent marker with a fine point.
- Dried bay leaves (one for each word you want to use for the ritual).
- A fireproof dish to burn the leaves in.
- A black candle or another way to burn the leaves.
- A stable surface (perhaps the floor or a table) on which you will set your burning candle and lit leaves.
- Optional: A hat pin or ritual blade to carve your candle. Carving the name of Daphne on the candle will help channel her energy.
- Optional: Oil to anoint your candle. Consider infusing oil with rose for self-esteem or rosemary for protection.

CIRCLE UP: Visualize a bright blue circle around you and your sacred space. Blue is a powerful spiritual color and strengthens your authentic internal voice. Know that you are protected inside this circle and that only correct energetic forces can join you. Affirm this by saying, "So mote it be."

SPELL WORK: Light your candle. Sit calmly for a few moments and think about the journaling work you did as well as your keywords that symbolize what (or who) you want to release. When you feel ready, write your keywords on the bay leaves using a permanent marker.

Once you've finished writing your keywords, burn the bay leaves one at a time, putting them in a fireproof dish after they catch fire. Only burn one leaf at a time so that your fire doesn't grow too big. As the bay leaves burn, chant, "Like Daphne, may my change release me."

CLOSE UP SHOP: Extinguish your candle and make sure your fireproof dish has gone cold. Pour a little water in it if necessary. When you're ready to leave your sacred space, open the circle by visualizing the blue circle fading into the earth. Know that it will carry the remaining energy of the bay leaves into the earth for recycling and grounding. Say, "The circle is open. Blessed be."

If for some reason you chose not to burn the bay leaves, release them and their energy as soon as you can. Toss them in a stream, bury them in the earth, or simply crumble them up in your hands before letting them blow away in the wind.

· · · · · · · ·

Beyond releasing the negativity we harbor for ourselves, womxyn need to check the baggage we carry around about one another. Womxyn have been set up to compete for resources, whether they are limited or not. Low self-esteem is closely connected to jealousy. It's never a bad idea to address the knotty issue of jealousy head-on.

Jealousy and Competition Between Womxyn

Jealousy is romanticized by American culture as a sign of "real" love. If we think of the idea of love as a recipe, jealousy has been sifted into passion until the two ingredients are hard to pull apart. How do we sort this out?

It helps to acknowledge jealousy as a normal human emotion while still holding everyone accountable for how they express said feeling. If you become possessive as a form of jealousy, for instance, then you are treating another person like a possession or object and not, um, a person. Not good.

Not all jealousy is connected to romance. It can be a strong factor in any environment where womxyn are forced to compete with one another. Marginalized groups are encouraged to compete with one another for limited resources in a hierarchical society. This is sometimes called "horizontal hostility."

In horizontal hostility, people of a certain lot in life are encouraged to battle it out amongst themselves rather than to challenge the entitlements that enable other social groups to lead a cushier lifestyle. This functions to make things easier for those in positions of power and privilege. But because many of us are indoctrinated to think in this way, we are enforcing our own oppression. A major element of this is jealousy.

For instance, if a business has only one or two affirmative action or diversity opportunities made available for womxyn or minorities, folks must compete with one another for those opportunities. This encourages jealousy and enmity rather than the collective action that could be a powerful force for social change.

Once womxyn and people placed in minority positions do start talking and uniting, great changes happen. Collective action has led to things like voting rights, labor unions, and other civil liberties. This, in turn, gives us more opportunities for personal happiness.

But there is also a dark side to communication: the little slimy, spiky monster known as *gossip*. Gossip is one of the most destructive little monsters once set loose into groups of people. It's a symptom of oppressive hierarchies in which most people haven't felt safe using direct communication. Instead, people whisper their grievances about one another to trusted friends. This breeds frenemies, backstabbing, paranoia, and feuds. Again, it all benefits the powers that be. I can't tell you how many groups of womxyn I've been part of that have been fractured and sometimes even broken to smithereens by the gossip monster.

Womxyn, we have to get over this stuff. The way to squelch the gossip monster is through direct and ethical communication. There are books and workshops on this. In general, it means:

- Talk directly to people you have grievances with. A good guideline is to practice this conversation once or twice with a trusted confidant before having it. Beyond that, you're drifting into gossip.
- Speak of your own experience when talking about a grievance.
- Ask about things you don't understand; don't make assumptions.
- If the two of you are making a good-faith effort to resolve the issue, do your part. Don't pick up your grievance again and discuss it with other friends. This is gossip.
- Apologize and try again when you screw up. Allow others to do the same.
- Be kind to yourself and others. This is tricky stuff.

Being kind to yourself and others will go a long way when it comes to combating jealousy, gossip, and horizontal hostility. When you feel resentment of some sort toward other people—and particularly toward other womxyn—you should ask yourself why. Journaling can be a good tool for this. Building empathy for other people, just as you build empathy for yourself, is bound to lead to healing.

Cut Out the Drama
Spell to Release Jealousy

A similar word for empathy is *sympathy*. We're going to employ a type of sympathetic magick in this spell to release jealousy. We'll be working with poppets or effigies, otherwise known as dolls. You may think of these little critters as tools for cursing due to stereotypes about voodoo dolls, but in fact, this type of craft has been used for healing and blessing just as much as—if not more than—for gnarly intent.

IDEAL TIME: The waning moon or a Saturday.

PREPARATION AND ITEMS TO GATHER:

- Place some salt and water in a chalice (cup or bowl). You'll be using this to cast your sacred space.

- Construction paper for a paper poppet. (You could also use note paper, although construction paper holds its shape better.) Choose any color and then choose colored pencils or pens accordingly; you want to be able to read what you write on the poppet.

- Scissors so you can cut out your poppet.

- Stones from your natural environment to place on your altar or around your circle. These will help you stay grounded and will help release the difficult energies we'll interacting with during the first part of the spell. While stones like hematite, shungite, lepidolite, and jet will help you draw out jealousy, rose quartz and amethyst help with the healing portion of the work.

CIRCLE UP: Take your chalice of salt water and affirm that the blend is both sacred and protective. Use your fingers to sprinkle a bit of salt water around your sacred space in a circular shape, preferably clockwise. Say, "This sacred circle will protect me and strengthen my magick for the good of all. Blessed be."

SPELL WORK: On a sheet of paper, draw a large poppet that represents womxyn who trigger feelings of jealousy or resentment. The poppet can represent all womxyn or one or more womxyn in your life. This poppet can be very simple or as elaborate as you like; just make sure it is big enough to hold the writing you will do for the spell.

Cut the poppet out so that you can write on each side of her silhouette. Consecrate the poppet by holding her in your hand and saying, "Henceforth, this form represents real womxyn in my culture and my life who give me jealous feelings. I thank her for holding this energy so that I may learn and heal. With harm to none and for the good of all, so shall it be."

On one side of your poppet, write down the jealous feelings you have had against other womxyn. These might be trigger words like "superficial," "bossy," or "conceited," or you can be more specific. For example, you might write, "She's always showing off by being the first to answer in class so the rest of us never get a word in," or, "My coworker is always complaining about how she looks even though she knows that she's gorgeous." The more you let yourself think about this topic, the easier it will be to fill up your poppet with trigger words and statements. If you run out of space, don't flip the poppet over and keep writing—we're going to use the other side next.

Once you are done writing down as many jealousy triggers as you can think of, take a minute to check in with yourself. Do some deep breathing. How do you feel? Did doing this exercise make you angry? Are you holding tension in a part of your body? Do you have a headache, stomachache, or pain in your back? Take note of any symptoms like these. Knowing where jealousy settles in your body can help you be more aware of it in your daily life.

Put your hands over your belly, which is the area that houses your solar plexus chakra. This is an important area for confidence and self-esteem. Wish good energy into this area as you say, "I acknowledge and forgive myself for my jealousies and resentments. I understand I have been encouraged to feel this way about other womxyn and myself. From now on, I want to work on having more empathy for all of us, including myself. Whenever I feel these jealousies and resentments, I affirm that my solar plexus will be strengthened and will empower me to rise above all negative, limiting thoughts. With harm to none and for the good of all, so shall it be."

When you feel ready, turn your poppet over and prepare to do more writing. Write down phrases that will help you build more compassion for yourself and other womxyn when your jealousies and resentments are triggered. For example, to counter the resentments I listed previously, I could write, "Many womxyn feel that they have to prove their intelligence. Sometimes they might come on too strong," or, "I understand that all womxyn—

even the ones I perceive as very beautiful—face the same body shame and self-criticism that I do. Being anxious to be liked may present as seeming obsessed with looks. I can understand and relate to that anxiety." You can also use keywords to counter jealousy. Some examples include "empathy," "kindness," "love," "acceptance," "strength," "character," or similar.

Fill up this side of your poppet with these types of messages. Again, check in with yourself. How have your feelings changed? Are you breathing easier? Do you feel less anxious? Are any aches or pains reduced?

Place your hands on your chest, where your heart chakra is located. This is a spiritual energy center for compassion and love. Feel positive energy entering your heart chakra as you say, "I affirm that there is enough love to go around. I send love to myself and to all womxyn who have ever intentionally or accidentally triggered my feelings of resentment or jealousy. I understand that we have been taught to compete with one another. While the womxyn around me may not know this, I now do. I affirm that I will counter the feelings of jealousy and resentment that only hurt me and limit me on my own life's path. With harm to none and for the good of all, blessed be."

It is okay to repeat this spell periodically. Womxyn receive regular messages that it's normal and perhaps even beneficial for us to be jealous of and competitive toward each other. Remember that and take it easy on yourself if you have recurring feelings of jealousy and resentment. If you make this spell a habit, you may feel your positive messages start to kick in automatically whenever feelings of jealousy are triggered.

CLOSE UP SHOP: Use your fingers to sprinkle salt water around the perimeter of your sacred circle again, preferably counterclockwise. Visualize the energy of the circle being grounded as you say, "The circle is open though unbroken. I affirm that the energy of this circle will be returned to the earth and be used for some good purpose. Blessed be."

The final phase of your spell work is the destruction of your poppet. When you do this, you release the energy that entered the effigy and allow it to do its manifestation work in the world. Burn the poppet, tear it up and release it into the wind, or destroy it in whatever way makes sense to you.

chapter three

BEAUTY, GLAMOUR, AND MAGICK FOR FEELING GOOD

Glamour sometimes gets a bad rep. It can be seen as deceptive or superfluous. But glamour can be a good thing; it can boost your self-esteem and remind you that you rock. As with many other types of craft, you could look at beauty magick scientifically and recognize that it is about changing your *neural pathways*, the ways you automatically think and feel about something.

Whether or not you have previously struggled with your self-esteem, glamour can create a little bit of joy and self-love that will gradually grow. Self-esteem is a powerful tool. Strong feelings—both positive and negative—draw in similar energies. In other words, it's better to feel like hot shit than total crap.

I think it's important to mention that glamour isn't about being femme—it's about embracing whatever makes you feel your best. You can use a plaid jacket or a pair of Dr. Martens to anchor yourself in your own personal glam. Or, if you prefer, you can use lip gloss and mascara. It totally depends on you!

PERSONAL POWER JEWELRY

The first spell in this chapter anchors you in your self-esteem using a piece of jewelry. You will create a talisman that serves as a focal point for your self-esteem. Your jewelry will become a battery to boost your positive, self-love energy. I will refer to your item as "jewelry" throughout the spell, but feel free to be creative. You could choose something traditional, like a set of earrings, or another accessory (a watch, a belt, etc.). It doesn't matter if you choose an expensive ring, a meaningful heirloom, or a plastic piece from a toy store. You could also use a gemstone as your jewelry. If you choose to use a stone, I'm a fan of the hardworking and versatile emerald. A stone known for its self-love powers is rose quartz. Your birthstone would also work great. Regardless of what item you choose, it should cheer you up whenever you look at it.

IDEAL TIME: The waxing moon, the full moon, or a Monday.

PREPARATION AND ITEMS TO GATHER:
- A piece of jewelry, another accessory, or a gemstone. Before the ritual, rinse the item in cold tap water and visualize any incorrect energies being washed away. If you are worried that water will damage the item, cleanse it by blowing on it and willing the incorrect energies to be blown away.
- The presence of rose quartz or other examples of the color pink would be helpful in your sacred space.
- If you'd like to incorporate flowers, geraniums, lilies, or roses (fresh or dry) would be great.
- If you'd like to incorporate mood music, make sure you choose music that gives you a positive emotional boost.

CIRCLE UP: Chant some "Om" sounds while you visualize your sacred space being encircled by soft pink light.

SPELL WORK: Hold the jewelry in your hand and ask for the energies of the circle to flow into it as you say, "I charge this talisman with the essence of the elements. I fill this jewelry with empowering energy. Whenever I wear it, I will remember that I spin my own reality. I choose to spin the reality of self-acceptance and self-love. I know that I am lovable. I know my soul is precious and strong. This energy will live within my jewelry and power my positive thoughts. Let this magick be fixed. Let it be done. Whenever I wear this jewelry, I know that my energetic levels will peak. The correct opportunities will come to me. I will be seen in the best possible light. I can and I will manifest my goals, with harm to none and for the good of all."

When you finish the spell, put the jewelry on and say, "Blessed be."

CLOSE UP SHOP: Chant more "Om" tones while you visualize the pink light rising to the skies, returning the energy you have called back to the elements. Know that some of your energy is going along and will be manifested even after your spell work is done.

• • • • • • •

As a working girl, I appreciate spells that are quick and functional. If you have makeup that you use as part of your daily routine (or skincare such as sunscreen, moisturizer, etc.), this glamour blessing will help you get the most beauty out of that buck.

QUICK MAKEUP GLAMOUR BLESSING

Many of us wear a beauty product every day, even if it's just moisturizer or lip balm. In this quick blessing, you can ask a love goddess like Venus or Aphrodite to give your cosmetics a magickal makeover.

IDEAL TIME: Do your blessing on a Friday or during the waxing or full moon for an extra punch.

SPELL WORK: Hold one of your cosmetics in your hands. Blow a gust of breath over it. Visualize your breath in the shape of a pentacle. Then say, "Spirits of beauty and love, hear me now. May I see my true beauty whenever I wear this. May I feel empowered. May those around me see my true beauty as well. I thank you, and I dedicate the fruits of this beauty and love to your purposes. Blessed be."

BUILD YOUR INNER BEAUTY BLESSING

Beauty usually is connected to how you feel. Have you ever started a new romance, gotten into a great school, or had something else make you very happy, only to have lots of people say, "You look great! You're glowing! What's going on?" This is no coincidence. When energy levels vibrate at a "love" or "bliss" frequency, this also translates to beauty.

The following spell is a great way to tweak your beautiful vibrations. It includes the use of a gemstone, but you can find a nice stone outside if you prefer. Another option that works well for this blessing is a piece of gemstone jewelry, like a pendant. I have a nice rose quartz pendant that I placed in the brew and then wore, charged to this purpose.

IDEAL TIME: Do this blessing whenever you need to. I prefer a waxing moon or the full moon to increase positive vibes, but you can also use a waning or new moon and focus on removing negativity. Or do both!

PREPARATION AND ITEMS TO GATHER:
- A container such as a glass bowl, mason jar, or non-metal chalice.
- At least one cup of spring water.
- At least two of the following herbs: vervain, rose petal, catnip, lemon balm, orris root, or mugwort. Harvest fresh and local when possible.
- Two or three drops of at least one of the following essential oils: rose, jasmine, or spikenard.
- A gemstone (or piece of jewelry) that you feel corresponds to beauty. Examples include rose quartz, clear quartz, fluorite, diamond, or emerald.

SPELL WORK: Add the water, herbs, essential oils, and gemstone to your container and leave it to charge under the moon, indoors or out. After your container has charged, anoint yourself with splashes of water while saying, "I anoint myself with beauty. I attune myself to the most gorgeous vibrations of the moon. I reflect beauty back to myself and to the world. I share beauty with everyone. Blessed be."

After you've finished anointing your body with some of the water, pour the rest of the container out, making sure to hold on to the gemstone. You can decide where to pour; perhaps the tub or shower (strain the herbs so they don't clog your drain), the sacred circle at your altar, a potted plant, or the great outdoors. Give thanks to the moon and its energy.

Keep the gemstone in your pocket, on your altar, or on your person (especially if it's jewelry).

Repeat as desired. You may want to follow the blessing with a full ritual like the one that's up next. Whether separate or together, these spells are great for boosting self-love.

• • • • • • •

In the craft and in the lives of most womxyn, the mirror can hold both wonderful and terrible powers. Like the queen in Snow White, we can get a little obsessed. Looking into a mirror and building self-esteem is an important step for those of us hoping to manifest our major life goals. This notion is based on what has recently been called the *law of attraction*. It makes sense that we will do a better job with our manifestation magick if we truly believe that we deserve what we want!

The following spell will help you tame that scary mirror monster and make your reflection your own. You deserve everything you want in life, and the mirror is a powerful tool that will help you realize that.

Mirror, Mirror Self-Esteem Glamour

Unlike many of these types of spells, I am not going to start by asking you to smile at your reflection. Some of us have had such a difficult relationship with mirrors that forcing a smile can be too much of a struggle and distract you from the work you are trying to do. I don't care what face you make when you look in your mirror. All I ask is that you respect the person looking back at you.

If it helps (or if you think it's more beneficial), you can approach this whole thing in a more playful way. Give your inner maiden another shot at self-esteem by bringing her presence to the mirror. Break out items like a feather boa, plastic gems, or a toy tiara. Say things into the mirror that your inner maiden needs and wants to hear.

IDEAL TIME: The waxing or full moon on a Monday or Friday.

PREPARATION AND ITEMS TO GATHER:

- Pick a mirror that you enjoy looking into. It can be vintage, kitschy, or minimalist. Tabletop, wall-mounted, or handheld styles will all work. Just pick something you feel comfortable spending several minutes at a time sitting or standing in front of.
- You can't go wrong having some rose quartz, amethyst, or emerald nearby.

CIRCLE UP: Harness blessings from a goddess of love by visualizing a bower of beautiful roses climbing up to form your circle. Say, "By perfume and by thorn, only the energies of love and light are welcomed here."

SPELL WORK: The first step is to consecrate your mirror with healing and empowering energies. Hold both hands over the mirror glass and say, "I bless this surface with kind and healing vibrations. May all who gaze upon it receive joy from the reflection. Blessed be."

If you work with power symbols (sigils) like the pentacle or Reiki symbols, you can put the positive image on the glass with your mind's eye. Affirm that this consecration is fixed and will remain on the glass for as long as you need it.

Face your mirror and close your eyes. Prepare yourself to be kind and loving to the person you see looking back at you—yourself! When you feel ready, open your eyes. Gaze into the mirror and know that this person is good. This person is deserving. This person is lucky to be alive. Tell the person in the mirror that you love them.

If it doesn't feel right to say, "I love you," try something like, "I respect you. I know you work hard, and you are doing great." It's important that whatever you say is positive, kind, and something you really believe. Practice until you find the right mantra and then repeat it to yourself several times. When you are done working with your own mantra, repeat this spell several times: "Mirror, mirror, self-esteem glamour, I send love to me."

CLOSE UP SHOP: Allow the bower of roses that you created to recede back into the earth, grounding your energies.

People develop relationships with mirrors and with their reflection over many years, and it won't be completely reprogrammed in one night. Repeat this spell at least once a month. Every full moon would be a great time.

SELF-ACCEPTANCE SELFIE SPELL

Lately, I've decided to work on my hatred of selfies. I'd attempted this before, but I never quite made it work. This year I had some success. I think persistence is key. If you are like me and have developed photo phobia, know that it can be overcome. Taking photos of yourself is the sort of thing that you have to get used to if you've been avoiding the camera. Give it a chance.

"Why bother?" you may ask. Well, just think about it this way: In twenty years if you look at a picture of yourself today, you'll probably say something like, "I was so young! What a beautiful day that was! There's my best friend. I never see her anymore. I remember that I *hated* how I looked in that top/ those pants/short sleeves. I wish I'd had more fun."

I am using the word *selfie* in the spell, but you could choose to have someone else take photos of you as well. I've tried both ways. Personally, I felt that posing for other folks was too difficult at first, even if they were people I love and trust. I had to fight this through on my own, but you might feel differently.

You will want to be fully prepped for your photo shoot. Before you get started, you may want to check a few websites for tips on camera angles and lighting. For example, selfie sticks are awesome because most people look better if the camera is higher than them, and when using a selfie stick, you are looking up (and probably a bit to one side). For lighting, being outdoors is better than in. Early or later in the daytime you get nice, soft light. Turn until you don't see any shadows.[12]

If you need more help than that, you need someone with more expertise than me. But I swear by one thing, and that's practice.

IDEAL TIME: The full moon or a Friday.

PREPARATION AND ITEMS TO GATHER:
- Clothes, makeup, jewelry, props, and a location that make you feel comfortable. With that being said, don't be too much of a perfectionist. If you don't like what you do this time, try again.
- A smartphone or camera. If you'd like, you can also bring equipment like a selfie stick, tripod, etc.

---

12. Saltzman and Rosenstein, "How to Take a Good Selfie."

- If you're very anxious about photos, you may want to incorporate a grounding stone like hematite, kyanite, or lepidolite.
- Depending on where you are taking selfies, you could use a self-esteem altar. Correspondences might include the color pink, the color white, the color green, the color gold, roses, jasmine, lavender, rose quartz, amethyst, or emerald.

CIRCLE UP: Visualize a pink or gold circle around yourself and your working space.

SPELL WORK: Say, "I affirm these energies raise the vibrations of my love and self-esteem. May I see only good when I gaze within. May I see only beauty when I gaze at my image. Thank you and blessed be."

If you cast the circle around your photography space, leave it in place while you do your photo shoot. Take a bunch of pictures. Play with angles, lighting, poses, and faces. Do at least two things you don't normally do in photos, like a certain pose or expression. You don't have to show these to anyone, but you might love them!

CLOSE UP SHOP: When you are done, if you haven't opened the circle yet, let your gold or pink energy dissolve and say, "I give thanks for the blessings of the energetic boost. May you take a bit of my beauty and grace back to the spiritual source as my gift. Thank you for your help. Blessed be."

Don't delete any of the pictures you took for at least twenty-four hours. Let them "cool off" before you decide which ones you love and which ones you hate. I strongly suggest you keep at least a couple pictures from each photo session. Repeat often, especially if you are still uncomfortable with being photographed. Believe me, it gets better with time!

If, on the other hand, you have some images you already love, share them with friends and family! Let the affirmations roll in and just say "Thank you" without self-deprecating.

• • • • • • •

Ready for your close-up now? If not, you may need to bask in the glow of the following queens of glam. All from the era of black-and-white film, these womxyn knew that beauty and brains go together like peanut butter and jelly.

Glam Dames to Search Immediately

It's easy, given mainstream culture, to feel like womxyn have to choose either beauty or brains. Glamorous womxyn are often trivialized. Meanwhile, smart and productive womxyn are pigeonholed as frumpy or uninterested in how they look. To each her own, but I'm here to say, you don't have to choose!

These divas of glam teach the lessons of style *and* substance. All of these womxyn belong on your dressing table or mirror to serve as powerful reminders. Consider including their images in your glam or personal power altar. Drink deep at the well!

- **Greta Garbo (1905–1990):** This silver screen siren was one of the few actresses to see her fame follow her from silent films to "talkies" in the thirties and forties. Originally from Sweden, Garbo (née Gustafsson) did it her way. Disdaining the tabloids and hubbub of Hollywood (which only made her more attractive to the press), she was dubbed "the Swedish Sphinx." Reputedly dating both womxyn and men, Garbo never wed. Perhaps she paid a price, since letters later auctioned off by her estate revealed her loneliness and isolation in America. Yet, as an avatar for independent womxyn, Garbo made her mark. Her legacy in film was due to her ability to portray sexy vulnerability and a nuanced, complex type of female who just wouldn't be pinned down.[13]

- **Hedy Lamarr (1914–2000):** This vintage film diva reputedly drugged her maid and then escaped her castle in disguise in order to launch her film career and resume single life; she did this to escape her wildly controlling husband. Her stunning good looks were the prototype for the first Disney *Snow White* and also the first *Catwoman*. But this looker was more than skin-deep. She had a hobby—she loved to invent things. One of the things she helped invent was the magickal techy tech found in modern Bluetooth; she gave her patent to the US Navy at no cost. Not only did she have perfect brows and lashes, but

---

13. Bret, *Greta Garbo*.

we wouldn't have modern internet without her. She was a legit glam genius. Look her up on the smartphone you can thank her for.[14]

- **Josephine Baker (1906–1975):** Josephine Baker was an African American singer and dancer born in Missouri who moved to Paris. Schooled in the American stage craft known as vaudeville, she flourished in Paris as a very "modern" entertainer. Romanced and romanticized, the French worshiped her as a "Creole goddess." She was famous in Europe (and eventually in the states) for her glorious jazz and her amazing dancing (which was usually performed mostly nude). When France was occupied by the Nazis in World War II, she used her status as a celebrity and pinup to spy for the Allies. She sold her jewelry to buy food for war refugees and engaged in activism for the Parisians suffering under Hitler. After the war ended, Josephine was granted high military honors including the *Croix de Guerre* (an award for heroic deeds during the war) and the *Rosette de la Résistance* (given for "remarkable acts of faith and courage" on behalf of the French resistance). Josephine was also named a *Chevalier de Légion d'honneur*. This was a *literal* knighthood. It is France's highest order of merit for both military and civil action, going back to the days of Napoleon. Not bad for a girl who started out struggling with discrimination and segregation. She was a goddess, indeed.[15]

- **Lili Elbe (1882–1931):** Lili Elbe was a transgender womxyn born in Denmark who became a successful painter under her birth name, Einar Magnus Andreas Wegener. Being transgender and openly developing her authentic identity at that point in history was incredibly brave of Lili. It helped a bit that she was part of the progressive artistic community of her time. Her then-wife, Gerda Gottlieb, was also an artist. The two remained committed to each other throughout Lili's transition. Gerda painted many beautiful portraits of Lili that epitomize glam. Lili wrote her own memoirs, though many names and details were changed to protect people. She died from medical complications following a uterus transplant. Her story was adapted

---

14. Dean, *Bombshell*.
15. Baker and Chase, *Josephine*.

into the scripted drama *The Danish Girl*, released in 2015. Her bravery, beauty, and glam should inspire us all.[16]

High Priestess Beauty Oil

This oil can be used to anoint your body or your jewelry and to paint glam sigils on a mirror. You will need:

- ⅛ cup base oil (I recommend almond, but coconut would make a lovely solid that you could use in the bath)
- 6 to 8 drops of spikenard essential oil (you can substitute jasmine)
- 6 drops rose absolute
- A clear quartz stone
- A half-pint mason jar with a lid or a similar jar

Combine the oils and rose absolute in your jar. Add the clear quartz stone.

Bless your beauty oil by holding your hands over the jar and focusing on it while saying, "By the blessing of the goddess and the moon, I charge this oil. May the divine intelligence anoint me with the blessing of High Priestess when I receive these vibrations. As High Priestess I am beautiful, I am powerful, I am wise, and I am good. Blessed be."

Charge the jar under the full moon.

This oil is great for anointing your body, jewelry, candles, or other altar tools. When not in use, make sure the jar's lid is on tight and store in a cool, dry place.

---

16. Elbe, *Man into Woman*.

chapter four

LOVE, MONEY, AND MAGICK TO ALLOW FOR ALL GOOD THINGS

I like to hang out in Salem, Massachusetts, when I have a little time off. When you hang around enough witchy shops, you hear the professionals talk. People in Salem's magick biz agree that tourists come to witches for two things: love or money.

This is hardly a surprise. Most of us know that it's hard to live well without those two things. People often relate to love and money in similar ways. How do *you* relate to love and money? Here are some possibilities:

- You worry all the time about how to keep what you have, or how to get more.

- You jealously guard your treasured funds or lovers lest someone comes to steal them away.

- You spend love and/or money "fast and loose," trusting that more will come.

- You carefully steward what you have with gratitude, always making a plan before you try something new.

- You believe love and money are there to enjoy. You use your values about family or social responsibility to guide how you spend these resources.

There is no judgment attached to any of these techniques. These are just a few examples of the connections between emotional and financial wealth. Thinking about love and money as resources makes a lot of sense; at different times in your life, you will probably have more or less of these resources. Sometimes these resources become unexpectedly depleted by crisis or heartbreak.

Experiencing hardships can shift how an individual relates to love and money resources over time. You may move between carefree trust and fearful attentiveness at different points in your lives. This is understandable. What matters most when working the craft is whether you are happy with how you *currently* relate to love or money, and whether you should be using your spinstress practices to shift these relationships in one way or another.

Before you try out the goodies in this chapter, it may help for you to spend some time thinking about your relationship to love and money at this moment. I recommend grabbing your journal and working through these questions:

- How do you feel about love and money? Are you afraid to lose what you have or afraid you'll never get more? Are you blissed out and blessed? Often, it's going to be somewhere in between.

- Are you the person others rely on to share your resources? Is this always okay with you? How do you deal with it if it isn't?

- Do you remember a time when you had very different relationships with love or money, for better or worse? What changed?

In the pages within, you will have a chance to mull this stuff over as you work on self-esteem, finding the love you want, and even knowing when to call it quits in a relationship. We'll also talk about money and getting needs met without having to tie love and money together for survival, if possible. I've also tossed in some fun sections on Victorian flower flirting and brewing up prosperi-tea.

First, let's spend some time valuing ourselves. To be abundant in love and money, you have to believe you're worth it.

WRITING A LOVE LETTER (TO YOURSELF)

The wise spinstress realizes that self-respect is the key to happiness. The more you work to attune your own energies to love and respect (for yourself), the more able you will be to draw a partnership where that same energy is at play.

This may seem like a step that you can skip over. It may seem selfish. It may even feel too hard if you have negative feelings about yourself that seem insurmountable. Nothing is insurmountable with time and—dare I say it—love.

Plus, these love letters aren't meant to be sappy, self-love glitter bombs. These letters are that moment when you finally sit down with yourself and give yourself some respect. This is the love letter from someone who knows you inside out—you! "I know all your messes, your mistakes, your betrayals, your disappointments, your spoiled hopes, and false starts. I know every part of your body, and how it looks at every age and every stage. I know all of this, and I love you still." I hope that everyone gets a chance to be loved like that by someone else. Regardless, you can give this gift to yourself.

IDEAL TIME: The waxing moon, the full moon, or any Friday.

PREPARATION AND ITEMS TO GATHER:
- You will need a mirror that fits inside your sacred circle.
- You may want to investigate some old-school writing supplies. They used to sell letter paper of every style you could imagine. The same goes for pens, pencils, calligraphy kits, and colored inks. (Some craft or specialty shops still do.) If this type of thing appeals to you, go for it. If not, any paper and writing utensil will do. The message (and the messenger) are most important.
- Your personal power altar from chapter 2 would be a great spot to do this work since you've already built it up to represent your strong and authentic self. If you haven't tackled that project yet, just make your sacred space reflect what you really respect about yourself; represent things like your style, activism, family, or tenacious ability to survive.
- If you'd like to incorporate flowers, white or pink roses match the vibration. You could also turn to lavender for spiritual clarity, healing,

and all good things. Any type of lavender will do: fresh, dried, potpourri, essential oil, etc.

- If you'd like to incorporate gemstones, I recommend rose quartz. We've done a lot with rose quartz, but that's because this little rosy workhorse provides the spiritual and healing type of love that womxyn need to reclaim and receive. You could also incorporate amethyst, the lavender of the quartz world.

- If you'd like to incorporate candles, tapers would work well in white, pink, purple, or gold. Just don't leave them unattended near the paper (especially if you have pets).

CIRCLE UP: Visualize pink or gold light circling your sacred space as you say the following invocation:

"North, I honor the earth that gives me my life. I am grateful for the body that carries and nurtures my spirit.

"East, I honor the air that gives me breath. I give thanks for the blessing of experience and of life, even though it is sometimes hard.

"South, I honor the fire that warms us from the distant and mighty sun. Thank you for our planet and for all growing things.

"West, I honor the waters that birthed us all. I am grateful for all life, including my own.

"Spirit, I honor you for being the unending source of all that lives and dies and is reborn. I ask you to help me see the gifts of this life, and to learn from them the lessons that will go on beyond the person I see in the mirror today.

"With harm to none and for the good of all, the sacred circle is cast, and bears witness to my spell. Blessed be."

SPELL WORK: Gather your writing supplies. Before you start, look into your mirror and say, "I see you. I honor you. You don't have to be perfect. I love how you try. I love how you hang in there. I love who you are."

Spend some time writing one or more letters to yourself. You may want to do your letter writing in more than one session. Pace yourself; it can be emotionally draining work. Multiple letters could deal with different parts of yourself that you love. One letter could be about your mistakes and what you forgive in yourself; another could be about your strength and what a miracle it is that you've survived the trials of life. Be creative and send loving respect to yourself in every way that you can think of.

When you are done with your letter(s), put it in an envelope for safekeeping. There is no need to seal the envelope, unless you want to. How would you spruce up a letter you were sending to someone you adored? Consider placing some dried flower petals in the envelope or spraying a bit of your favorite scent on the pages. Don't use essential oils, though, because it might erode the pages.

CLOSE UP SHOP: Visualize the energetic light you have cast around your sacred circle and allow it to fade back into the elements as you say, "North, east, south, west, spirit, I give honor to you once again. I thank you for your blessed presence in my sacred circle. As you return to the elements that bore you, I affirm that you will carry my positive energy and that you will manifest it in my life. With harm to none and for the good of all, so shall it be."

After this ritual work is done, store your love letter(s) in a safe place so you can revisit them when you need a boost.

This is a good exercise to do in group work as well. It's a great way to model self-respect to younger womxyn and girls.

• • • • • • •

When you begin manifestations that involve major life changes (like welcoming a new partner into your life), it is probable that your life and habits will begin to shift and change. This will likely happen before you even meet your new squeeze; divine intelligence will be preparing you for what you asked to receive.

RIDE THE TIDE: SPELL TO PREP FOR MANIFESTATION

When you are calling a new relationship into your life, you want to take your time. This spell, based on the phases of one moon cycle, gives you a month to practice. In the interim you have a chance to journal, meditate, think, learn, and otherwise prepare to make the most of your spell. During this time, fill your life with the grace and beauty of love. Flowers, music, movement, your personal sexual practice, and bodywork are a few examples.

This spell has two parts, which I've called low and high tide. During the final phase of the waning moon and new/dark moon (low tide), you will fill a jar of water with things you feel no longer serve you. You will charge another jar of water in the final phases of the waxing and full moon (high tide) with the new things you wish to add to your life.

IDEAL TIME: Three days around the new/dark moon (low tide) and three days around the full moon (high tide).

PREPARATION AND ITEMS TO GATHER:
- Two jars or bottles of water that are safe for drinking.
- Journaling materials.
- Materials that will raise your love vibration, such as flowers, music, or gemstones.
- Timely altars for each phase of the spell.

LOW TIDE: CASTING AWAY WHAT DOES NOT SERVE YOU

Two nights before the new/dark moon, set out a jar of water so it can receive the energy of the moon. You could set the jar on a windowsill, your porch, the dashboard of your car, or wherever makes sense to you. Just make sure it is a flat surface so the jar does not tip over.

For the two nights before the new/dark moon, visit your jar before you head to bed. Take it in your hands and spend some time focusing on it while thinking about what you want to get rid of in the patterns of your life. Visualize the energies of these patterns entering the water in the jar, knowing that they will be diminished by the powers of the moon. Typical thoughts and patterns might have to do with:

- Low self-esteem
- Trauma
- Poverty
- Addiction

- Bitterness or jealousy

- Depression

- Pessimism

- Anxiety

- Fear

- Poor boundaries

- Sexual dysfunction or inhibitions

- Unhealthy anger or coping mechanisms

Journal or make lists about the items you are casting off and why. Also note anything you learn about yourself or your environment during this process. As the days progress, do you start to feel changes in your mood, health, relationships, or other areas? Is there any resistance (particularly from friends, family, or yourself) to the changes you are making? How are you handling that?

On the night of the new/dark moon, prepare an altar. Autumnal colors (deep blues, browns, greens, or even black) can be a feature. Stones that support diminishment include onyx, jet, hematite, kyanite, and shungite. Scents might include dragon's blood or copal, pine pitch (all tree resins), or a smudge of sage. Goddesses with the appropriate energy are of the badass variety; think Kali, Hecate, Morrigan, Sekhmet, or someone a little more chill like the Black Madonna. Of course, make sure to add any journaling or listing you have done to your altar. Finally, place your jar of water on your altar.

CIRCLE UP: Cast a clear, silver, or gold circle around yourself and your sacred space. You may want to cast a protective symbol, such as the pentacle or an equal-armed cross inside a circle.

SPELL WORK: Once more, visualize all the outgoing energy you put into the water. Say, "As the tide washes out into the sea, I release into this water all that doesn't serve me. The moon pulls the water in its courses, according to natural law. I release these energies back into nature's care so that they can serve a better purpose. Blessed be."

CLOSE UP SHOP: When you are finished thinking about the energies you are releasing (and perhaps why you are releasing them, using your writings if needed), let your circle ground into the earth.

Sometime soon after the ritual, take your water and dispose of it somewhere that seems fitting; you could use it to water a plant, pour it on the grass, or release it into a natural body of water. If you're getting rid of some particularly toxic sludge, you may even want to flush it down the toilet! Do whatever seems the most fitting and liberating for you.

HIGH TIDE: DRAWING IN WHAT YOU DESIRE

Just the way you set up the first jar of water, do so with the second. This time, however, you are working with the last two days of waxing moon that lead up to the full moon. As the moon phase charges the water, spend time each night focusing on all the great things that you wish to draw into your life. They might include:

- Romantic love
- A pregnancy
- Healthy eating habits
- An exercise routine
- Drinking more water
- Better sleep
- Healthy ways to cope with stress
- A better sexual practice (with others or self-partnered)
- Optimism
- Healthy boundaries
- The ability to use "yes" and "no" safely and successfully
- Forgiveness

Journal about what you would like to welcome into your life and why. In the meantime, do what "fills you up" with the things you want more of. Take baths, or at least soak your feet! Try some bodywork or a mani-pedi. Move or meditate to your favorite music. Work on your sexual practices and find what satisfies you (there is support for this in the next chapter).

Create an altar for what you wish to draw in. It should include symbols of the work you have done, perhaps including flowers, a kick-ass playlist, soothing scents, and so on. Color schemes might include gold, silver, pink, or green. Corresponding stones could be emerald, rose quartz, lepidolite, or fluorite. Scents I would use include rose, vanilla, vetiver, lavender, or citrus. The most important thing, though, is that you work with things that boost your own powerful sense of connection to all you wish to draw in. Don't forget your journal or your jar of waxing moon water!

CIRCLE UP: On the night of the full moon, create your sacred space in a way that makes sense to you. I might cast a light green circle of energy in the shape of a pentacle (my go-to sigil). Again, use what makes sense for you; a simple circle around yourself and your sacred space is just fine.

Take time to raise energy around the work you've been doing the past couple of days. Hold the jar of water and do some more work, reflecting on what you have filled it with and adding some more juicy positivity.

SPELL WORK: When you feel ready, say, "As the tide flows in, bringing all life-giving things, so I call to myself all the positive energies I have manifested."

If you are comfortable doing so, take a few sips of your water. Take your time with this. Allow yourself to feel hopeful. Let yourself feel, as much as you can, the way you will feel when these manifestations are yours. Express your gratitude for them.

CLOSE UP SHOP: When you feel ready, ground your circle by letting the protective energy either sink into the earth or rise into the heavens. Say, "I thank the divine intelligence and spiritual powers who work with me that my goals are met, perfectly and with harm to none. Blessed be."

Since this water is full of good vibes, you don't have to throw it out like you did with the new/dark moon water. You can drink as much of this water as you like or add it to a ritual bath. However you choose to use it, visualize yourself taking in all the energies of your moon-cycle manifestation.

• • • • • • •

Now that you're well grounded in self-respect, you can spend some time tuning up the love you share with others. The following spell is great for drawing a new relationship into your life. If you are already partnered, you could also tweak it to draw in positive change with the lover(s) you already have.

PUZZLE OF LOVE RITUAL

One of my coworkers came up with the "puzzle" analogy for starting a new relationship. When we first meet someone, we see an overall picture that we like. Getting to know each other is the phase where we're each trying to put the puzzle together, so to speak. We see pieces that fit easily and pieces we don't quite understand yet. When we see a piece that bothers us, we have to decide whether to stick with the puzzle because we still like the sum of the parts or if it's a deal-breaker.

Before you do this ritual, use the waxing moon to plan and construct your physical puzzle of love. Make your puzzle fun! I'm talking about a sort of collage that uses words, photos, magazine clips, or whatever inspires you to represent the love you desire. Include activities you like to do, imagining how your lover will support your activities and/or join you. I suggest using a piece of construction paper or stock paper as the base so your puzzle is solid enough to be cut into pieces. Bear in mind, this isn't strictly required; you could visualize your puzzle in meditation if you feel constructing the real thing is too much of a barrier.

IDEAL TIME: The waxing into full moon.

PREPARATION AND ITEMS TO GATHER:
- To make your collage, use construction or stock paper. You might also want glue, scissors, markers, glitter, photographs, bits of writing, magazine clippings, or sigils. Let your love desires play and have fun.
- Design an altar, leaving room for the puzzle as a centerpiece. Choose love correspondences of pink and green cloths, candles, and gemstones. Roses are the queen of love spells, but check out the section on flowers in this chapter for other ideas.
- Create or find a playlist that includes songs that excite you about love; the songs should make you feel good and upbeat.

- Anointing candles or gemstones with a love oil (like the Love Goddess Oil later in this chapter) would be beneficial. If you use wax candles, try carving some symbols such as the astrological sign for Venus or the classic Valentine's heart.

CIRCLE UP: Light any candles or LED lights and incense. Visualize a big heart creating an energetic field around you. If you're not feeling the heart, use whatever symbol you like, such as an ankh or pentacle.

Say, "I cast this circle so that all the correct energies and forces will join me in manifesting my ideal relationship. Blessed be."

SPELL WORK: Get comfortable in front of your altar and prepare to enter a light, meditative state. Close your eyes and count yourself down into a meditative state from five. Again; five, four, three, two, one. To draw in the correct energies for your love manifestation, say:

"Powers of earth, I call in the physical person of my beloved. Powers of air, use the ideas and inspirations to draw my beloved and I together. Powers of fire, ignite our passion and sexual desire for one another. Powers of water, align and activate our souls for uniting in this life. Powers of spirit, guide us to our correct relationship according to your highest wisdom and spiritual resonance. Blessed be."

Spend some time focusing on your puzzle of love. Go over the images that you assembled and what they mean to you. Inside the circle, discuss your desires and goals out loud. Saying what you want out loud is a step toward welcoming the reality into your life. Inside the sacred space of your circle, have an honest conversation with the spiritual and elemental powers you are asking to bring this manifestation to you. Have fun with it; let it raise your mood.

Take your time. Spend as much time as you need thinking about the relationship that you want to manifest. If you pick up pieces of your puzzle and handle them as you talk about why they are there, say something like "I call this to me" when you put them back on the altar.

All this emotion and all these thoughts will be empowered by your circle. When you feel finished, say affirmatively, "I have this relationship. Blessed be."

CLOSE UP SHOP: Extinguish any candles before visualizing the energetic symbol that forms your circle fading back into its source. Affirm that this energy will continue to help you manifest your goals. Express gratitude from your heart. Say, "The circle is open, yet the magick remains."

I recommend leaving your love altar assembled for the entire upcoming moon cycle. If you can't, just put your puzzle in a safe place. While manifestation begins immediately, it may take some time to call the right love in, so you may want to repeat this ritual periodically. If you eventually decide to free the energies, you can burn the puzzle or dispose of it in another way that you feel releases the energies. Another option is to keep the puzzle forever to remember what you asked for. It can remind you of the power you have to manifest your desires!

If it takes some time for your beloved to appear, work on other stuff! Stay positive and know that your beloved is coming. As my spirit guides have advised me, "Now is now, but now is also a process."

Keep notes on the effects of love spells, especially during the next moon phase. Be aware of potential partners who pop up as well as spirit messages about your love journey. These may come from nature, art, dreams, or other sources. Pay attention to repetitive symbols or other synchronicities.

QUICK DRAW CRUSH SPELL

If you meet someone and you think you really click, here's a quick spell you can do in order to get the gears turning. It uses a birthday candle or something else very small so that the whole candle can burn out very quickly.

IDEAL TIME: Whenever you meet someone! If you can wait until a Friday to do the spell, that is the best day of the week for love-based workings.

PREPARATION AND ITEMS TO GATHER:
- A birthday candle, preferably pink or white. Also, keep a chalice or bottle of water nearby when you burn a candle, no matter how small.
- Some ritual oil for anointing the candle.
- A dish of sand or salt to hold the candle safely while it burns.

• A quick altar with whatever juicy love correspondences you would like to add. You could grab items from your other love altars to connect more literally to the spells you've already done.

CIRCLE UP: Visualize an energetic heart (pink or red) around your ritual space and say, "I seek love, and I ask for the correct energies of the spiritual source to assist me."

SPELL WORK: Think about your new crush and picture them as clearly as possible. Say, "Love energies, deities, and guides, help me in this work. If there is something there, let it be found. Bring all correct energies and opportunities to bear. I love you and I thank you. Blessed be."

CLOSE UP SHOP: Let your energetic heart dissipate back into the spiritual source. Say, "I thank you for your assistance. I affirm that you are carrying my spell into the source elements for manifestation. So shall it be."

Now pay attention to synchronicities, opportunities, and other good things. Perk yourself up by revisiting chapter 3 and doing activities that make you feel really confident and good about yourself. Then see what comes your way!

• • • • • • •

I love flowers. It's probably because I live in New England and they bloom in our environment for such a short time each year. During the winter, I buy flowers from the store almost weekly to keep my spirits up. The following section will help you make the most of flowers, no matter the time of year.

Flowers: The Old-School Emoji

Back in the age of horse and buggies, flowers were basically an emoji. Your great- and great-great-grandparents got their flirt on by sending meaningful flowers to their sweeties or displaying said bouquets in the parlor during a visit. You may think this sounds really complicated, but they learned their shorthand just like we do.

When I was a weird romantigoth kid in high school, I preferred shopping at antique stores rather than malls. My dad loved to antique, so we often went together. He got me the book *The Language of Flowers* by Louise Cortambert, which was hot off the presses in 1835.[17] I've still got this little tome, so I thought it might be fun to resurrect some of the old romantic ideas about what flowers mean. Here's what they did with blossoms way, way back in the day:

- **Roses:** Reigning supreme in flower-land, the rose means love—not just one type of love, but the whole enchilada: grace, spirituality, and of course romance (and though the Victorians didn't say it, definitely sex). Though my old-school book didn't break it down like this, I've heard it said that white roses are for spiritual love, pink for self-esteem, and red for romance and sex. There are plenty more colors of roses; assign your own meanings if you'd like.

- **Violets:** Purple violets were for modesty (shyness) and white for candor (good at keeping secrets).

- **Daisies:** Innocence, childlike fun, and friendship. Perhaps you could send daisies to a new paramour to set up your first, ahem, playdate.

- **Carnations:** Pure and ardent (very hot) love. These also come in a variety of colors, so mix and match to make a statement about exactly what is making you feel ardent.

- **Lilies:** Perfect for getting your flirt on, although back in the day they called it "coquetry." How's that for a word?

- **Tulips:** A declaration of love. New love, especially, with this flower's springtime energy.

- **Daffodils:** Shockingly, the old-timers thought this sunny little flower stood for regret. This was because the flowers come and go so quickly on an early spring landscape, usually well before other flowers decide to show up. I prefer to alter the meaning while keeping the springtime metaphor; like, "Hey, I'm glad I just made it through a really tough time. Things are about to get better!"

- **Sunflowers:** Sunflowers represented … umm, the sun. Also, abundance and riches (like gold).

- **Hyacinth:** The flower for playing games. *The Language of Flowers* didn't specify whether this was a good or bad thing—you do the math.

---

17. Cortambert, *The Language of Flowers.*

- **Lilac:** The purple and lavender lilacs mean the first bloom of love (like that moment you realize you're in love). The white lilacs represented purity (resembling the spirit of a child).

- **Vervain:** Enchantment (that means magick)! Vervain lets them know, "I put a spell on you"—theoretically, of course! Even the churchy Victorians gave props to vervain as a druid herb, used throughout ancient times and cultures for divination and consecration.

- **Mugwort or St. John's Wort:** Happiness. *The Language of Flowers* specifically mentioned the folklore that St. John's wort casts away evil spirits, so sticking this in a bouquet signifies you're coming out of a funk.

According to *The Language of Flowers*, Victorian folks used to put a bouquet together in a way that would form a sentence. For instance, violets and lilies combined could mean, "I'm a little shy, but I think I really like you!"

If you feel inspired to, come up with some flower language of your own. You can make your flower language a whole lot racier than the old-timers dared to.

Here's a quick little blessing for your new bouquet, whether it's fresh-cut or from the market.

THREE-STEP FLOWER BLESSING

1. Trim the stems of your flowers and put them in a vase of fresh water. If your flowers came with a packet of vitamins to lengthen their life inside, add it to the water.

2. Before you display your flowers wherever you plan to give them a home, use your finger to draw a pentacle (or your symbol of choice) over the blooms. Perhaps you'd like to blow these types of symbols over the flowers with your breath to introduce your own energy.

3. Say, "I thank these blossoms for contributing their life force to my home and craft. May their loving and positive vibrations be a blessing to us all."

Consider keeping dried petals from your bouquets in a dish. Later, you can use the dried petals as ingredients in spell bags, potpourri, incense, or a smudge.

• • • • • • • •

Working with fresh ingredients like flowers and herbs always seems to add an extra bit of power to my spells. I like to work the following divination with a fresh apple. When you're done with the magick, you have a snack!

LOVE-LY APPLE DIVINATION

There were lots of old divination techniques (often masked as party games) that our European ancestors used to try to work love spells. In those days, the spells usually encouraged young girls to use apples to try and catch a glimpse of their future husband, or at least to learn the first letter of their name.

In spinstress craft, we like to be a little more proactive. The best way to find a great relationship is to take time to figure out exactly who you are. Otherwise, how can you know exactly what you want out of a lover? Therefore, I suggest the following meditation. The apple will help you find love by giving you a hint about how to do your own work.

Take an apple and a knife sharp enough to cut fruit. If you have an athame, you may want to use that instead. Then get into a proper space and posture for meditation. If you typically lie down when meditating, sit upright instead since you're going to be using a knife.

First, hold the apple in both your hands and say, "Maiden goddesses of love and light, show me how to find love and delight."

Cut the apple in half across its middle. A five-pointed star should be visible at the core. Don't brush the seeds aside if any have come dislodged—this is what you want to see. Work with whichever half of the apple has more visible seeds. If they both look good, you can divine with each half in turn.

The apple seeds are your divination tool. Turn one half of your apple clockwise just far enough for one of the points of the star to point straight up. This is the point witches tend to think of as the spirit point. The point directly to the left of the spirit point will represent north, earth, and body.

The one left of that will be east, air, and ideas. After that comes south, fire, and strength. The final point represents west, water, and love.

Pay attention to where seeds have been dislodged from the pentacle (the core) and have drifted away from the star. Which direction are they closest to? Each one of these seeds is literally giving you a direction for your journey toward true love.

Though I am now going to suggest some possible interpretations, you should always feel free to let your own intuition guide you. If the seeds are drifting toward:

- **North:** Work on body acceptance and self-esteem. This could mean things like working magick, buying some outfits, or joining a gym.
- **East:** Join a meditation circle or a book club. Choose something that inspires you and puts you in spaces with like-minded people.
- **South:** Conquer something that scares you. Take a class or have someone you know mentor you. For instance, you might choose to learn how to repair your car or practice self-defense.
- **West:** Get involved in a charitable cause that calls to you. This will boost your self-esteem and broaden your perspective on love.
- **Spirit:** Take some time to study your chosen spiritual path or patron deities through books or a class.

Love Goddess Oil

Feeling pretty tuned up in the love department? There's one thing that will make it even better! Nothing says "love goddess" like a heavenly scented oil blend to slather on your skin. This oil generates self-esteem and sexy feelings. Use it to massage yourself or put it on after you get out of the shower. It's also great for anointing candles before you cast love spells. This is my blend, but feel free to tweak the proportions of the ingredients until you find your perfect blend.

- ⅛ cup base oil (olive, almond, grapeseed, sunflower, etc.)
- 6 drops rose absolute essential oil
- 1–2 drops patchouli essential oil

- 3 drops orange essential oil
- An orange citrine crystal (can substitute clear or rose quartz)
- Optional: 1–2 small dried rosebuds or a pinch of crumbled rose petals from one of your love spells

Combine ingredients and store in a half-pint jelly jar. Charge under the light of a full moon. Before using or storing, say a blessing over the oil. Hold your hands over the jar and focus on the oil. Say something like, "I charge this oil by the energy of the moon, by the powers of the divine intelligence, and by my own arts to draw in powerful love." Store in a cool, dry place with the lid secure.

• • • • • • •

Unfortunately, the pieces in a puzzle of love don't always fit the way we hoped. There is no point in beating yourself up over this; the process of dating is about finding this stuff out. Sometimes you can be in a relationship for quite a long time before you realize that the things you were trying to work around are too much to deal with, and sometimes they are downright dangerous.

Calling It Quits: When and How to Break Up

In heteronormative relationships, womxyn/femmes often get the message that we are "lucky" to have whatever relationship we've landed in, and break-ups are often the partner's decision. Spinstress craft seeks to make you more empowered throughout this process. A spinstress must decide how to balance the needs of her partner with her overall happiness and life goals. She not only asks whether her relationship is working, she also asks if her own authentic purpose is being fulfilled.

Ending a relationship when you feel like you aren't getting what you need is hard enough. And sometimes no one is to blame, but it just isn't working. But deciding when a relationship is toxic—even abusive—brings its own challenges.

Loves Me, Loves Me Not: Warning Signs of Partner Abuse

I have worked in the intimate partner abuse prevention movement for twenty years, and I've learned a ton from survivors and peers. In general, womxyn are very giving in relationships. When we start to think we might be experiencing abuse, it's usually because we've tried to explain it every other way under the sun.

Therefore, if you think it's a problem, you should trust yourself. At the bare minimum, reach out to local professionals to get some advice. This can be done anonymously online or by phone. For starters, here are some tips to consider when you're trying to figure this out.

Do you think it's okay if the person you're dating tells you when your skirt is too short? Or when they tell you your friends take too much of your time? Is a little jealousy okay? How much is a little? We all have different comfort levels around these issues. That's okay. What isn't okay is the point where one person in a relationship is not comfortable anymore.

Intimate partner violence occurs when one person in the relationship uses a pattern of controlling behaviors to remove the autonomy of their partner. Here are some practical examples:

- They tell you who to be friends with.
- They regulate your time with your family.
- They monitor your activities, the way a parent might monitor a child.
- They punish you when you are wrong (and they decide when you're wrong, of course). The "punishment" could be anything from the silent treatment to hurting you, your kids, or your pets.
- They control your money or your ability to work.
- They demand sex when you don't want sex, or they demand a type of sex you don't want.
- They hit you, your kids, your family, or your pets.
- They threaten to hit you, your kids, your family, or your pets.

These are just examples, of course. Each relationship is different, and each controlling person's tactics are different. A controlling person does tend to be controlling no matter how many times they change partners. Controllers develop an almost innate sense of what it takes to get what they want, and they act accordingly.

Relationships are important. You may have worked long and hard to make your relationship work. That is what we are taught to do by society; we believe we should make compromises, be loyal, and hang in there with the ones we love. Of course, all of this is true—in the right relationship. A controlling partner will not respond to your trust, loyalty, or hard work by no longer being controlling; they like their control just the way it is, thank you very much. You may reach a point in the relationship where your well-being or even your physical safety is at stake. If you've ended a relationship that left you feeling burned, the following ritual may help you assess how you're dealing with it all and help you speed up the healing process.

To Hex or Not to Hex?

Before we dive into ritual work around the end of a relationship, I want to address the topic of hexing. While researching love magick, I found that many spells regarding an ex-relationship are framed as hexes. I just don't think this is the way to go. I believe all craft contains the potential for a full spectrum of positive and negative forces, but I almost never contemplate hexing. And even when I do contemplate it, I never do it. I just don't think it's necessary.

No matter how badly a relationship ends, you can reclaim your self-esteem and tend to your personal safety without risking any karmic blowback from attempting a hex. When dealing with the type of raw emotions and unfinished business often associated with a breakup, you must be especially careful to make sure you don't throw any boomerang hexes at your exes, because you will surely be the one who ultimately gets clobbered. Those spells are very tricky. Plus, you don't want to dabble when you're already hurting.

Magickal systems and religions often allow for a lot of personal responsibility when it comes to defining personal ethics. It's important for each spinstress to weave her own ethical foundation. I'll leave you to study the ethical suggestions of your path of choice. Just be aware that we magickal folks are no less accountable to spiritual realities than members of any other philosophy or religion. You can call it the Golden Rule, the Threefold Law, karma, or whatever you like, but the bottom line for nearly any group of people who study spiritual matters is that unseen energies and forces are part of our ecosystem. The energies that manifest all seen and unseen realities ebb and flow in ceaseless rhythms. Energies are never destroyed, only repurposed. With every cause comes an effect, and with every effect comes another cause. This ripple effect is an aspect of natural law.

I suggest that you ask yourself the following questions whenever you find yourself contemplating a hex:

- Do I feel the need for self-defense or am I mostly hurt and angry?
- If I feel the need for self-defense, what safety plans have I made prior to working a spell?
- Are there trusted friends, family members, or peers who can help me plan for my emotional and physical safety?
- What about my safety plan isn't meeting all my needs?
- Are there other types of spell work that might better fill this need, like a spell to build up my self-esteem and my energetic defenses?

If you go through this checklist and hexing still seems to be an important part of your strategy, then doing this advance work will help you clear up why you need a hex and how to craft that spell. It's generally best to stay within the realm of defensive magick rather than offensive whenever possible.

If you do decide to hex, try to frame it in a defensive way, such as "Stay away and do no harm." Casting harm won't be of any help to anyone in the long run. It will wound your own spiritual core and, if it works on your target, may cause unintended consequences to your own safety should this person be wounded and lash out.

In short, ideas about witches and wizards hexing their enemies are more from the outside world and from dabblers. People who really understand the energetic echoes of crafty work in terms of the rule of returns and cause and effect are too smart to throw curses and hexes at random.

"THANK YOU, NEXT!" RITUAL TO RELEASE AN EX (WITHOUT A HEX)

However a relationship ended, it can hurt. Even if the breakup was your choice and a great decision, it can cause haunting regrets. This ritual is meant to help you cut those cords and move on.

IDEAL TIME: Begin your prep work a day or two prior to the new moon.

PREPARATION AND ITEMS TO GATHER:

- An altar containing items that represent yourself, your ex, and your relationship history. The tone of your altar will depend on the context of the relationship you are letting go. It may be moody and beautiful or Gothic and pissed. Go with what feels cathartic, healing, and helpful for you. Consider including the symbol for Mars, the planet of strength, sex, curse-breaking, and even vengeance (better framed as self-defense).

- The colors of Mars are red and orange. Other colors you could include are black, which absorbs negativity and is common in banishing, or purple, which can evoke strong healing and even exorcism. Blue and green are good colors for healing and moving on.

- Three one-foot lengths of twine or yarn. I recommend choosing a different color for each length of twine.

- Scissors or your athame to cut the twine. Scissors will probably be best—at least have some as backup if your blade can't, well, cut it.

- If you'd like to incorporate oils, you may want to have a healing/protective blend on hand for anointing yourself or your candles. Lavender, orange, cypress, and myrrh are some popular choices. Follow your own intuition.

- If you'd like to incorporate gemstones, I recommend emerald, hematite, jet, kyanite, shungite, or onyx.

CIRCLE UP: Visualize a black or red pentacle protecting your sacred space. Say, "I affirm my craft is powerful and good. As I work this spell, protect all involved and let my will be done. So shall it be."

SPELL WORK: Braid your three pieces of twine together as you say, "Past, present, future. All interwoven, all in my hands. I take from the past to inform my present. I claim my power to shape what lies ahead." Chant this as you braid, saying it at least six times. When you've finished braiding, hold your braid and feel the heat of your energy building up in the braid.

When you feel ready, take the scissors or athame and prepare to cut your braid in half. Before you do so, say, "Past cut from present, cut from future. I celebrate the opportunities the universe will provide me. I give thanks for the lessons of the past as I ground myself in the present and prepare for the future. I release what is no longer needed. Divine wisdom guides me by the hand. Help me make my ideal future. For the good of all, so mote it be."

CLOSE UP SHOP: Dissolve the pentacle around your sacred space while saying, "I give thanks that my work has been done correctly and with harm to none. I look forward to a bright future and the best possible of new beginnings. So shall it be."

I recommend disposing of the braid by burning, burying, or another safe method that makes sense to you. As the moon darkens and then begins to wax back full, be prepared for wonderful things!

Picking Up the Pieces

Mainstream culture does a great job of celebrating marriage and commitment. However, idealizing marriage as perhaps the most important marker in one's life can lead to certain pitfalls like the following:

- You aren't a "real" adult (or even a successful person) until and unless you've been married.
- Marriage can fix the problems lurking within the relationship.
- Loyal and virtuous people never "give up" on a commitment like marriage, which is a failure if it isn't "till death do us part."

Most of us can easily identify the problems with these deeply seated cultural beliefs. Using marriage as a "fix" for relationship problems is often an explosive disaster. In some cases, trying to make a relationship work no matter how toxic or violent it becomes creates untold damage and danger. In all too many cases, "till death do us part" takes on the worst possible meaning.

Slowing our pace when it comes to wedding bells would ameliorate some of these issues. But society also needs to be better at acknowledging a simple reality: People change. Relationships change, too.

Ultimately, we have to learn to forgive ourselves (and others) when our relationships don't turn out the way we'd hoped. Communities of womxyn also need to support one another in this process. Spinstress craft celebrates both the thoughtful and loving creation of relationships and the thoughtful and loving dissolution of relationships. We must acknowledge that relationships may evolve (or devolve) to the point where they should be reframed or ended entirely.

STRONGER IN THE BROKEN PLACES: RITUAL FOR AFTER DIVORCE

The following ritual can be performed alone or with a group of supportive sisters. Feel free to adapt the ritual to help you heal from any rough breakup.

We will be making use of an effigy that is commonly known as a poppet. The poppet work to heal your broken places after an important relationship ends may be done in solitude or incorporated into a public hand-parting ceremony. Do whatever feels right to support your own healing.

IDEAL TIME: The new moon or a Sunday.

PREPARATION AND ITEMS TO GATHER:
- A magickal doll (poppet) that represents you. This can be a homemade paper doll, a corn doll, or a Barbie doll—whatever works for you. Ideally, whatever poppet you use to represent yourself as you heal and move forward should give you a positive feeling. Let it represent aspects of yourself that you love and respect.

- When choosing colors to use on your altar, aim for colors that represent healing, compassion, and unconditional positive regard. The color pink has corresponding energy for this sort of energetic work. White pulls out and repels energies, making it good for rituals that remove incorrect energies and forces. Incorporate pink or white candles, gemstones like rose quartz or clear quartz, or actual flowers like rose or Sweet William.

- Have a dish of salt on your altar that you can use while casting the protective circle. If you'd like, add some rose petals to the salt.

CIRCLE UP: Take your dish of salt and turn with it in a clockwise (deosil) direction as you say, "I cleanse this space of all incorrect energies and forces. With harm to none and for the good of all, so shall it be."

SPELL WORK: In energy work, the left and right hands are widely believed to have opposite energetic currents. The left draws in energy and is for receiving; the right projects energy out and is for casting.

Sit comfortably with your poppet held in front of you or cradled in your lap. Hold your left hand up toward the sky. As you say the incantation, touch the poppet's corresponding body part with your right hand. Say, "I acknowledge that endings can be painful. Yet, I myself am always being renewed. I affirm that the spiritual force is healing me in the broken places following this painful transition. Let this poppet serve as the conduit through which I receive my blessing. Head be blessed with inspiration and with healing thoughts. Throat be empowered to speak my own truth. Heart be healed from old wounds and made open to new blessings. Belly be nourished by what is healthy and be a source of empowerment for my body. Sex be healed of all that was deficient and empowered to accept what is worthy. Legs be strong to carry me on my forward journey. Feet be blessed to stand always on holy ground."

Now, turn the palm of your left hand toward the floor (or touch the floor, if you are sitting low enough). Still touching the poppet with your right hand, say, "I claim the grounding and healing influence of the earth energies to aid me in thriving on my journey. I am grateful for the life I have within me and all the time that I have yet to claim. With harm to none and for the good of all, may I be blessed."

CLOSE UP SHOP: Pick up your dish of salt and turn counterclockwise (widdershins) to open your circle. As you do so, say, "I affirm that this ritual will continue its healing work even after it has returned to the spiritual source. This circle is open, though the magick continues. With harm to none and for the good of all, so shall it be."

Leave your dish of salt on your altar or in another prominent place for up to one month (one full moon cycle) before disposing of it. One way to remove ritual salt is to mix it with water and apply it in pavement cracks, which will remove weeds.

Abundance Magick

Part of the decision to remain in a relationship or to end it is usually financial. Your romantic partner is likely also a partner when it comes to things like rent, groceries, transportation, and more. One of the toughest parts of independence is making ends meet. It sucks, but money matters. The following spell invites abundance while ensuring you can make independent decisions.

"IT'S NOT EASY NEEDING GREEN" PROSPERITY SPELL

This spell is going to help you work on how you think and feel about money. Many of us have feelings of guilt tied to money. Wealth and poverty are loaded concepts in society, and they leave a psychic mark.

This ritual will develop your money mantras so that you have more control over your relationship with wealth. In magick, it is often said that "energy follows thought." How you think about money isn't everything, but it does matter. From now on, try to catch yourself when you use what I call *language of lack*. Language of lack might sound like, "I can't afford that" or, "I don't have any money." Instead of "I can't afford that," I recommend something like, "I don't want to spend my money on that right now." See the difference? The second phrase gives you more power. It acknowledges that you have money (even if it isn't as much as you want or need). It also expresses your power over the money you do have.

This spell brews up some financial abundance to help support your daily hustle. As with other magick, this spell can and should be partnered with a plan of action.

IDEAL TIME: The waxing moon, the full moon, or a Thursday.

PREPARATION AND ITEMS TO GATHER:
- An altar cloth in green or gold, the colors that correspond to wealth magick.
- The largest denomination of paper money that you can bear to set aside for this work. The money will need to stay in the offering dish for about a month.

- An offering dish to hold the money on your altar. This can be as simple or as fancy as you'd like it to be.
- If possible, use a wax candle that is green, yellow, or gold. If you can't use a real candle, green, yellow, or gold LED lights will also help set the mood.
- Almond oil draws abundance, so anointing candles with this would be a great idea. Carve pentacles or the symbol for the money god, Mercury, into the candle wax for an extra energetic burst.
- A smudge stick or incense. I recommend frankincense, myrrh, amber, or patchouli.
- If you'd like to incorporate flowers, marigolds and carnations are good options.
- If you'd like to incorporate herbs, sprinkle chamomile, sage, or cinnamon into your offering dish.
- Optional: Lodestone is included in many financial spells.

CIRCLE UP: Place your money in the offering dish. Use a fragrant incense or smudge stick to consecrate your sacred space. This form of casting may leave a residual scent on your money that lingers even after it reenters your wallet later, which will reinforce the spell in your mind. As you smudge, say something like, "I consecrate this sacred space. Let this be a space of abundance and wealth. So mote it be."

SPELL WORK: Light any candles you're using and get into a comfortable position to meditate. This will be a light meditative state.

Gaze at the money in your offering dish and think about a positive money mantra you can use. I suggest something like, "I have enough. I will receive and am receiving enough. I do good for myself and others with my cash."

Hold the money in your hand and say, "I have money. It is mine to keep or to spend as I choose. I am good with money. I can help others and myself with my money. There is always enough money for me to tend to my own needs as well as to do good. When I spend money, it returns to me with abundance to spare. Money is good for me to have and to use. I am grateful for the money in my life."

Say any money-positive mantras you can think of. When you feel ready, end with, "With harm to none and for the good of all, so mote it be."

CLOSE UP SHOP: Use your incense or smoke again. As the smoke dissipates, visualize the energy of the circle also clearing. Thank the powers for helping you with this work.

Keep the money in your offering dish for at least one cycle of the moon. You can return to the altar, cast your circle, and repeat positive money mantras as many times as you'd like during this time period. After the moon cycles back to the same phase that it was when you first performed the ritual, you are free to spend the money in your offering dish. When you spend it, you are releasing it back into the elements for your will to be fully manifested.

Since the cash on your altar is now extra-magickal money, be thoughtful about how you choose to spend it. If you need to use it to pay a bill or buy some food, that's fine. If you can give this money to a charitable cause, affirm that you will always have enough money for yourself and for others and express gratitude for this. No matter when or how you use the money, remind yourself as you spend it that your needs are always met.

Repeat this spell as needed and continue to hone your money-positivity mantras.

JOURNAL PROMPT

Write down some of your previous attitudes about money. Your relationship with money has likely changed over the years, depending on what challenges you were facing at the time. Then answer the following questions:

- Has your attitude about money changed?
- What are some of your current money mantras?
- List the positive things you already do with your money. What else would you like to do?

PROSPERI-TEA

A little kitchen witchery can help with any goal. While you are waiting for your personal abundance to manifest, have a sip of this moneymaker tea.

Mix a base of green or white tea with a teaspoon of dried parsley. Parsley corresponds with love, money, and lots of other good things. Sweeten your tea with maple syrup or maple sugar. Maple draws in sweetness and abundance. If the abundance you seek is more of the emotional, romantic, or sexual type, add some dried rose petal.

As you drink your prosperi-tea, say, "As I draw in the nourishment of this tea, my life draws in abundance. There is enough of everything that I need freely available in nature. Blessed be."

MAGICKAL FLOWER POWER PARTY

Drawing in more abundance in life is also about celebrating what you already have. This ritual is meant to be done with a group of like-minded friends and family. I picture this being a house party–size crowd (a dozen people or less), but it can be adapted for larger groups or worship services.

The sharing of flowers draws in the beauty of community. Everyone's offering is diverse yet equally sweet, and the final product is always amazing!

IDEAL TIME: The waxing moon, the full moon, or a Friday. Since fresh flowers are used, it will be easiest if this event is held during the peak growing season for flowers in your area. That way, people can bring wildflowers from their yard if they wish.

PREPARATION AND ITEMS TO GATHER:
- Plan what music you will use during the spell work. Depending on the resources of your group, you could invite a member to play live music, choose a song for the group to sing, or play recorded music selections. Make sure you have song lyrics printed and that at least one group member has learned the tune in advance and is willing to lead the singing.
- Set your altar with items that increase the energies of love and compassion. For gemstones, rose quartz, clear quartz, and amethyst are great gems. I also recommend incorporating floral herbs like rose or calendula petals and lavender buds.

- Scent the air appropriately. Spritzing rose water is probably a better option than burning heavy incense. Alternatively, you could use an essential oil diffuser and add rose, lavender, or jasmine essential oils.

- Each person who attends the party should bring a flower (or a bouquet) in a vase of water. The more flowers, the merrier. One way to set up the room is to put one flower from each person in a big vase and then spread any remaining flowers around the room. Follow your intuition; celebrate the diversity and beauty of your flowers in the way you put them around the room.

CIRCLE UP: Circle up and, looking to one another for your cues, cast a circle of sound by having everyone chant their own name. The tone doesn't matter; it will sound great if everyone participates. Have one person lead this process so participants know when to begin and end.

Allow the sound of the chanting to grow gradually louder. It doesn't have to become a shout, but you want energy to be raised around your circle.

After the leader ends the chant, the leader or another designee says, "Through the beauty and power of our combined names, the sacred circle is cast. Let this be a space filled with self-acceptance and sisterly love. Blessed be."

SPELL WORK: One designee reads the following:

"Like the flowers of the earth, each one of us is beautiful and perfect in our own way. Like the flowers of the field, we all give gifts of beauty and nourishment to the creatures of earth. Flowers pollinate the planet. Flowers create beauty and joy. As womxyn and girls, we create life. As womxyn and girls, we manifest love. In this spirit, I invite each of those gathered here to now select one flower and take it back to your place in the circle."

Play music while you allow time for people to select a flower and return to their spot. If you want to sing a group song, this is a good time to do so.

Once everyone has selected a flower and returned to the circle, one designee says, "Like these flowers, each one of us is beautiful and unique. Look at your flower and think of one unique quality that it has. As you value the uniqueness of your flower, also value the uniqueness of others.'"

Invite each circle member to briefly share what they admire about their flower. Also invite them to share a quality that they share with their flower.

Make it known that all circle members have the option to pass if they'd rather not share.

CLOSE UP SHOP: As you did while opening the circle, have each attendee chant their name. This time, let the sound of the chanting dissipate gradually into silence. Once there is silence, one designee says, "The energy of this circle now returns to the elements. We affirm that it carries with it the positive vibrations of our love. Go forth into the world, but remember that you, like a flower, are beautiful and unique. Blessed be."

After the ritual, encourage people to sample from the different flower arrangements and to take home bouquets that represent the shared energy of the group. If flowers are left over, one or more attendees can leave them out as a nature offering or gift them to someone.

chapter five

HAVING SEX (AND NOT HAVING SEX) ON YOUR OWN HOT TERMS

Okay, let's talk about sex. It's something grown people need to learn how to do. Vast amounts of media about sex are largely problematic because of uncritical biases about sexual and gender identity, size diversity, race, religion, and so much more. Yet, the media's messages wash over us and often influence an individual's feelings about sex.

If you can't talk about sex, you and your partners (if you choose to have partners) miss out. It's like walking into a great restaurant and, without benefit of a menu, feeling confined to whatever entrée you saw in a commercial the night before. From available partners to sex positions, frequency, and the negotiation of relationship roles, everything can and should be wonderfully up to debate.

With that being said, you can get sexy without a partner. The trendy term for masturbation is *self-partnering*. It's the new name for the oldest sex in the books. Far from being a shameful act or the last choice you should have to make, self-love is actually essential. Modern sex educators and therapists are on the ball (pun intended) by pointing out that you have to experiment on your own before you can communicate what kind of sex you like with your partner(s).

Yes, I said *communicate*. It's a great time to be alive, girls. Talking dirty is in. Not only is it in, it's the sexually mature and responsible thing to do. The boring (but also accurate) terminology for this is *active consent*. In other words, you should talk about sex with your potential partners—and your established partners. A lot. Some examples of active consent include:

- Do you like this?
- Would you like to (do this)?
- I like it when you (do that).
- Could you (do this)?
- Show me how you like (this).
- Can I watch you (do this)?

Not rocket science, is it? But many people are terrified to talk to their partners about what they want. As long as you are choosing partners who are safe and caring people, these nerves are usually due to a lack of role modeling and a lack of practice. Sometimes it's also because you don't really know what you like; that brings us back to self-partnering. Think of it as the best homework ever!

In this chapter you will find rituals, spells, and other helpful tidbits that celebrate—and perhaps even help you begin—a super-steamy sex life that you love. Not only does sex feel good, sex does good. It tones your body, regulates your hormones, and helps stabilize your mood. Sex is magickal, and I don't just mean that good sex feels supernatural. Sex is a powerful manifesting machine! Remember the Cone of Power Ritual from chapter 1? Well, one very effective way to raise that pointy hat high is through sex. We will discuss sex magick in this chapter as well. You'll get a couple of chances to try it out so that you'll be equipped to design your own sexy rituals. Is all of this sex talk making you nervous? Wait until I get to the wonderful world of sex toys.

When prepping for a sexy spinstress journey, you may find that you have some old baggage you'd like to exchange. This could be sexual trauma. It could also be the toxic sludge that accumulates in people after years of being exposed to sexist, heterosexist, and other unhealthy sexual cultural tropes.

The more a culture exploits and abuses sexuality itself, the more that important aspect of yourself is taken away from you or weaponized against you. It's time, my sisters, for all that shit to *stop*. You may not be able to change the whole world (at least, not in one spell), but you can damn well do something about your sex life. It's time to learn how to love and unleash the power of your passion.

First, however, let's check some of our sex baggage at the door. Be kind to yourself during this process, and don't give up. Womxyn, you're worth it.

I'm Your Venus: Rites for Sexual Healing

There are a ton of ways that womxyn experience wounding of their sexuality. By sexuality, I am referring to several qualities, including but not limited to:

- How you see yourself as a sexual person
- How you think others see you (what type of partners you "deserve" or are "in your league")
- Whether you think you can or should ever say no to a sexual request or demand
- Whether you think you can or should ever say yes to a sexual request or demand
- How vulnerable you can or will be with your sexual partners (how much you allow yourself to be present and emotionally honest)
- How honest you feel you can be about your own wants and needs (turn ons/turnoffs)
- Whether you feel you have the right to ask for safer sex
- Whether you feel safe to express your authentic sexual identity
- How relaxed you can be in an intimate or sexual moment (which has a lot to do with your—and even your partner's—enjoyment of that moment)

Womxyn's sexuality can be wounded because of sexual abuse or sexual assault. It's also possible to be quite wounded by social pressures. This might include familial pressure and societal pressure that can be as overt as bullying but as covert as advertising, rude jokes, or the secondary trauma of observing the sexual wounding of our friends and loved ones.

The most wounding social messages are often oppressive ones that include some combination of racism, sizeism, ableism, heterosexism, ageism, and so on. These types of messages are so insidious because they function to limit oppressed people not only by empowering bullies, but also by teaching these targeted folks to self-limit. Those of us who get ongoing oppressive messages absorb them in ways that impact our chosen professions, hobbies, and health, including sexual health.

The spinstress path empowers you to be a whirling dervish who recognizes and rejects these insidious limiting messages. Not that it's quick and easy. It's part of your journey, and it may take active effort for your entire lifetime. Yet, if we support one another and do the work, there will be victories and moments of absolute bliss that make that journey worthwhile.

Venus (Aphrodite) is a particular goddess concerned with this topic. As a goddess of love and beauty, she is often minimized by being associated with hearts and flowers. But she had provenance in Roman culture over punishing pedophiles. Over centuries of working with witches, she moved beyond baby-making and love potions to take charge of healing for victims of sexual trauma.[18] Venus knows that healing, strength, and self-esteem are keys to real love.

Harness your Venus energy in a quick and easy way by looking in a mirror and visualizing a pink or gold pentacle (a symbol sacred to Venus) surrounding your reflection. Say something out loud that is positive and authentic to yourself. Yes, it has to be out loud. Practice makes perfect.

You could say something like "You are beautiful" or "You have great eyes." If it's a struggle at first, at least say, "I respect you. I love you. We're going to be okay." Allow your mirror affirmations to change over time. When you're done, absorb the energy of your pentacle into your body and thank Venus for infusing it with some healing self-confidence.

Besides the spells and rituals that this book recommends, there are basic daily activities that a savvy spinstress will recognize as more healing rites. To

---

18. Monaghan, *Encyclopedia of Goddesses and Heroines.*

work on issues of body shame and sexual wounding, try any of the following rites and practices:

- The colors pink, gold, and green all correspond to love and healing. Collect items in these colors like clothing, snuggly blankets, candles, and novelty light bulbs to throw some healing shade.

- Get a massage or other bodywork. If you have experienced sexual wounding, being touched by someone else might be extremely stressful. A massage is one rite you can undertake to start to spin a new framework related to touch. Bear in mind, you could start with a hand massage or a foot massage from a trusted friend. Reiki or another type of light touch energy work is a less invasive option. Diving right into the towel-clad spa experience is not required. Think about what might be a reasonable first, second, and third step in getting some bodywork done.

- Get (or give) mani-pedis with a friend. As mentioned with bodywork, starting with fingers or toes might be a less intense way to get used to letting other people into your personal space. Caring for and decorating your fingers and toes, which you can easily look at and enjoy, is a way to increase your feelings of body positivity and positive touch.

- Change up your wardrobe. You could do this in an economical way, like taking part in a neighborhood clothing swap. Look for colors and styles that make you feel sexy, happy, and like the real you. It isn't necessary to take a wrecking ball to your whole closet; you could just clear out a few things you never wear and add one or two new pieces of spectacular spinstress regalia.

- Try a new hairstyle. Your hairstyle is an aspect of yourself that is an indicator of personal flair and self-love. Getting your hair done isn't as invasive as some other types of bodywork.

- Take classes about sex positivity or attend groups that focus on it. There are increasing options for this type of work, either in your locale or online. Do this on your own, with your honey, or with a pal. Due to the very nature of sex positivity, most of these opportunities are open to people of all sexualities, but do some research before diving in. If a business isn't trying to be open and inclusive, it probably isn't all it was cracked up to be.

- Visit a sex-positive sex toy shop. Again, this could be in your town, on the web, on your own, or with someone you love. Get referrals for these types of places through a sex-positive hub.

- Investigate sex-positive books and programs that reflect diverse sexualities and body types. Look for educational and artistic materials that represent folks who resemble you and folks who don't. Diversity tends to reflect equality, which is a must-have on the path to positivity. Seeing the beauty in a vast array of people and aesthetics will help you value your own.

- Do love magick for yourself. On a waxing moon or a Friday, anoint yourself in emotionally loving scents like rose, vanilla, or amber. Soak in a tub infused with these scents or use the oils in an essential oil diffuser. Visualize yourself surrounded by soft, pink light. Choose a self-healing and self-loving mantra like, "I respect myself. I love myself. I am deserving of every good thing, and good things are coming to me."

These are some everyday places to start when you want to celebrate the rites of sexual healing.

Morning Yoni Scan

Many of us have less than a passing familiarity with our lady parts. Society may have left you feeling shame about your body, plus they are really hard to see without a mirror. But did you know you can talk to your sex organs? The following body scan technique can help you develop this practice if you'd like to.

For ease of discussion, I'll call the whole package the yoni. No matter what procedures you have had or what anatomy may have been altered or removed, your spiritual and energetic yoni is still there.[19]

---

19. Lister, *Love Your Lady Landscape.*

First thing in the morning, or maybe right before bed, try developing a practice where you check in with your yoni. You can access this area in a few different ways:

- Cup your vulva in the palm of one hand.
- Rest one or both hands over your lower belly so that your energy and focus goes within.
- Let the fingers of both hands form a triangle that rests over your pubic triangle (the area surrounding your clit).

Now let your consciousness go to the area under your hand. Do you hear, see, smell, or feel anything? Try humming or singing to see if your womb has a tune.

In chapter 7, I talk about spirit prayer, where I let my voice do things I'm not consciously planning as a sort of energetic prayer offering. Sometimes it is a sort of language and sometimes it is musical. I had the sudden inspiration during my practice one day to put my hands over my womb area and see if that part of my body wanted to "pray." I immediately found myself singing in a particular type of vocalization that I now know only comes from my womb.

If this idea appeals to you, experiment with it. Perhaps your yoni will want to express itself in some other way. Does it yell? Giggle? Cry? Sculpt? Paint? Your yoni is powerful. No matter what stage of life you are in and what your yoni has or hasn't been doing, she's a core part of you who has something to communicate.

BLESSED BATH SOAK FOR SEXUAL HEALING

One of the most common tricks when you need a little self-love is to take a warm bath. That sudsy water can feel like a hug. Boost the magick of your soak with the following recipe.

PREPARATION AND ITEMS TO GATHER:
- A cloth drawstring bag often sold for making tea, or any mesh/cloth drawstring bag that will keep herbs from leaking.

- A pinch of dried seaweed, either bought or collected locally (bladder wrack is ideal).
- Dried rose petals.
- Four apple seeds.
- A small seashell and/or a small quartz point.

SPELL WORK: Fill the cloth bag with your ingredients. The size of bag will dictate the amount of ingredients, so use your intuition. Tie the bag securely closed.

The next time you take a bath, place the bag in the water, as if you were making a big cup of tea with you in it! While you soak, spend some time chanting the following: "In the name of Venus, I am renewed. By the power of three, blessed be."

Look at your body in the tub and know that it is renewed. You are whole. Your future sexual life is yours to define and enjoy. When you are finished with the bath, stay in the tub while the water drains. Know that all you wish to release from your sexual past is draining away with the water to be reused and renewed by the elemental powers. So mote it be.

A History of Sex

Soon we'll be getting into some very sexy magick. This may feel very new to you. It's important to note, however, that the idea of sex for pleasure is not a new one. Modern people did not invent sex toys. Greco-Roman culture was filled with phalluses, as you will see if you visit virtually any museum of ancient history.[20]

A realistic stone dildo, for instance, was found in Germany. It is thought to be about twenty-eight thousand years old. Archaeologists had trouble admitting this was clearly a dildo. They even suggested that it could have been used for sparking flint and starting fires.[21] Well, it probably did start fires—in the bedroom. Anyhow, the embarrassment modern historians have about the sex toys of old are because of modern norms, not our ancestors'.

---

20. See Eisler, *Sacred Pleasure* for more information on phalluses throughout history.
21. Amos, "Ancient Phallus Unearthed in Cave."

Another seminal example, if you will, are all the stone and ceramic man parts on display in remains of places like Pompeii. The trove of penises made the moderns who discovered them clutch their pearls. But phalluses, yoni eggs, strap-ons, and anal plugs were in use during ancient times across many cultures. And while some were purely artistic, many others were *not* for show.[22]

Archaeologist Marija Gimbutas documented Neolithic sculptures (about six thousand years old) showing masked men and womxyn (interpreted as priests and priestesses) enacting sexual rites. You can trace sacred sex through time. By the time modern occultists like the British Wiccans of the 1970s got hold of this "great rite," it was already way old-school.[23]

It seems ironic to me that modern culture doesn't mind exploiting bodies and sex (particularly womxyn's bodies and sexuality, though not exclusively) to sell everything from barbecues to automobiles, but it's often seen as offensive to talk about vaginas, penises, or sex in healthy and empowering ways.

For instance, my rural town produced *The Vagina Monologues* as a fundraiser for local domestic violence and sexual assault agencies. A few vocal locals went nuts about the word *vagina* being on the theater marquee. They said it was offensive and that it put them in a horrible position because they had to explain the word *vagina* to their kids. (By the way, that was the point, and *you're welcome.*) American culture has such double standards about sex, especially for womxyn and girls.

I've encountered this double standard repeatedly in my work in the violence prevention field. It's at the core of what we in the field refer to as our "victim-blaming society." People have spent so long listening to society's messages that womxyn's bodies can and should be exploited that there is now a deeply held belief that womxyn and girls are actually morally or intellectually unable to make those judgment calls for themselves. Our bodies are treated like things (objects) that womxyn are not smart enough, or good enough, to wield ourselves.

In workshops and retreats that I have attended about sexual empowerment and sex positivity, I've realized that womxyn are treated as though our

---

22. McKennett, "Bizarre History of Sex Toys."
23. Eisler, *Sacred Pleasure*, 63–64.

sexuality (and our bodies) are dangerous weapons. It's as if womxyn's bodies "cause" violence. Our bodies "cause" sex crime. Our bodies "cause" child abuse. Our bodies and our sexuality "cause" the murders of many womxyn. There is a toxic—and entirely untrue—idea that womxyn "cause" bad things to happen to themselves (think about when victims of sexual assault are asked, "What were you wearing?"). But this idea extends into womxyn's families and into society as a whole. Since this is taught generationally and culturally—subconsciously or otherwise—there is no visible end to the loop. We believe it, we receive it, and we pass it on. That's a heavy burden, sisters. Let's set it down.

I tell you this because I really believe that healing your sexual self is a huge starting point for doing all the rest of your loving and important work. This could be the topic of an entire book, but I am only introducing you to a few sexy concepts that you can try out. Beyond that, check out the recommended reading section at the end of the book for other resources.

There are many womxyn and men doing the good work of sexual healing. You can do sexual healing regardless of what age or stage you are in. You can do sexual healing whether you have partners or are self-partnering. If you have some sort of physical or emotional trauma that remains a barrier to your healthy sexual self, seek out a trusted professional. There is help out there to overcome any obstacle. Sisters, you don't have to do it alone.

If you take what I have to offer you in this chapter, the world is your sexy, sexy oyster. The first rule of healthy sex is to be loving and kind to your hot self. Okay? As the maiden says, "Play."

Your Sexy Wonderland

You're probably about to receive your greatest homework assignment ever. I want you to look into the following list of sex toys and consider adding something new to your repertoire. I'm not saying you need to break the bank buying everything on this list, but explore what's out there. And if you are already well supplied with sexy toys and gadgets, it may be fun to spice things up. Some of the sexy toys and tools you may want to gather include:

- **Vibrators or Dildos:** These are the tools that people tend to think of first. But don't underestimate them! Dildos, as we learned in our history lesson, can be made of many materials and have been used throughout human civilization. Nowadays you can buy them with handles for easier reach, with attachments that allow for clitoral stimulation, or with two phalluses so two partners can have simultaneous penetration. They even sell dildos for long-distance use for partners in different locations, usually controlled via a smartphone app. With vibrators there are even more options. You can use a vibrator on a clitoris, a prostate, and a penis (erect or flaccid).

• **Rings:** Cock rings go at the base of the penis, beneath the scrotum. They keep the blood in a penis longer and often increase sensation. If you have sex with a partner that has a penis, this may help both of you! They also sell cock rings with vibrator attachments that hit the clit during vaginal penetration sex. You can attach one of these little buzzers to a dildo to turn it into a vibrator.

• **G-Spot Barbells:** These odd-looking creatures are usually made of stainless steel (or sometimes of stone) and are built to curve inside the vagina and apply steady pressure to the G-spot. These are good toys to use if you are trying to increase your vaginal sensitivity or chase the holy grail of female ejaculation. Check out yoni eggs for many of the same effects.

• **Anal Plugs:** These toys are built to penetrate and stimulate the anus. Both men and womxyn find this pleasurable, and it can deepen orgasms. Some vibrate or work by remote control! If you have men in your life, encourage them to use anal toys to engage in prostate massage that can tone their organs, regulate hormones, and otherwise protect their health.

• **Gemstone Eggs, Plugs, and Wands:** We will explore the use of the yoni egg later in this chapter. For now, suffice to say that some sex toys are made of gemstones and allow for an additional layer of sex magick. Any gemstones you put in your body should have a Gemological Institute of America (GIA) certification so that you know what they're really made of. Harmful chemical dyes and certain minerals can be absorbed if you insert unsafe gemstones into the vagina or rectum. For example, you should never use tiger's eye, moonstone, lepidolite, or sodalite as sex tools or toys. Make sure you research the proper way to clean your gemstone toys.

- **Harnesses:** Harnesses have many uses. They are commonly used with dildos to penetrate a partner. Womxyn can use this setup to penetrate partners of any gender. People with penises use harnesses and strap-ons too! Some folks wear a strap-on kit for the way it makes them feel, not for sex with someone else. The harness's options are limitless!

- **Sex Furniture:** Cushions, benches, swings, and pillows designed for sex improve the ability to reach your or your partner's sexy areas. They also improve comfort—and therefore stamina. Sex furniture is made for people of all sizes. It's great for self-partnering as well as partnered sex.

Remember that lube is a sex toy too. It is often very important for a safe and pleasurable experience, especially if you have a condition like vaginismus. There's a trick to it, though. We magickal folks like to use our special oils; I've put several of them in this very book. I want to point out that oils and latex *do not* mix. If you use any oils—including oil lube—condoms will break or lose effectiveness. Latex toys will deteriorate. Did you know an oil massage you had several hours earlier can damage latex, even if you have showered? This is because oil can cling to your body (not to mention if you've used it internally). In summary: Use non-oil lubes or non-latex everything else. So, as you prepare the following consecration ritual, avoid the impulse to anoint your latex toys with any oils.

One more thing: always clean your toys after use (and before, if they're new or haven't been used in a while). Research the proper way to clean your toys; most waterproof toys can be cleaned with water and special soap.

Okay. You've now inventoried your sex toolkit. Maybe you have added something new. The following sex toy consecration will give you a chance to add an extra blast of power to those little beauties.

SEX TOY AND TOOL CONSECRATION

You may want to use your toys (have sex, self-partnered or otherwise) during this ritual. I'm leaving the option open! If you are having sex with another person, make sure you both brainstorm your magickal goals in advance so you are working together with full consent. And if you decide to use your toys during this ritual, you will obviously want to arrange your sacred space accordingly.

IDEAL TIME: The full moon is ideal, but you can really do this anytime. Spend the moon phase prior researching toys and tools, perhaps adding some to your collection.

PREPARATION AND ITEMS TO GATHER:
- Plan your sacred space around physical comfort for whatever you plan to do in this ritual. You may have to work around a couch or your bed. If you invested in new sex furniture—or pulled some old out of storage—set it up in advance.
- You don't have to set up a full altar. Instead, create a kit of sexy goods for yourself. Include your toys, lube, lotion, and a few clean towels. If you aren't sure where to store your toys, I recommend a nice wicker laundry basket lined with satin sheets.
- If you choose to incorporate color magick, consider the use of receptive black or fiery red. Ultimately, though, it's about what makes *you* feel sexy.
- Sexy correspondences include red roses, garnet gems, and incense featuring vanilla or musk. Remember, don't use oils with any latex toys or prophylactics.
- As always, be ready to journal about your insights or experience.

CIRCLE UP: Visualize a rosy pin or red circle of energy surrounding your entire ritual space. Say, "I cast this sacred space, within which I will consecrate and empower my sexual practice. May all energies that love me unconditionally support me in this. Blessed be."

SPELL WORK: Pick up and honor the toys and tools you have gathered. Or, if you prefer, pass your hands over the collection to infuse them with your blessing. Say, "I honor and celebrate my sexuality with these gifts. I give thanks for them. May these sacred objects enhance my sexual practice and therefore increase my joy and my power."

You can spend some time singing or chanting in order to raise energy over these toys. What would be even more fun is to use at least one and have sex inside the sacred circle. Set your magickal intention ahead of time, which is to charge these tools and toys with the sacred energy you deserve in your sexual temple.

When you are done raising energy in whatever way you do it, take some centering breaths and prepare to open the circle.

CLOSE UP SHOP: Let the sacred circle dissipate back into the spiritual source while you say, "I thank you for participating in my sacred work. Please carry the positivity of my casting back to the spiritual source. I know that as I share good energy, more will be returned to me. Blessed be."

Spend some time journaling if you wish. Now that you have your toys and tools prepped, work on developing a regular sexual practice, however that fits into your life. This could be tantric meditation, sex solo or with a partner, or something else. Decide for yourself how often you will do this practice and make a commitment to it.

• • • • • • •

One of the coolest sex practices out there involves crystal eggs made specifically for vaginal use. These magickal creatures have been used to treat bladder incontinence, painful penetration, vaginal dryness, and all sorts of things. The use of a gemstone in this way can also invite your whole glorious body into the manifestation of your spells.

Bear in mind as you read about these eggs that I am not a doctor. I suggest that you read my thoughts about these little gems and then follow it up with some research of your own. If you find that a yoni egg works for you, it can be a real gift for body and soul.

The Magickal, Marvelous Yoni Egg

You may have seen the term *yoni egg* in my earlier writings. Yoni eggs originated thousands of years ago. Based on archaeology, they may have originated in China.[24] Essentially, yoni eggs are little polished gemstones that go

---

24. Diaz, *How to Use the Yoni Egg for Sensual Healing.*

in your vagina. They come in different sizes and different stones, but jade is considered the queen.

This may seem like little more than a wacky trend. Believe me, sisters, these little gems are a gift. They are great both physically and spiritually. Some yogis and Reiki masters incorporate them into their practice. The medical benefits of yoni eggs are gaining notoriety as well. Both emotionally and physically, yoni eggs are being used to treat sexual dysfunction, tone and heal the vagina after pregnancy, help with incontinence, and more. Yoni eggs are not only medicinal; they help womxyn with vaginal lubrication and sensation and increase pleasure during sex.[25] Yoni eggs are also used to treat conditions related to menopause, menstruation, and sexual trauma.[26] Of course, if you are incorporating a yoni egg, use common sense and get medical advice as needed.

I want to discuss one condition these gems help with because it was part of my journey, and I think this may be important information for some of my sisters. Have you ever heard of the condition vaginismus? It basically means that the vagina clenches involuntarily. It leads to painful penetration and makes that kind of sex difficult, scary, or even impossible. Some womxyn have it so severely that they cannot insert a tampon or have a full gynecological exam.[27]

I struggled with this condition for most of my life due to childhood sexual trauma. The problem was that I didn't know that's what I was struggling with; I just felt broken. Lots of things helped me with this condition over time, including my spirituality. Another tool has been the yoni egg. If you are dealing with issues where you know or suspect that your sexuality is a factor, it may be worth giving yoni eggs a try.

Of course, most of the community using yoni eggs has gotten into them around holistic or even allopathic (mainstream) healing. But gemstones have a full range of ritual correspondences. You can engage your sexual energies and those parts of your body by trying yoni eggs. Incorporating yoni eggs

---

25. Diaz, *How to Use the Yoni Egg for Sensual Healing*.
26. Starr and Lemmon, *How to Use Jade Eggs*.
27. Stachel-Williamson, *Stop Painful Sex*.

into your practice is a great way to connect mind, heart, and womb/sex. You may find that this heals you on many levels and produces powerful results.

It's important to know that not all stones are safe to insert in your body. Due to mineral composition, the following stones should not be used as sex tools or toys: tiger's eye, moonstone, lepidolite, and sodalite. Make sure you purchase your yoni egg(s) from a verified seller who is not using chemical dyes to fool you into buying a cheaper stone. The certification body for gemstones of this type is the Gemological Institute of America (GIA). Look for GIA verification when buying your stone.[28]

Also, please remember yoni eggs are not to be used in the rectum. They will not get lost in a vagina, but they can get lost in the rectum—you don't want to have that conversation with your doctor. Check out gemstone anal plugs and prostate wands if that's more your thing.

I highly recommend you do some additional research on these babies if you plan to try them out. No need to reinvent the wheel (or the egg).

Now, on to some practice!

YONI EGG FULL MOON MANIFESTATION

This ritual is designed to help you dedicate yourself and open yourself to your own sexual empowerment and joy. I therefore suggest using either a rose quartz or jade egg. Acquire and practice with a yoni egg beforehand if you are going to try this ritual; this shouldn't be the first time you are using your egg. With that being said, you can put your yoni eggs on your altar and practice using them as altar amplifiers while you are trying them out.

IDEAL TIME: The full moon.

PREPARATION AND ITEMS TO GATHER:
- Your altar can incorporate healing and self-loving correspondences like pinks, whites, golds, and greens. The rainbow works great also. Add statues, art, and sex toys that celebrate your body. Let your altar push you toward the sexy, empowered place you would like to get, even if you aren't there yet.

---

28. Diaz, *How to Use the Yoni Egg for Sensual Healing.*

- Your yoni egg (again, I recommend rose quartz or jade).

- You will be "birthing" your egg in some way. Since you have been practicing with it for a while, you should know by now what works for you. Decide whether you want to remove the egg in the bathroom before you cast a circle or whether you would like to do this in the circle (and how). Consider what you might need, like hand wipes or a towel. It is optional to clean your *amrita* (the tantric term for vaginal fluid) from a yoni egg during sex practices; do what seems right for you.

- Have a place of honor for your yoni egg to sit on the altar after you remove (birth) it from your body. Eggs rest well on the tops of certain candleholders or vases. The stands they sell for a scrying/crystal ball may work. You may even be able to find a vintage egg cup at an antique store. If you like, you can build a "nest" for your egg out of herbs and flowers; store your nest in a cup or dish. Do what seems fun; let yourself play.

- As part of the ritual, you will be invited to spend some time celebrating your sexual energy. You might like to dance, drum, create art, or do something else that seems authentic for you. Prepare what you need accordingly.

- Your journal should be nearby, along with stuff to write with.

- If you'd like to incorporate scents, roses, jasmine, or lilies are great flowers to include. You could also use rose, jasmine, or lily incense or essential oil. Spikenard essential oil has a high spiritual vibration that can really bless this work.

CIRCLE UP: Visualize a cosmic egg shielding and defining your space. Make it whatever color you like, or let it be a rainbow. Say, "I celebrate the cosmic mother egg. Protect and incubate my magick and myself within this sacred space. Blessed be."

SPELL WORK: If you haven't already "birthed" your egg prior to casting the circle, do it now in whatever way you have chosen. Say, "I give honor to this gemstone egg and to my own sexual being."

Once the egg is in its place of honor on the altar, spend some time praying, singing, or chanting over it. Remember it has fused its energy with that of your vagina and womb. It is a link to those parts of yourself. Spend some time feeling what you need to feel and saying what you need to say. You can stop and journal at any point.

When you are ready for the spell, say, "I open myself to be in full relationship with my sexual self. I receive my sexual dreams, sexual desires, and sexual feelings. I reawaken to and welcome my sexual body. I love and accept all of my sexual body, especially all that has been denigrated or wounded by others or me. I love and accept all that I am. To my sexual being, I say that we are strong now. We can be safe coming out to play. I will take care of us. It is time for power and pleasure now. I open to receiving, giving, and being within this high-vibrational sex energy. Blessed be."

Again, spend some time singing, chanting, drumming, dancing, creating art, journaling, or whatever feels right for you.

CLOSE UP SHOP: Allow the cosmic egg that you cast around your space to "crack" and dissipate. Say, "I affirm that my manifestation is born! That which my egg and I incubated will now be manifested. Blessed be."

Over the rest of this moon cycle, pay attention and journal about any manifestations from your spell. When you are ready to take your altar down and put your yoni egg back into active duty, consider charging it by the light of the next full moon. Clean it well with warm, soapy water before storing (or reusing).

Over time you can adapt this same idea in other spell work. For instance, you could use the new moon and an onyx egg to expel unwanted sexual energies. There's no limit to how you can design spells and rituals that include yoni eggs.

• • • • • • •

Okay, we've got a nice collection of sacred sex toys and tools by this point in the chapter. It's time to think about safer sex. This is an ethical imperative for yourself and your partner(s), should you choose to have them.

SAFER SEX SELF-DEDICATION

Womxyn need to set healthy and well-informed limits around sex. Whether your relationships with partners are long-term or casual, the use of latex (or latex-free) gloves, condoms, or medical contraceptives are the responsibility of both partners. Getting safer sex items is easier than ever with the technology and resources now available.

Family planning and womxyn's health centers usually provide safer sex education and supplies for a sliding scale fee, or even for free! If you haven't yet, consider setting up an appointment to go over the best types of safer sex precautions and pregnancy prophylactics that may apply to your life. Go with a trusted friend or family member if this is a difficult issue for you to discuss due to trauma, bullying, or abuse. The more forthcoming you are with the healthcare provider, the more on-point his or her suggestions will be.

When you have decided what your safer sex routine will be, it's time to do your self-dedication ritual. The surest way to crystallize safer sex habits is to clearly decide what they are and then dedicate yourself to these boundaries. You're basically making a promise to yourself; to the best of your ability, you'll make sure your sex is safe.

IDEAL TIME: The waxing moon, the full moon, or a Friday.

PREPARATION AND ITEMS TO GATHER:
- A bell or wind chimes.
- A safer sex go-bag with the types of items you want to use (or already use). You can include your gloves, dams, condoms, lubes, toys, or anything else you would like to consecrate as part of this dedication to sexual self-care. Remember to go with non-latex protection if you plan to use any kinds of oils in sex or ritual. Whatever you gather for your safer sex dedication, lay these items out on your working surface (altar, bed, table, floor) in the shape of a circle (a shield).
- Seashells, amethyst, or rose quartz are good additions to your sacred space.
- If you've survived a secular Valentine's Day, you already know that red and pink are powerful colors for both love and sex. Mix in whatever colors correspond with the energy you want to raise. Green is a common healing color. Feel free to rock your rainbow pride as well.
- Lavender is a sacred herb that corresponds to higher spiritual energies and helps to attune to your spiritual source.

- If you like incense, something containing amber and/or rose has a very warm, healing feel that works wonderfully in love spells.
- Go for brassy bonus points by performing this ritual in sexy negligee or similar boudoir garb.

CIRCLE UP: Use a bell or wind chimes to cast a sound circle. As you listen to the tones, affirm that their vibrations are defining your sacred space.

SPELL WORK: Visualize your safer sex aides as both a physical and spiritual shield that will protect you as you enjoy the gifts of your sexuality. Say, "I charge these items to serve as my shield of knowledge and safety. I commit myself to safer sex practices for my own good and for the good of others." (Say a few words about the safer sex habits to which you are committing.) "I thank the spiritual powers for giving us the gifts of our sexuality. With harm to none and for the good of all, so shall it be."

CLOSE UP SHOP: Use your bells or chimes again and as the sound fades away, know that the circle has dissipated as well. Say, "The circle is open. Blessed be."

Sex Magick and a Ritual to Own Your Sexy Powers

So, you've got your sex toys consecrated, and maybe you're literally rocking it with a yoni egg or two. You've got your lube on lock. You know some good tunes for your sexy playlist. You may have played with ritual sex when you consecrated your tools and toys. Now let's really get into it! I want to help you bless and commit your own practice of sex magick. Sex practices in sacred space can be complex and highly ritualistic or simple and au naturel.

Erotic energy packs a very powerful magickal punch, but the idea of having sex (self-partnered or otherwise) might leave you feeling embarrassed or ashamed. If you're feeling really nervous about engaging with the spirituality of sex, you may want to check out some simple tantric breath work. Trying a yoni egg is another way to "wake up" your sexual body and start developing a greater sense of your whole self. Your sexuality is a part of you. A healthy and self-honoring sexual practice will help you tune in to all your sexy powers.

Sex magick isn't simply getting off. It isn't like the stereotypical visit to the sperm bank where a guy is given some racy magazines and asked to go fill a jar. Magickal sex has to be focused, just like any other casting. At least, it's supposed to be. There are times when sex itself is considered sufficient magick; for instance, *eco-sensuality* encourages having sex (solo or partnered) in nature as an energetic offering to the planet as well as for your own benefit.

It takes practice to hold a ritual (or any) intention while having sex. Therefore, there is a lot to be said for using a sigil for sex casting. (I go into detail about drawing sigils in chapter 9.) When you create a sigil, you are boiling your intention down into a representative artistic form. Keeping your sigil near you or somehow drawing it on yourself (or your lover) for a ritual is also effective.

Instead of crafting a sigil, you could create some artwork, use a photo, or write a brief and concrete intention down on a piece of paper. Look at any of these visual cues during the sexual practice in order to trigger your intention. Keep the verbiage low. For instance, if you are casting for some cash, you might want to say, "Money comes" (pun intended). It's okay to have fun!

Sexy Self-Dedication

This ritual is written for you to do solo. (Remember, if you do sex spells with a partner, both of you have to know what you are casting for.) It is meant to help you inaugurate (or recommit to) your sex practices. The intent is "My sexuality is powerful and good." Short and sweet!

If you need to wrap your head around this idea, spend some time journaling about it prior to the ritual. Does the phrase seem silly to you, or is it empowering? Does it seem hokey or absolutely true? Does the idea of your sex being powerful or good excite you? Scare you? Anger you? There's no judgment on any of these responses. Take the time you need to think about it, but don't be afraid to push yourself a little. You don't have to be totally certain that your sex is good and powerful in order to do this ritual—you just need to *want* to be totally certain. If that's true for you, give it a try.

IDEAL TIME: The full moon or a Friday.

PREPARATION AND ITEMS TO GATHER:

- Design a sigil, scroll, symbol, or other artistic representation of the intention "My sex is powerful and good." If you use a sigil, you can draw it on paper or on your body using nontoxic paint or makeup. You could also trace it on yourself with oil (as long as you're not planning on using latex anytime soon).

- Have your sex supplies ready to go. You've got a sexy bag of tricks if you've worked your way through the chapter.

- If you use playlists, pick tunes that resonate with you. As I've said before, lyrics may not help you retain your focus. Music should not trigger self-criticism or any other negative feelings; sexy, good vibes only.

- On your altar or in your bedroom, incorporate love colors like pink, gold, red, or whatever works for you. Flowers might include roses, geranium, or lilies. Consider including Venus incense (ingredients can be found later in this chapter).

- Make sure you also have some drinking water handy.

CIRCLE UP: Cast a five-pointed star inside a circle in honor of Venus. A hot pink or red pentacle is recommended. Say, "I honor my own body and the powerful gift of sex. I know that my sex is good. It feels good and it does good for me and others. I claim this as safe, sacred space."

SPELL WORK: Have your sigil or goal present. Say, "I affirm that my sex is powerful and good. Venus (or divine intelligence), thank you for helping in this sacred work. As my sexual energy climaxes, I affirm that my goal is sent to you for full manifestation."

Meditate or listen to music for a while while periodically looking at your sigil or other artistic representation. Repeatedly affirm aloud, "My sex is powerful and good." If negative thoughts intrude on you, say, "No thanks." Push them away by repeating again, "My sex is powerful and good."

When you feel ready, raise your sexual energy however you like, whatever that means to you. Many folks like to try to focus the rising sexual energy up toward their third eye chakra. Follow your intuition. Remember, you have already set the intention that your climax will complete the spell.

After you have climaxed, spend some time meditating or journaling before opening the circle. Drink some water also. If you do not experience climax, that is fine. Simply raise energy for as long as you like and then say something like, "I offer this energy to the spiritual powers in order to manifest my intent."

CLOSE UP SHOP: Let the pentacle dissolve back into the spiritual source. Say, "I give thanks that my sex is powerful and good. May Venus (or divine intelligence) use this offering in correct and loving ways. From now on, I know that you will honor and empower my sexuality as well as my craft. Blessed be."

• • • • • • •

Sometimes it is your sexual identity that requires a little affirmation. The following ritual gives you space to celebrate who you are and how this informs your special place on this earth.

"BORN THIS WAY" RITUAL TO CLAIM AND NAME YOUR SEXUALITY

Whether you are living the dream with the identity you were born with or you have decided to claim another, this ritual and spell work will help you honor the true you. This ritual uses a birthday candle, symbolically bringing you a fresh start. You may even wish to perform this ritual on your legal birthday or a new birth date of your choosing.

IDEAL TIME: The waxing moon, the full moon, your birthday, or a new birthday of your choosing.

PREPARATION AND ITEMS TO GATHER:
- Prior to beginning the ritual, take some time to journal about your authentic identity. It may be a good idea to journal through the moon's waxing phase and perform the ritual when it's full. Your journaling may be focused primarily on your sexuality, gender identity, spiritual beliefs, or something else. Some questions you might want to ponder

include: What name do you wish to be called? Is it the one you were given by your parents or something else? How have you come to realize what feels authentic for you? What identity markers are important for you: hair, makeup, clothing, body art? Is your identity closely tied to your spirituality and faith, romance and dating, and/or creativity and art?

- Prepare for the ritual by choosing your wardrobe, your music, and what to place on your altar. If you already built a personal power altar, you're mostly there. Add photos, art, statues, gemstones, and powerful items of any type that represent your authentic self.

- Have a mirror on hand. This could be the mirror you used in chapter 3 or one chosen specifically for this ritual.

- Grab a birthday candle and matches or a lighter. The birthday candle's color is personal preference. This is all about you!

- Have a dish of salt or sand to hold the birthday candle after it has been lit.

CIRCLE UP: Chant "Om" three times in order to stimulate all your energetic centers and ground yourself in your body. As you finish chanting, visualize a circle of your favorite color casting a sacred space. Affirm, "My circle is cast. Only correct and loving energy may enter here."

SPELL WORK: Light your birthday candle and place it in a dish of salt or sand to hold it upright. As it burns, review your journal entry by looking at what you wrote or using your memory. Look into your mirror and affirm your identity by saying, "My true self is correct. My true self is good. My true self is benevolent. My true self is sexy. My true self is funny. My true self is a great companion." Add any other affirmations that are important to you.

Look into your mirror and call yourself by your chosen name three times. Say, "I am committed to loving and living my authentic self. I affirm that my world will be remade and will be populated by people, circumstances, and opportunities that honor and love me as I am. Blessed be."

If your birthday candle hasn't burned itself out yet, meditate and enjoy your chosen music until it does. As the smoke of the candle dissipates, know that your spell has been cast and is going forth to manifest itself through the spiritual source.

CLOSE UP SHOP: Chant "Om" three more times and visualize the circle dissipating back into the spiritual source. Safely dispose of your candle and matches, if you used them.

• • • • • • • •

We've been clocking a lot of hours on sexy spells and rituals. The following incense recipe, dedicated to one of the most famous love goddesses, is a great addition to any of the work in this chapter.

VENUS INCENSE

Venus is often seen as little more than a Roman knockoff of the Greek love goddess, Aphrodite. It's true that they were both sort of combined over time, as often happens with deities and myths. But Venus definitely has her own thing going on.

Blend up this incense when you are looking to add more sex and passion into your life. One of Venus's symbols is the five-pointed star. As an additional shout-out to Venus, you could challenge yourself to use five ingredients in your incense.

All of the following ingredients are associated with Venus. If any of the flowers listed are in season and growing in your yard, using your own stuff is optimal. Gemstones are optional. Choose from:

- Apple blossom
- Damiana
- Emerald
- Evening primrose
- Hyacinth essential oil
- Jasmine essential oil
- Jasper
- Lemon verbena
- Rose
- Rose absolute essential oil
- Sandalwood essential oil

- Spikenard essential oil
- Thyme
- Tonka bean
- Turquoise
- Vanilla bean
- Vanilla essential oil
- Vervain

If desired, loosely process your herbal ingredients with a mortar and pestle. Combine your ingredients in a dish, dream pillow, or red pouch. Place your hands over the incense and focus your energy on it as you say, "Magickal elements, be joined in sacred union to create a blissful and life-giving new thing. May these sweet and lusty scents create this same energy in my life."

Use this blend as potpourri or an offering (indoors or out), or burn it as incense once everything dries. Don't burn your gemstones, of course; you can reuse them for similar work later or put them out in nature as an offering. Fridays are the best day to do this because that is Venus's sacred day of the week.

• • • • • • •

The last tool in your sexy new kit is a magickal mascot. Far more than a horny horse, the unicorn adds empowerment as well as fun to our craft.

Magickal Creatures 101: Unicorns

Lots of kids nowadays go through a unicorn phase. Add magick and fantasy to the already-appealing horse and you've got daydreams on steroids! Like dragons, unicorns are beloved because of the inspiration that they evoke. The fact that we have never seen one isn't a deterrent. In fact, it's part of their allure.

People see unicorns in many ways. They may be creatures from faerie realms or even the purely imaginary trappings of fantasy books. But it doesn't matter if you see them as nature spirits or angels; they remain precious to us because they evoke the feeling that enchantment is afoot (on four feet, in fact). They represent the power and potential of belief.

In today's slang, the word *unicorn* often sarcastically refers to an unattainable ideal. I have heard it applied to adult virgins, a winning lottery ticket, a parking space in Manhattan, and even to the concept of "humane" meat. And though these applications are modern, they get to an ancient idea: Chasing the unicorn means to chase an ideal. And the prize that you desire is often an intangible one like love, happiness, or spiritual enlightenment.

Unicorns go *waaay* back in human history. Like dragons, they were once believed to be quite real. They were included in the literature, art, and natural histories of many different cultures. Four thousand years ago in the Mesopotamian cradle of civilization, unicorns were portrayed as one-horned bulls. Descriptions of them in the Hebrew testaments made them sound like either cattle or rams. The explorer Marco Polo described a creature that sounded closer to a rhino. Only in India did the ancients seem to think it was at least part horse, though Strabo reported in 24 CE that these Indian creatures had the head of a mono-horned stag.[29]

Perhaps all this shape-shifting is a necessary part of the unicorn. As a spirit animal, they represent transformation. Even the ones that look like horses seem to be a bit of animal cracker soup. You may have seen medieval tapestries that depicted a white, horse-like unicorn. But if you look closely, you will see that many of them bear cloven hooves, a billy-goat beard, or even a lion's tail. Some look more like deer than horses.

But there are themes. For instance, the creature is most often portrayed chained to the ground in a pen or lying on the lap of a pretty girl. What's up with that? Why is the medieval unicorn so often asleep in the lap of a young woman? Perhaps it is symbolic of the idea that pure and well-meaning humans can befriend wild, even supernatural, beings. This is a good train of thought, but the historical artwork has a different meaning. In the medieval period, this imagery had layers of meaning. A lot of it had to do with the civilizing virtues of a well-behaved, chaste woman. This wasn't a feminist sentiment; it actually used the societal ideals of a virginal, innocent, obedient, and conforming female as a cudgel to keep all womxyn in line. The unicorn as a creature was always described as incorrigible and wild. To tame one meant

---

29. Zell-Ravenheart, *Grimoire for the Apprentice Wizard*, 330; Matthews and Matthews, *Element Encyclopedia of Magical Creatures.*

you were perfectly civilized. Nature dominated by culture; the primal tamed by the chaste. These were monarchical, patriarchal ideals from the European Christianity of the times.

But religion has often floated above a cultural undercurrent of sex. During this same period, the unicorn in the lap of the lady came to represent concepts of courtly love and faithful marriage. A beautifully dressed noblewoman entices the horny horse (otherwise known as a stud). I know I don't have to draw you a map, or even weave you a tapestry. In fact, medieval mythology held that there were *only* male unicorns. In a rigid patriarchy, this makes sense.

A unicorn, half horse and half something else, endures in mythology as a perfect psychopomp. A psychopomp is a guide or messenger between realms. Typically, this means between the realms of life and death (or this world and spirit world). Ravens, crows, vultures, and some other creepy critters have historically been seen as psychopomps. The unicorn is a realm-crosser as well. As a psychopomp with traits of physical, ethereal, and overt sexual overtones within its human mythologies, the unicorn is a powerful partner in sex magick—but we need to get past the old-fashioned stuff about kings and virgins.

After reading this section, I bet you are full of more information about the mythology and symbolism of the unicorn than you ever expected. Now what? Here are some of my takeaways:

- As a spirit guide, the unicorn can empower you to embrace the sexuality you want. The unicorn is also a good partner who can help carry your wishes across the realms.

- The hunt for the unicorn teaches you to be clear about your goals. When you seek the spiritual, are you looking for personal enlightenment or personal power? Mind you, power isn't inherently negative. But if you do seek power, you should also ask why. How do you intend to use it?

- As the ultimate symbol of wildness, the unicorn also informs your relationship with nature. Perhaps it is one function of the unicorn's shape-shifting appearance to teach us that it represents all animals.

- If you were to meet a unicorn in a quiet glade, would you commune with it for a while and then go your separate ways, or would you pen it up and tether it to the ground? If you summon the unicorn, is it for partnership or to capture a prize? The quest for this self-knowledge is part of the quest for the unicorn.

• You rock the energy of the unicorn when you dress how you want, say what you want (kindly, when possible), stand up for others when you see they need it, claim your authentic identity, and push back against racism, sexism, heterosexism, ableism, etc., in your quest to treat others fairly.

There is a growing market of people interested in using gemstone wands for sexual healing and magick. Some of these wands are twisted to form something similar to a unicorn horn. This is a great tool to use in your healing sexual practice as well as your sex practices for self and others. If it appeals to you, think about working with the powers of the unicorn to claim the sexuality that you want.

Journal Prompt

What does a unicorn look like to you? What animal(s) does it resemble? What color(s) is it? You may have heard the phrase "Always be a unicorn." What does that mean to you? Perhaps it means to always be your own enchanted, special, unique self. Maybe you interpret it to mean that the shape-shifting unicorn is telling us not to fear change or to hold true to our ideals. How can you embody the energy of the unicorn?

part two

MOTHER: PASSION

The mother births more than children, although this role remains very important to a vast array of womxyn. Mother energy empowers womxyn who raise kids, care for elders, engage with their communities, and support others. "Mama bears" are fiercely protective of others when their intuition tells them it is warranted. The roles of the creatrix and activist highlight other common uses of mother energy. In these roles, they "birth" creative projects, political systems, social services, and spirituality. Activists use the protective mother energy to defend the ecosystem, creatures, and their loved ones. Womxyn of all ages embody these traits when they change the world, protect life, and provide for future generations.

> *The message of the mother is: "Remember passion." The mother calls you to creativity, whether you birth children, activism, art, or all three. This is the time to give your gifts to the world.*

In most mainstream cultures, motherhood is equated only with childbearing. Certainly, this aspect of the phase is very important. Without it, none of us would exist! I am going to touch on traditional mothering in this chapter since it is something that many spinstress womxyn do. (If you'd like more than a brief exploration into motherhood, there are *so* many books out there, including in Pagan circles.) Statistics show that single motherhood has greatly increased in recent decades, which is no shock as strict societal norms about monogamy, marriage, and housebound mothers are eroded.

Generally, evolving societal norms are a good thing. However, the blowback is that womxyn have to bear the full responsibility of parenting more and more often. Recent Pew Research Center studies indicate that the United States—where I am writing from—has the highest global percentage of single-parent households. And when it comes to single parents, the mother is the primary custodial parent in more of these arrangements.[30] Therefore, I'm including spells and rituals about parenting in this chapter, including how to empower magickal kiddos and talk to youth about gender diversity. But the area I think we really need more conversation about is womxyn who don't bear or otherwise raise children.

Womxyn without Children

Womxyn who do not have children are a rising demographic in the developed world. I have sat with other childless womxyn from around the world (since I myself am one). Here are some of the reasons we discussed for both chosen and unchosen childlessness:

- Medical issues, including those to do with sexual abuse, assault, and trauma

- Sexual wounding or trauma that delayed sexual partnering with others and/or made us not wish to bring children into the world

- Unstable and/or violent relationships took up many of our childbearing years

- The choice to terminate the pregnancies that were a result of assault or domestic violence or to place the child for adoption

- Legal loss of custody of children to partners or child welfare services (often due to domestic violence, addiction, mental health, and/or poverty issues for one or both parents)

---

30. Pew Research Center, "Religion and Living Arrangements."

- Lack of economic resources to support children during our childbearing years, in partnered or unpartnered households
- War, global politics, and/or refugee/immigration status issues that separate womxyn from their children, lead to the death of their children, or otherwise prevent them from raising families
- Need or desire to focus on career instead of childbearing
- Lack of desire to bear children, as a single person or as a partnered/shared decision
- Desire/calling to spend our lives focusing on other forms of creativity and "mothering" (often to do with religion, art, and/or activism)

Wow! Did you ever stop to think about all those reasons? And there are more. It really shouldn't come as a surprise that so many womxyn are pouring creativity and love into endeavors besides childbearing or child-rearing. Some womxyn I have spoken with feel this is part of the divine plan for their lives.

When I sat in a circle with other childless womxyn, it was with womxyn from the United States, England, Germany, Sweden, Australia, Portugal, and who knows where else. Yet the stories were so often the same. More than this, the pain and heaviness in that space was immense. I think this has a lot to do with the pressure womxyn still feel to make children the core of our lives. Another possible reason is that this topic simply isn't discussed often enough—or openly enough—to find the blessings and joy in addition to the guilt and sorrow. That is why I am holding space for the topic in this section.

It's plain to see that mother energy is crucially important for our own lives and for the well-being of everyone. If you never have, never plan to, or are no longer parenting kids, know that the mother is still there for each of us. The mother will always be a part of all womxyn.

This section contains rituals, recipes, meditations, and tips for bringing mother magick more fully into your life. There are spells for a better night's sleep, connecting with Mother Nature, and sparking your creativity. Kitchen witchery gives you tips for brewing up fun and empowerment. May you be nurtured as you nurture those in your world.

Goddesses with Mother Energy

• **Demeter:** The Greek earth mother wasn't having it when the god of the underworld, Hades, took her daughter, Persephone, down under. Whether we choose to think of this as a consensual elopement or an abduction, Demeter thought that Hades needed to understand that no means no. She asked the god king, Zeus, to intervene, but he seemed to think that what went on between another god and some nubile maiden was private business. So what did Demeter do? She went on strike. No crops grew and the whole land was pitched into endless winter until her daughter was returned to her. It turns out that hell (or Hades, as the case may be) hath no fury like a mama scorned. Demeter may have originated the truism that it's a bad idea to mess with Mother Nature.

• **Isis:** Also known as the "Goddess of Ten Thousand Names," Isis is sometimes treated as a catch-all for the energy of the female divine, and this seems to have been true in ancient times as well. She was carried all over the world through commerce and immigration, sometimes being syncretized (combined) with the goddesses local to far-flung regions. Statues of her holding her baby, Horus, have been suggested as the template for later ones representing Mary and Jesus. After a treacherous power play took place in the Egyptian pantheon, Isis had to resurrect her hubby Osiris using her epic brand of badass spell craft. She is so powerful that she has been called the world-soul, meaning the totality of the spiritual source.

• **Macha:** Her lout of a royal husband bet his buddies that Macha could win a footrace against the fastest horses they could find. This, mind you, while she was full-term in her pregnancy. Macha ran in the race, won the damn thing, and had her baby right after she crossed the finish line. Royally pissed, she cursed the king and his entire boys club to suffer the pangs of childbirth from that moment on. Now that's badass.

• **Mary:** Mary pops up across the globe, much like Hecate and Isis. She has a polarity of identities from light (vanilla, nurturing, virginal) to dark (racy, sexy, sovereign).[31] Her color polarity tends to have more to do with the aspects of her that cultures (mostly Christianized) try to suppress, taking certain parts of her and turning them into "shadow." But all of us have polarity! No one is only light or only dark.[32]

31. Belloni, *Healing Journeys with the Black Madonna.*
32. Monaghan, *Encyclopedia of Goddesses and Heroines.*

chapter six

NURTURING YOURSELF AND OTHERS

ost of us are familiar with the stereotype of a warm, nurturing, powerful mother, even if we didn't have one of our own. Your idea of the perfect mother might be influenced by society, peers, or religion—even patriarchal religions have the loving mother in their sacred stories. In Paganism, we have the flexibility and intellectual (as well as spiritual) freedom to relate to gods and goddesses as we like. Sometimes, we don't relate to them at all. Our divine moms are as likely to be sword-wielding badasses as they are rosy-cheeked bakers. The mom is pretty complex. I think she's better that way, and much closer to the truth.

Whether you have children or not, we've gotta give props to parents everywhere. Parenting can be *hard*. Especially when, as we discussed, so many womxyn are parenting alone, whether by happenstance or choice. There is a great deal of pressure to be the perfect parent. (News flash: There is no such thing!) And parents aren't just trying to raise healthy, smart, well-adjusted, successful kids. They're also earning money, cultivating a spiritual life, being responsible members of the larger community, and maybe even making time for romance! Crazy, right? But it's happening. Womxyn are kicking ass! This chapter is here to help you give yourself a little bit of the love you give to others.

This chapter is for womxyn with and without children. We start with a focus on self-care. I serve up empowering practices, relaxation tools, a ritual for decent sleep, and soothing tea and potpourri blends. I will include some work you can do if you'd like to connect with the divine energies of both mother and father; I know they sound binary, but all of us have both (whether they are present in our lives or not), and kids do as well.

The chapter will end with two sections on motherhood. The first section, "Mothering without Children," includes a ritual to honor your nest, whatever that looks like for you. The final section in this chapter includes parenting rituals. One involves your kiddos themselves, if they are old enough to decide to participate. Feel free to read one or the other, neither, or both sections.

ME-TIME MAGICKAL SOAK AND BLESSING

I decided to put this soak first in the chapter so you could refer back to it while you work through the other practices. It's common to take a magickal bath before you perform rituals in order to cleanse your energy field. Beyond that, a good soak is imperative for re-centering and self-care.

PREPARATION AND ITEMS TO GATHER:
- Mason jar with lid.
- ½ cup Epsom salt.
- 2 tablespoons baking soda.
- About ten drops of essential oils of your choice. I recommend mixing rose and orange or lavender and lemon. Floral and citrus blends lift the mood and comfort the soul.

SPELL WORK: Combine the salt and soda in a mason jar. Then add the essential oils, capping and shaking the mix periodically to blend it. Add the oils slowly so you can make the mix as fragrant as you'd like. If you add too many oils and your mix becomes too strong, move it to a larger jar and dilute the oils by adding more salt and soda.

To add an extra charge to this blend, let it sit on a windowsill to soak up the energy of a waxing moon. On the night of the full moon, give this blessing:

"May the mother energy of the goddess infuse these ingredients with positive energies. As I soak in soothing bathwater, may I be healed of any stress or discomfort. Support me in my mother work, great mother of all. In the correct way and with harm to none, blessed be."

Your bath soak is now ready to go whenever you'd like to take a bath. I recommend adding half of the mixture (about a fourth of a cup) per bath. Use this soak whenever you need a powerful boost!

QUEENING RITUAL

The motherhood phase of life isn't only for creating babies. Lots of womxyn do not take this path, by circumstance or by choice. It is important to honor the gifts that all womxyn bring to the spinstress community. Womxyn's work on social issues, neighborhood improvement, education, and the arts makes the world a better place for kids and for everyone else.

A queening ritual is a celebration for womxyn of all genders who are bearing the responsibility of nurturing their communities. This could certainly mean raising children, but it doesn't have to mean that. Queening is also for womxyn who are creating in other ways that deserve honor, including activism or art. The following ritual is about celebrating womxyn owning their power. Womxyn are queens no matter what type of work they do. In short, this is one big and well-deserved shout-out to womxyn everywhere.

This ceremony could be held for one individual or for several womxyn at once. It's up to the honorees and may also be influenced by the size or resources of your group. Guest lists should be agreed upon by the honorees and usually include close friends, family, and the like.

IDEAL TIME: The full moon or a Sunday.

PREPARATION AND ITEMS TO GATHER:
- Ask all the queens to bring a crown that will be symbolically blessed and placed on their head as part of the ritual. This crown may be something they already own, or they could make or buy something representative of their own personality. Sometimes a queen's family will buy or make a crown for them as a gift prior to the ritual.
- The color purple is a good one for your altar and accessories since it corresponds with personal empowerment. Gold as a color of spirituality and power will also work well.

- Place every queen's crown on the altar (or on the floor around the outer edge of the altar) for easy access during the ritual.

- Buy red roses or a similar flower and put them in a vase on the altar. Make sure you have at least one flower for each queen.

- There should be space for a banquet. The queens should be seated with honor and waited on by others, if possible. It would be great to have a side table with pictures of the queens. There could also be cards that attendees have written loving messages in.

- If you'd like to incorporate correspondences, lavender essential oil and amethyst stones are appropriate. As always, our old friend emerald is a gem that corresponds to this work.

CIRCLE UP: Designate one attendee as the officiant and ritual leader. The officiant says:

"North, we welcome you. Bless the earth on which we stand and the bodies that carry us through this life. We lovingly thank you for your gifts.

"East, we welcome you. Bless the air that we breathe and empower our individual voices. We lovingly thank you for your gifts.

"South, we welcome you. Bless the sun that warms us and makes the foods that nourish us. We lovingly thank you for your gifts.

"West, we welcome you. Bless the water that flows through the earth and through our bodies. We lovingly thank you for your gifts.

"Center, we welcome you. Let us be grounded now in the core, deep authenticity of our highest selves. As these womxyn come to accept the crown of their sovereignty, anoint them with their spiritual power."

SPELL WORK: Have each queen come to the altar one at a time. The officiant places the crown on her head while saying something individualized for each honoree. Example: "(Name), I crown you in thanks for the gifts you bring to our community." (Then say something individual for this queen.) Hand each queen her flower before she rejoins the circle.

It would be nice to have a musical offering of some kind after this spell work. It could be drumming, singing, a recording, or similar.

CLOSE UP SHOP: The officiant says:

"Center, we thank you for your blessings and gifts. May the highest spiritual intelligence of these womxyn continue to give them strength and council.

"West, we thank you for your blessings and gifts. Please continue to nourish and sustain all present here.

"South, we thank you for your blessings and gifts. Please continue to warm us and to feed us.

"East, we thank you for your blessings and gifts. Please continue to sustain our individual voices.

"North, we thank you for your blessings and gifts. Please continue to strengthen and renew our physical bodies."

After the circle ends, it's time to serve refreshments and wait on your queens hand and foot! Remember, happy queens make for a happy community.

• • • • • • •

Everyone deserves to feel well rested, especially hardworking womxyn. The following sleeping spell, potpourri, and tea are great for relaxation and good sleep. They will work for womxyn of any age or stage. Enjoy!

Sleeping Beauty

Independent womxyn carry their fair share of responsibility—and often, womxyn carry more than their fair share. It's exhausting! It may feel like the weight of the world is on the shoulders of womxyn everywhere. In that case, Sleeping Beauty of fairy tale fame didn't get off half bad with her curse of unending sleep. The goal of this section is to help you experience the ever-elusive good night's sleep.

Insomnia, being unable to sleep, is super common. Do your thoughts start racing as soon as your head hits the pillow? Do the hamster wheels of time and space spin in your head all night? Often when someone experiences nighttime anxiety it's because they're dwelling on the past or dreading the future. To function and live your best life, you've gotta nip this junk in the bud.

A technique to combat insomnia is to create a grounding mantra. While these skills abound in many philosophies, they are well described in Buddhist teachings about mindfulness. Cognitive behavioral therapy (CBT) is a clinical discipline that takes the lessons of Buddhism to heart. CBT states that an individual can manage their anxiety by retraining how the brain responds to stressful cues.[33] People using the program are encouraged to find healthy coping strategies to combat negative ones. Little by little, the healthy and productive overshadows the harmful and negative. If you are interested in CBT (or Buddhism, for that matter), self-help books abound.

In both cases, coming up with an affirmation or a mantra is the key form of mindfulness exercise. Like doing weight reps in a gym, the more you use your mantra, the stronger it gets. You might even start putting your anxiety and negative coping skills in their place while hardly being conscious that you're doing it.

Practicing a nighttime mantra that makes sense to you is key. You might like to use one from a spiritual document or a religious teaching that you already rely on. It could also be an adapted form of a lullaby or a hymn. It should be something you can easily memorize and use when under stress. Above all else, your mantra must feel natural. Experiment until you develop a personalized mantra that makes sense to you. It could be as simple as "I'm okay" if that feels right to you, or it could be something like "I'm safe in my bed and I'm grateful for my peaceful place to sleep." Take your time developing at least one mantra that seems to help with your night terrors. You will use this mantra in the following spell.

In addition to finding your mantra (or the strongest one of several), assemble other sleeping aides for a better night's sleep. Clean your bedroom and have a nightstand or dresser available to hold some gemstones, statues, relaxing images, or a bowl of potpourri.

Sleep relies on ritual (the witchy kind or not). Set a bedtime routine that tells your body that it's time to recharge. Use scent, sound, light, or dark in any combination that works for you. While common sense suggests silence is better than noise and total darkness is better than light (especially the light of electronic screens), what matters is *your* preference. If listening to your television drone on helps you sleep but the light of the screen keeps you up, add an eye mask to the mix. You could even try an eye mask that is stuffed with herbs like lavender. If you don't want to incorporate herbs that way, consider

---

33. Riggenbach, *CBT Toolbox.*

adding a bowl of potpourri or an essential oil diffuser to your bag of tricks. Keep experimenting with your surroundings until you get it right.

INSOMNIA  SPELL

This ritual will help you inaugurate your mantra and sleep routine. In the future, use as little or as much of this ritual as you need to help you ease into sleep. Keep practicing your mantra when anxiety and night terrors arise. Above all, be patient with yourself. If the process doesn't seem to be working, you may simply need a little extra help. Seek advice from your primary physician, your therapist, and/or your spiritual guides of choice.

IDEAL TIME: Anytime you are experiencing insomnia or interrupted sleep or a Monday.

PREPARATION AND ITEMS TO GATHER:
- Items for your sleep space like images, gemstones, flowers, a relaxing light, a dream journal, water or herbal tea, music, a white noise machine, an eye mask, an essential oil diffuser, special pillows or blankets, your dog or cat (or partner), a ticking clock, etc.
- Gemstones to encourage relaxation and sleep include rose quartz, amethyst, shungite, and moonstone.
- Herbal teas to induce sleep often include chamomile, lavender, or valerian. Rather than consuming these herbs (always heed allergies and follow medical advice), you could also incorporate the herbs into a sachet or dish of potpourri.
- Essential oils can be very relaxing. The typical scents for sleep include the herbs mentioned above as well as clary sage, sweet marjoram, and bergamot.

CIRCLE UP: Visualize a protective aura of light surrounding your entire sleeping area. It can be any color that you find soothing. Common protective colors are gold, blue, or green. Ask any spiritual guides you regularly work with to help you in this work and to protect you during sleep. Say, "I affirm that my sleeping space is safe and sound. Blessed be."

SPELL WORK: Say, "Bless my sleep. May the correct energies and forces be present in my sleeping space so that I can relax and recharge. Whenever it is needed, I affirm that my mantra will recalibrate my mind and aura with the correct energies and forces that will heal and protect me. Many thanks and blessed be."

Repeat your mantra several times, letting it become a habit.

CLOSE UP SHOP: In this case, simply say thanks to any guides you have called in and then float off to dreamland. Sleep well!

APHRODITE'S NIGHTIE POTPOURRI

When you create your ideal sleep environment, a sweet scent may help you settle in. This potpourri may be just the ticket. It's one of my favorites.

PREPARATION AND ITEMS TO GATHER:
- ¼ cup dried rose petals.
- ¼ cup dried lavender buds.
- 2 tablespoons dried patchouli leaves.
- 1 dried vanilla bean.
- A bowl or sachet.

SPELL WORK: Crush these lovely herbs, flowers, and spices together in a bag or with a mortar and pestle. Bless them by saying, "Aphrodite, goddess of love, bless this potpourri. With its scent, infuse this space with your energy and presence. Let my bedroom be a space of comfort, passion, health, and rest. May I be supported in caring for myself and accepting the love of others. When I smell this blend, may I remember your presence and its meaning. With harm to none and for the good of all, so mote it be."

Store the potpourri in your bedroom in a decorative bowl or sachet. To periodically refresh the scent, crush the ingredients again.

CAMBRIC TEA FOR THE WHOLE FAMILY

When you really need to slow things down and get ready for bed, the old-school remedy is a glass of warm milk. Dress that up a bit with a vintage throwback, Cambric tea. My grandma Hester used to make this classic for my mom and me. It was big in the nineteenth century; it was probably a way for country families to stretch their milk supply. Named after an old-fashioned fabric that was this same creamy color, this is a little bit of herbal decaf tea in a whole lotta milk. The old-timers also called it *nursery tea*.[34]

PREPARATION AND ITEMS TO GATHER:
- Hot water.
- Milk of your choice.
- Your fave herbal tea.
- Optional: Sweetener of your choice.

Fill each cup about halfway with hot water and steep a bag or bell of your fave herbal tea. After removing the tea leaves, fill the cup up with a milk of your choice. Sweeten to taste. You can mix the ratios to please yourself.

Drinking this before bedtime would be a great addition to your nighttime ritual. If you're not quite ready for bed yet, don't drink this—it will knock you out!

• • • • • • •

Okay, let's spend a bit of time connecting with healing masculine energies. You might be wondering what this is doing in a chapter focused on nurturing yourself and others. I think it is important to mention that healing your understanding of masculinity will also help heal you. Though we've spent our fair share of time talking about what to do when relationships get toxic, that conversation is by no means connected to masculinity itself. People of all sexual and gender identities can be abusive. The good news is, they can also be awesome. There is plenty of healing energy to be found in masculinity.

Connecting with Healing Male Energies

For better or worse, our understanding of male deity ("god") strongly informs how we relate to the men and boys around us. You might have experienced toxic religion in your life that was just as damaging to your view of masculinity as an abusive partner might be.

---

34. Troy, "What Is Cambric Tea?"

Doing some spiritual work with your understanding of masculinity in the form of the god is one way to heal your relationships with men and boys. It can help you pave the way for healthy relationships with the lovers, fathers, brothers, and sons already in your life and the ones that are yet to come.

Let's get to know this guy a little. Positive attributes of the god include being loving, generous, wise, patient, brave, just, kind, powerful, loyal, accepting, healing, compassionate, and nurturing. Do any of these traits surprise you? If so, you probably experienced toxic patriarchal religion and/or a toxic relationship in the past. It's important to heal these internalized messages.

Of all the traits mentioned above, physical force is not mentioned. That doesn't mean it has no place in healthy masculinity. The god may be a warrior, but this connotes more than the violence and force you may immediately think of. Remember that other traits of the warrior include wisdom, prudence, strategy, and a commitment to justice. Both gods and goddesses often carry this type of warrior energy.

Though the god-form varies from culture to culture, certain trends echo across regions and eras. In general, a powerful god is consort to a powerful goddess. At some point, the god is killed and then resurrected.

Just as the god is both matter and spirit, so is the goddess. He is her partner and co-creator, though his form changes. In many ancient stories, this was described in the god's journey between being child, lover, and later sage equal to the goddess. While his form moves through the body of the world, his spirit moves through the essence of the world-soul.

The goddess, as the earth that we live on and the body of the god (indeed, the bodies of all of us), is ever-present with us at our matter and our core. The god is the accessible form of divinity with which humankind can relate to and learn from; he is more of an example for us to follow.

How might it change your relationship to the god-form if you were able to see him as your peer or your mentor rather than your judge or taskmaster? What if we emphasized the god's role as nurturer, lover, or teacher rather than warrior, disciplinarian, or boss?

Oh, My God! Meditation

This ritual and guided meditation will connect you with positive male energies through the personhood of a god. If the concept of a deity is simply too loaded for you to work with, you can pick another male archetype or thoughtform for the work. It could be your father or another man in your life; just make sure to choose a male figure who is a positive presence. Ultimately, this meditation should strengthen your relationships with the men and boys in your daily life.

IDEAL TIME: The waxing moon, the full moon, or a Wednesday. Wednesdays correspond with messages, ideas, and Mercury. Along with his kindred gods Thoth, Hermes, and Lugh, Mercury is a god associated with wisdom and important spiritual truths. You may want to make one of these gods the focal point of your ritual, unless there is already another divine man in your life.

PREPARATION AND ITEMS TO GATHER:

- Find a statue or other image that evokes your god (or other male archetype) of choice. You might use traditional religious imagery, a collage, poetry, your dad's old catcher's mitt, or anything that helps you to connect to the appropriate energy. Think about both traditional and nontraditional religious symbols of godhood. Some may include the cross, the ankh, antlers, a tree, a lamb, Thor's hammer, or Cernunnos's cauldron. Since this is a ritual to heal your relationship to the god, stick to things you view as positive.

- If you've chosen a specific god to relate to, do some research on the herbs, gemstones, and colors that correspond to his energy. For instance, Hermes corresponds to blue, opal, and the hawk or owl.

- This work includes a guided meditation. Prepare by dressing in comfortable clothes, finding a nice spot to relax in, and placing your journal nearby so you can write in it as soon as the meditation ends.

CIRCLE UP: Since the sun is strongly associated with the god, use sunlight in your circle-casting. Visualize the sun rising above your sacred space. Let the warm gold of this light cast a circle around you. Say, "I affirm that the healing and nourishing power of the god is empowering my circle. Blessed be."

SPELL WORK: When you feel ready to begin your meditation, take some deep and grounding breaths and let your body relax.

Allow yourself to visualize a door taking shape in front of you. If it has any symbols or words on it, notice them. Affirm that the journey awaiting you behind this door is for your own highest good and will do you no harm. When you're ready, open the door and walk through.

You find yourself on a descending set of steps. Climb down them one, two, three, four, five. You are entering the alpha state of meditation, where you will be most attuned to correct and healing messages from psyche and from spirit. Climb down steps six, seven, eight, nine, ten. At the bottom of the stairs, you find yourself in a place in nature where you feel safe and at peace. It may be a place you have really been to at some point in your life or a land of complete imagination.

Wherever you find yourself, you notice a comfy place to sit. Sit down, leaving room next to you. Say, "I invite (name of a deity/ancestor/divine male energy) to come and speak with me. I know this will be a positive experience. Thank you."

Take a breath and wait. The male energy appears, walking toward you. Is it who you expected? What does he look like? He sits or stands next to you.

Spend some time with this divine male figure and ask him any questions you have or just listen to what he has to say. Leave whatever you have that needs healing from your experiences with men with this divine male energy. He won't be offended; this is part of why he has come. He is very strong and very good. He can take it. If you have anything to say about the experiences you are releasing, now is the time.

When you are ready, tell this divine male energy what you wish for in your future relationships with men. This could include aspirations for your sons and grandsons or calling in a romantic relationship. You could discuss how you would like to relate to the divine male energy in your craft as well. Don't censor yourself—this divine figure has come here to help and support you.

When it feels like you have said and done all that you need, the divine male energy has a message for you. Be open to what he has to say. He may even offer you a symbolic gift. Take it if you like.

When the two of you have said what you need to and spent as much time together as you would like, the male energy leaves. Know that you can access him in thoughts, prayers, or rituals anytime that you wish.

Stand up and head back to your spiritual doorway. As you climb back up your set of steps, you ascend into your normal waking state. You climb up one, two, three, four, five, six, seven, eight, nine, ten steps. Open the door and step back into your meditation space.

As you enter your normal waking state, wiggle your fingers and toes and take some deep breaths. Drink some water or eat something to ground yourself.

CLOSE UP SHOP: Visualize the sunlight that you cast around your sacred circle. Now allow it to dissipate like the sun sets on the horizon. Say, "I give thanks to the god for empowering my craft. As this sacred sunlight returns to the spiritual source, may it continue to manifest my will. Blessed be."

JOURNAL PROMPT

Write about your guided meditation. What male energy showed up for you? What did the two of you talk about? What additional questions or insights did the meditation bring up? How did you feel when you returned to your normal waking state?

Remember that you can repeat this meditation multiple times and speak to one or more god-forms. If you choose to do so, journal about how the experiences differ.

Mothering without Children

Even when you are not mothering children, it is powerful and important to ritualize and honor your path. Perhaps you have never been a mother, or perhaps you are just not currently mothering a child, whether your child has moved out or due to another circumstance. Some folks in the goddess community call this being a *childless mother*. I know this may be a triggering term for some; since this topic isn't talked about enough, I suppose the right language hasn't been developed. I do think it is important to mention that when I have heard this term used in womxyn's circles, it is to celebrate the mothering phase of life for all womxyn.

Womxyn embrace motherhood in their own unique way and that should be honored regardless of whether or not they are raising children. There are countless reasons a womxyn may not be parenting; do not stereotype or limit anyone's experience. (Refer back to the "Womxyn without Children" section for more information.) Motherhood is about nurturing, providing, protecting, disciplining, teaching, and so much more. These traits tend to be thought of as part of the "mother" archetype, but all womxyn have these capabilities.

MANY DIFFERENT NESTS: RITUAL TO HONOR YOUR MOTHERING

This is a ritual that anyone can do. It is here to honor all womxyn reading this book and the many ways that we "mother." This ritual also holds space to honor the children you may or may not have with you. This can be triggering, so please have a plan for how you will take care of yourself when you take some of these issues on, perhaps with loving friends and family or even a therapist.

IDEAL TIME: The waxing moon, the full moon, or a Monday.

PREPARATION AND ITEMS TO GATHER:
- Make a "nest" to symbolize all that you mother (or once did or would like to). It could be an actual bird's nest that you found outside—just make sure it's an old and abandoned one, obviously! You can also purchase nests or nest-like birdfeeders at craft suppliers. A cup, bowl, or candy dish would work too.

- Inside your nest, place symbols of your motherhood. These could be quilt patches, gemstones, ornaments, photos, scraps of poetry, or any number of things. It doesn't have to be all warm and fuzzy. Tributes or mementos about children you lost or who are all grown up could be included. You could write lists of the bullshit about mothering that makes you angry, put them through a paper shredder, and line the nest with the shreds. Get creative!

- During the spell work section, you will have a chance to say something to lost children, your mother, your grandmother, etc. Read the spell ahead of time and see if you want to add something that will better suit your needs. Perhaps you would like to boost the spell work by listening to a playlist, singing a song, or writing and sharing how you are feeling.

- This ritual can be cathartic. Plan in advance by having tissues, a cozy blanket, and whatever you think you may need to handle your emotions nearby. You may want to let someone you trust know what you're up to. If you feel like it would be beneficial for you, plan on talking to a loved one after you've completed the ritual.

- Optional: Wear a yoni egg while visualizing the ways you have mothered, currently mother, or will mother. Then place the egg in the nest. You can put other symbolic eggs in, of course, but when used in this ritual, the yoni egg can bring a whole new layer of power and meaning.

CIRCLE UP: Visualize a nest of golden energy around you. Affirm that this energy is of the highest spiritual vibration and will hold you emotionally as well as protect your sacred space. Say, "I thank the spiritual source for this protective energy. As I mother, you mother me. Blessed be."

SPELL WORK: Spend some time with your nest. Talk to it, to the spiritual source or to your deities, to children in this realm or another, or to yourself. Talk about what mothering you have done, will do, or are doing. If you have anger or grief and need to purge those emotions, go for it. Read or perform anything that you have prepared.

At this time, offer a blessing to lost children if you would like. The following blessing can be replaced or adapted: "Sweet child, I love you and will always carry you within myself. I commend your spirit to the spiritual source with love and trust. I feel in many ways that we are together still and always. Be blessed."

When you feel ready, say the following motherhood blessing or adapt it in your own way: "I honor all the ways that I mother. I am a nurturer. I am a defender. I am a creator. I birth many important gifts into the world and into the fates' great tapestry. May my mothering remain all that I wish it to be. May my mothering be all that is needed from me. May I be mothered as well. Blessed be."

CLOSE UP SHOP: Allow the golden nest of energy around your sacred space to dissolve. Say, "I thank you for holding and protecting me during this sacred work. Please carry my words and wishes back into the spiritual source."

JOURNAL PROMPT

Journaling can be very helpful during this process. If you feel called to do so, answer the following questions: What was it like to create the nest and to perform the ritual? What have you learned about mothering? Did this ritual help you develop new goals or heal some old wounds?

Mothering with Children

Whether you take care of your own kids or someone else's, this section contains info to help you raise great kids. It takes a village; let's take a moment to appreciate the work child-rearing grown-ups take on.

Our Kids Are All Right: Teaching Youth about Gender

One of the preeminent parenting issues that current generations are addressing in very new ways is how we talk to younger generations about gender. Professionals in fields like therapy and sociology are calling it *gender expansion*. The way gender is viewed is evolving. Gender is fluid. It's expressive. It's connected to creativity, relationships, and the expression of personal power.

When it comes to rethinking gender roles, it feels like we're all sort of winging it together. Youth are making new rules that older generations are following. As a parent, teacher, or mentor, you may feel like you should be the one providing guidance and leading the conversation. But it is kind of exciting that there is a new frontier in front of us that youth and adults can co-create! Exciting, but daunting.

How youth use what they have learned is often out of the teacher's control. This is often a good thing. I believe that raising children to have an open, less-restrictive view of gender roles and gender identities will prepare them to elevate cultural views on these issues to a new level. It's a brave new world.

In the meantime, here are a few tips for teaching kids about gender:

- Challenge the gender stereotypes you learned. For instance, stay out of the pink/blue binary when it comes to decor, clothing, toys, etc.

Stay away from the gender binary altogether by using neutral terms like *kids* instead of *boys* or *girls* when possible.

- Encourage kids to play with toys that reject traditional gender roles. For instance, boys can play with dolls and girls can play with trucks! This doesn't mean kids need to be discouraged from engaging in more traditional play. Instead, use the moment to talk to them about all the things both boys and girls can do.

- Let youths see you model awareness of gender diversity in the way you speak across the board. For instance, you might ask an acquaintance if they have a partner instead of asking if they have a husband, wife, boyfriend, or girlfriend. Let the acquaintance demonstrate the appropriate language and go from there. When you meet a new person, tell them your pronouns. (Example: "I'm Leslie and my pronouns are she, her, and hers.")

- Speak openly to kids about the diversity they see around them. Encourage this by incorporating books and media that reflect diversity. Spread the message that different doesn't mean wrong. Draw kids into healthy conversations that model equality and acceptance.

- If you are raising a transgender or nonbinary child or simply want to learn more about how to support transgender and nonbinary youth, you can find Q+ organizations for youth and/or adults online or locally. Look for parenting groups that encourage these kinds of considerations.

- If your child talks about their gender identity with you, never contradict them. Seek out a therapist with the expertise to help you and your child be emotionally healthy as you move forward. When a child expresses a nonconforming gender identity, the advocates I've met consider empowering the child's choices to be the most emotionally healthy response. Allow them to wear what they want, change their hair as they want, or perhaps even change their name. Children will surely need your help to negotiate these changes at their school or in other community groups. Other parents and support groups can help.

- Seek help from diversity nonprofits (and possibly seek out legal counsel) if you or your youngsters are facing discrimination. This could be based on family structure, expressing gender identity at school, or any number of things.

I LIKE ME: RITUAL FOR MAGICKAL KIDS

This ritual provides a chance to teach your kids what you know about magick. Your child should be old enough to express interest in participating. Kids typically have a better connection to the playfulness and belief required to excel at the craft, so be prepared for them to be way better at it than you!

IDEAL TIME: The waxing moon, the full moon, or a Sunday.

PREPARATION AND ITEMS TO GATHER:

- In preparation for this spell, work with your child to think about who she/he/they feel that they are. Have them prepare a scroll on a piece of construction paper in their fave color that answers the following types of questions:
  - What makes you happy?
  - What do you like to do?
  - Do you have dreams for your future?
  - Who are your favorite people? Why?

  Children can either draw or write their answers on the scroll. Make sure to lend a helping hand as needed. Then, ask each child to come up with one wish and have them draw or write it on their scroll. It could be about anything!

- Help the child doing this work design a fun altar that represents them. Favorite toys, pictures of their idols, photos of them doing their favorite things, or artwork they've made are all great options. Make sure to represent their favorite colors as well.

- If your child wants to have the basic elements represented, work with them to figure this out. For example, a favorite plant or garden rock could represent north/earth, a feather or a balloon could be east/air, a candle or artwork of a fire-breathing dragon could be south/fire, and a set of goggles or the goldfish bowl could be west/water. For spirit, let the child choose something that they feel represents their own spirit.

This could be some of their artwork, a favorite stuffed animal, or even their favorite pair of pajamas.

CIRCLE UP: Kids usually like to cast the circle themselves by sweeping it into being with a broom or waving a wand. Discuss this in advance and have the necessary supplies on hand; a toy broom is fine. With the craft, it's the thought that counts!

As the child moves clockwise to point out the circle with the wand or to sweep it into being with their broom, have them say something like, "I cast this sacred circle now. My wishes will come true inside it. I am strong and good. I always wish for great, kind things. Blessed be."

SPELL WORK: Lead the spell by saying, "We have gathered in the circle to celebrate (name)." Help your kiddo work their way through their scroll aloud, saying their list of positive attributes, what and who they love, and finally, their wish. After they make their wish, everyone present in the circle should say, "You are magickal and good. Blessed be."

CLOSE UP SHOP: Have the child open the circle the same way they cast it, working counterclockwise this time. Have them say, "I open this circle. Thanks for helping me. Carry my spell back into the world and let my wishes come back to me. Blessed be."

chapter seven

ACTIVISM, ENVIRONMENTALISM, AND LOVING MOTHER EARTH

ots of womxyn use the mothering phase of life to birth social action. Womxyn are badass activists, social justice advocates, and environmental protectors. Some womxyn even take on these endeavors while raising a family of children! Those of us who don't have children still hold the powerful aspect of the mother within our spiritual selves. Loving mothering energy can be tapped into at any age or stage by:

- Setting up a neighborhood watch to protect yourself and your neighbors from predators

- Creating an art installation of your own work and/or the work of other talented souls who might need help "birthing" their voice

- Organizing a grassroots piece of activism or a group that does this regularly

- Parenting your children and/or mentoring other kiddos through peer groups, informational blogs, and more

- Caring for your elders and/or supporting others who do this critical work

- Creating a business that supports your family (and perhaps other families) while offering valuable contributions to the world
- Engaging in acts of environmental sustainability, like starting a composting project on your block or cleaning up trash on a beach

When you think about which actions you might like to take, you are exercising your personal ethics. You will probably consider your ideal relationship with the planet and the other beings around you. The following section is all about ethics, which I think of as the building blocks for boundaries.

Ethics: Your Personal Map

Have you ever heard the saying "If you don't stand for something, you will fall for anything"? I think there's something to that. Ethics are what you stand for. Your personal set of ethics might be influenced by society, religion, or your life experiences. Take some time to think about what morals and values you hold. Have they changed as you've aged? If you're feeling inspired to redevelop your ethics, you don't have to start over from scratch. Learn from others in the spinstress community via group membership or independent study (ideally, a little of each).

What's the point of a bunch of rulemaking and introspection? It may seem like a less-fun version of religion. Perhaps avoiding religious rules is what drew you to Paganism in the first place. Laying an ethical foundation that makes sense to you is an important part of the spinstress path. When you know what you stand for, you won't fall for anything. Ethics are helpful guides when you start a new job, a new relationship, or a new activism endeavor. It's also good to know what your firm "yes" and "no" moments are.

When I worked on developing my own set of ethics, I relied on the traditions and information that made the most sense to me. In your own work, it is important that you do the same. If you're feeling a bit lost with this one, review some of your favorite spiritual books or talk to some of your mentors. Spend some time journaling about your personal ethics. If you were raised in a religion where the rules chafed you, use this as a springboard and write about how you do things differently.

WHAT I STAND FOR ETHICAL DEDICATION

Before beginning this ritual, determine a few ethical statements that are important to you. Your ethical statements could simply explain what you believe, or you could write down sayings you learned from a faith tradition, advice from your family members or mentors, or quotes from books you are drawn to. If you're not sure where to start, there are philosophy books about ethics that focus on all sorts of specialized topics like feminism, race, environmentalism, animal rights, and more.

IDEAL TIME: The full moon or a Saturday.

PREPARATION AND ITEMS TO GATHER:
- If you'd like to incorporate color magick on your altar, lavender and gold have high vibrations associated with ethics.
- Set a blank piece of paper on the altar. During the ritual, you will use this piece of paper to summarize your ethics. (You can prepare it in advance and read it aloud during the spell if you prefer.) Set out pens and any craft supplies you would like. You will keep this "scroll" of ethics, so I recommend decorating it in a way you will enjoy.

CIRCLE UP: Visualize gold energy forming a four-armed cross inside a circle. This energy covers you and forms the barrier around your sacred space. Say, "May the balance of these elements ground and protect me as I consider my ethical foundation. Help me make this foundation solid and strong. Blessed be."

SPELL WORK: Gather your supplies and write or review your ethical scroll.

When you feel ready, read your ethical scroll aloud. If it is a long document, feel free to summarize. When you're finished reading, say, "I commit to these ethics, which I have chosen from my own power and wisdom. I am thankful for the privilege in this life to make such a choice. I give myself permission to let these ethics evolve over time, so long as they are still my choice. I will defend my right to my beliefs and those of others. Blessed be."

CLOSE UP SHOP: Allow the gold cross and circle to evaporate back to the source elements and energies. Say, "I thank you for balancing me and protecting me in my ethical work. Blessed be."

Keep your ethical scroll near your altar or in another location where you can easily refer back to it. If your ethics change over time, it is a good idea to write and consecrate a new scroll.

• • • • • • •

Now that you've got a rock-solid set of ethics, let's look at how you can boost your personal power source when you engage with issues that matter to you by creating the right altar.

Rooted in Place Altar

Activism may not always be about the environment, but it is deeply personal, so therefore it is always partly rooted in *your* personal environment. To tap into the strength of your home base, place this altar inside or in your yard, depending on practicality and preference.

PREPARATION AND ITEMS TO GATHER:
- Go on a scavenger hunt for items from your environment that can be placed on your altar: pine cones, stones, sticks, fallen feathers, shells, etc. I was lucky enough to find a shed stag horn on the forest floor while out for a walk! Whatever you gather, be mindful to only take things that cause no harm to the environment.

- Build this altar entirely from found objects or add items like an altar cloth, statues, gemstones, and so on. The point is to build something that triggers your love of your own environment and home.

- If this is an outdoor altar, it might look more like a hiking cairn. You could pile up stones or use one large boulder as a focal point. Make it a nice little spot that you can visit once in a while. Many people like to leave a small, biodegradable offering to the spirits of the place. If you do so, make sure it will do no harm to the ecosystem or any critters that may pass by.

SPELL WORK: When you've got your altar all set up, say this blessing (or one or your own):

"Spiritual powers of this place, I thank you for blessing and protecting me. I am honored to make my home here. I ask that you protect me and my family and lend energy to my personal endeavors. Blessed be."

Visit this altar whenever you need a little boost or to anchor yourself when you feel anxious.

• • • • • • • •

The following ritual for activism is very detailed; it's a great ritual to do before you organize a march, fundraiser, or other event.

Mother Energy and Activism

Mother energy is not only about creating the next generation, it's also about creating a world that is fit for the next generation to live in. Womxyn who embody mother energy in their activism pursuits are powerful agents for birthing change.

Tips for Effective Activism

- Sending written letters, petitions, or postcards is still thought to be more impactful than email campaigns.

- Focusing on your area's political representatives has more impact than reaching out to policymakers in other areas. If you really need to get the attention of a politician who is not your own elected official, engage in activism with that person's own constituents.

- Writing a letter to the editor in your local newspaper is still a great way to educate your fellow citizens on an issue that really matters to you.

BALANCING THE SCALES: AN ACTIVISM RITUAL

This spell is most suited for social justice issues because you will be visualizing a set of scales that you will bring into balance with your spell work. However, you could modify this ritual to apply to many types of activism.

IDEAL TIME: The waxing moon, the full moon, or a Sunday.

PREPARATION AND ITEMS TO GATHER:

- This ritual's guided visualization involves the scales of justice. If you have a set of scales, put them on your altar or within your sacred space.

- Gather yellow, orange, or gold items for your altar. Make sure to grab a few yellow or orange candles.

- Anoint your candles with orange or grapefruit essential oil.

- Grab your journal and a pen or pencil.

- If you'd like to incorporate incense, burn frankincense, amber resin, or a cinnamon blend. For putting some fire in your belly, try burning tobacco leaves or dragon's blood resin. Make sure you don't touch your eyes when you're working with feisty ingredients.

- If you'd like to incorporate gemstones, amber and diamonds are great. Garnet and red jasper will boost your courage, as will platinum, steel, or gold. If you collect high-wattage jewelry, this is a great time to put it to use!

- Optional: A fan or feather to move the air.

CIRCLE UP: If you're using incense, tobacco, or dragon's blood resin, purify your sacred space with the smoke. Spread the smoke around your circle using your hand, a fan, or a feather while saying, "May this sacred smoke mark my sacred space and protect me from all incorrect energies and forces. May all the magick I do in this space be well blessed. So shall it be."

If you don't want to work with smoke, move the air around your sacred space with a fan, feather, or your hand and say, "May this breath of spirit mark my sacred space and protect me from all incorrect energies and forces. May all the magick I do in this space be well blessed. So shall it be."

SPELL WORK: Open to a blank page in your journal and draw a line down the center so you have two columns. Think about current injustices, personally or globally. Make a list of these imbalances on the left side of the page. In the right-hand column, write down what you think will help bring aspects of injustice into balance. What types of activism might bring this scale into balance? What have you heard of being done already? What additional ideas do you have? For example, you might write "sexism" in the left column and "creating a feminist group" in the right column. This is a very simple example, but you should be as detailed and creative as possible.

What do you as an individual do with your activism? Which aspects of injustice and imbalance will your plans correct? Be specific with your initial action steps. For instance, maybe you decide to host a feminist art exhibit and invite womxyn to showcase their work. If you collect donations at your exhibit, perhaps you set up a treasury so you can host recurring events. If you don't want to manage money long-term, you could raise donations for existing feminist groups that share your goals, like your local family-planning clinic or domestic violence shelter.

When you've finished writing, take some centering breaths, close your eyes, and visualize a set of scales. On one side, heap items of injustice. It may be useful to visualize the energy of injustice. Is it an ugly pile of squirming, unpleasant bugs? Is it a big blob of stinky mud? Once you have these items in mind, say, "I affirm that with this spell, the scales will be balanced, and these incorrect energies or forces will be transformed. They will become correct and useful as they are put into appropriate balance. So shall it be."

Next, visualize the countermeasures that you created in your list. See them heaped on the other side of the scale, bringing the situation into balance. Are your countermeasures shining with the gold of truth? Are they liquid and blue with the energy of love and healing? Say, "I affirm that the measures I have conjured will bring this situation into a just and healthy balance. If other energies and actions are required in this work, I ask that you provide them. Let this situation be put into correct balance and be healed. With harm to none and for the good of all, so shall it be."

Take some time to enjoy the sight of the balanced scales. Be open to receiving insight about what other actions or ideas have been provided by the spiritual source in order to bring balance.

When you feel ready to end the spell work, say, "I affirm that this work is being manifested by the spiritual source in the correct way and at the correct time. Blessed be."

CLOSE UP SHOP: Move the air around the sacred space again or simply visualize the sacred smoke (or breath of spirit) that cast the circle dissipating back into the spiritual source. As you do this, say, "I give thanks that the sacred energy of this circle will carry my wish back to the spiritual source, where it will be manifest in a correct way with harm to none. Blessed be."

JOURNAL PROMPT

Record any insights or experiences you had while performing the spell. Did you learn anything about your activism while you were balancing the scales?

• • • • • • •

Not all activism has to take place in a picket line. Energetic healing and ritual are also forms of activism for those of us who truly believe in magick. Another word for energetic work that many of us are very familiar with is *prayer*. While some Pagans think prayer is strictly for other religions, there are those of us who use the practice, so I wanted to share a prayer practice for you to consider if you are interested.

Spiritual Prayer as Activism

This may seem a little unusual to those of you who have been practicing Paganism for a long time. While prayer in Paganism isn't unheard of, I may do it more than most. As you know by now, I had a unique relationship with religion. My father was a Christian minister, and at one point I took the academic training to follow in his footsteps. I attended Christian churches when I was growing up. Full disclosure: I hated it a good portion of the time, especially during my rageful teens.

Having done a lot of spiritual and religious questing of my own, I've come to terms with my very eclectic experiences. I now see the beauty in several aspects of evangelical Christian belief and practices. In evangelical traditions there is this thing called "praying in the spirit" or "speaking in tongues." The technical term is *glossolalia*. This just means speaking in words and/or vocalizations that are not part of any human language and are known to be commonly applied to a practice of fervent prayer. It's sometimes so fervent that it's classed as a form of possession! If anything, I prefer to think of it as channeling spiritual information.

How does spiritual prayer tie into this chapter? I wanted to offer it to you because I consider the practice of prayer part of my own activism. This often includes prayer in spiritual words and singing that I don't understand or feel the need to. In the spirit of perfect love and perfect trust, I am trusting the spiritual source and the deities I primarily work with to carry the energy and intent of my prayer into manifestation according to the divine intelligence. I'm acknowledging that I don't always know how to pray or craft a spell with the most efficacy for a situation; I am trusting them to do it for me.

I may use spiritual prayer when I'm too upset or overwhelmed by a topic to pray about it in my own words. In recent times, for example, I prayed in my spirit language about crimes against mothers and babies near and far. I prayed for kids in cages on the United States border. I prayed for the safety of protesters and for global healing.

The other time I like to pray in my spirit language is when I have a personal issue that I'm not sure how to solve. I feel like praying in a language only my spirit guides and I can understand is a way for me to completely take my hands off the steering wheel so they can guide me toward a solution.

How you feel about spiritual prayer will probably depend on how you feel about deities and/or the nature of divine spiritual intelligence. If you trust in something out there, you may wish to collaborate with it in this way. Prayer like this reminds me of a form of energy healing, like Reiki. You send the energy toward its goal and trust the spiritual source to use it. I suppose I see spiritual prayer as a verbal form of energy healing.

Feel like giving it a try? The following meditation will help you find a spiritual prayer language that feels comfortable to you. Don't put pressure on yourself—just try it out and go with the flow.

RITUAL TO FIND YOUR SPIRITUAL PRAYER LANGUAGE

This ritual is meant to help you feel safe and supported while you practice spiritual prayer. Once it's a habit, you can do it anywhere: while walking, in bed, while cooking, or even when stuck in traffic!

IDEAL TIME: Anytime!

PREPARATION AND ITEMS TO GATHER:
- Get comfy in a space that makes you feel safe and secure. It could be in front of your personal power altar, at your kitchen table, or even in bed!
- If you would like to construct an altar for this purpose, spiritual colors include purple/lavender, white, silver, and gold.
- If you'd like to incorporate scents, rose, lavender, and vervain are very sacred and spiritually opening herbs. Consider oils or incense that have these ingredients.
- If you use a playlist, it should be relaxing music that puts you in a meditative, spiritual space. Make sure it isn't playing too loudly—you want to hear your prayer language.
- Since spirit prayer can result in spirit messages, you may want to keep a journal nearby.

CIRCLE UP: Cast a circle of pure spiritual light around yourself. (It will probably be clear or gold.) Say, "I am safe in this space, and I am fully connected to the spiritual source."

SPELL WORK: Take some deep breaths and settle into a receptive, meditative state. Begin praying by stating this intention to your deities or to the spiritual source: "I am open to receiving the gift of a spiritual prayer language. I offer the energies of my voice to the divine intelligence to be correctly applied to any situation. In perfect love and perfect trust, I believe that you can meet my needs and those of others by correctly applying my prayers. I know that for all the energy you use toward the higher good, I will receive many times the blessing. I now offer you my voice. Please craft and use it accordingly."

Let your voice just say syllables, babble, or sing. If you feel uncomfortable, start with a whisper. As you become comfortable with this process, let your voice become more and more audible. Experiment with humming and singing. Remember that every sound you make is an energetic offering and is accomplishing your goals. You may not have a powerful first experience—it's okay to relax and just see this as practice. The energetic offering will be good no matter what.

You may only want to do this for a few moments on your first try. Don't give up! If you're on a roll, though, have fun with it. When you feel finished, say something to end your prayer that feels right to you. While many people say, "Amen," this word basically means "So be it"—that works too.

CLOSE UP SHOP: Thank the spiritual source for working with you and reciprocating your offering of prayer energy. Allow your circle of protective light to rise up to the heavens as you say, "I give thanks for your help. As you return to the spiritual source, I ask that you help to manifest these prayers."

You may want to journal about this experience. Take some time to jot down any impressions that came to you during prayer; you might forget if you don't write them down right away.

If you enjoyed this practice, I highly recommend continuing to experiment with spiritual prayer. I find that it is a nice addition to many rituals and spells.

Other Ideas for a Prayer Practice

- Use a goddess rosary in the gemstone(s) of your choice to make gratitude lists and literally count your blessings.

- Pick a spiritual song, chant, or playlist that puts you in the right frame of mind and use it regularly. It will trigger your prayerful state and help you time your session.

- Take your prayer activism online by offering silent meditation, drumming, chanting, or other opportunities to your tribe.

- Use your journal to document how your prayer practice evolves.

EASY SHIELDING DURING ACTIVISM

Whether you're taking your activism to the front line or praying from home, it's a good idea for the spinstress activist to practice shielding. I'm talking about an energetic force field that you can call upon whenever you need a little extra buffering from the world around you.

Energetic shielding is like any other type of exercise: your shield gets stronger with practice. At first, it may seem like you're just pretending. Remember, magickal systems believe that energy follows thought. If you believe the energy around you is stronger, it is. If you practice this over time, you will start to feel the difference when your own personal force field is in place.

Many folks use a clear shield because it's just pure energy. If you prefer, you can tinge it with your favorite color or the color of an energy you want to draw in; for instance, light pink for self-esteem if you're feeling raw. The shape of your field is also up to you: it might be as simple as an energy bubble or as complex as a cowcatcher. (Yes, you read that correctly. I once developed an energy shield for the front of my friend's car that was shaped like an old railroad cowcatcher, the snowplow-shaped frame they put on the front of a train to deflect obstacles.)

Don't stress out about shielding. All it takes is imagination and a little practice. After a while, you can just see your shield and it will be rock solid. It may even start amping itself up involuntarily when you are under stress.

For a quick shielding blessing, visualize your shield in whatever color you like. Say something like, "I call upon my protective shield to guard, protect, and soothe me."

You go, girl! You're titanium in that thing.

• • • • • • •

In a chapter all about speaking up and using your inner fire, I'd be remiss if I didn't mention the fabulous dragon. If you feel called to embrace it, this creature can be a badass bouncer. Dragons can also add a little steel to your backbone when you have to do something tough.

Magickal Creatures 101: Out There Be Dragons

Nothing says power quite like a dragon. They're big. They breathe fire. They do what they damn well please. Not all dragons fit that stereotype of flames and flying and stomping around, but all dragons are badass. Exploring dragons, including which ones you are most attracted to and which ones "come when you call," can teach you a lot about your own power. The dragons who show up for you may share your strengths. More likely, they are coming to give you a helping hand and to offer you a boost in an area where you could use some growth.

Dragons across cultures have varied traits and an array of both positive and negative relationships with the people who know them. In the ancient world, books about animals were called *bestiaries*. The people who wrote them compiled their information not only from seeing live creatures, but from oral interviews and, occasionally, from viewing ancient remains. It's likely that the dragon's physiology comes partly from long-ago discoveries of dinosaur fossils and bones. People who relied on a bestiary for their animal information had no reason to believe in the lion or the hippo and to disbelieve stories of the unicorn or dragon. And creatures as impressive as the dragon became heavily mythologized by those who read or heard about them.[35]

In Western cultures, dragons tend to absorb negative traits and religious anxieties. Dragons are seen as greedy, lustful, fiery, and violent. Stories about dragons often involve stealing and hoarding treasures, including the occasional virginal maiden. As Christianity syncretized and swallowed up the old tribal religions, dragons came to symbolize what Christian authors thought of as the bad old days and the bad old ways.[36]

Yet, as with the old religions, people retained a certain longing for and fascination with dragons. They—and now we—intuitively seem to know that dragons call us back to something deep and powerful within the earth and within ourselves. Many believe that these hot tickets are real elemental powers of the earth and heavens. As earth energies, dragons are the perfect partners for eco-friendly spells. As the guardians of living things (including us) they can also be called on for protection.

You may be struggling with your beliefs right about now. Are dragons real or make believe? As with many of life's great mysteries, I think the answer is probably a little bit of both. Calling a dragon involves opening your consciousness to their possibilities. You have already learned that the craft relies on the power of thoughts. You also know that energies are drawn to one another according to the power of correspondences. With these two key pieces of knowledge, you can find and partner with the right dragon(s). The enchanted beast who corresponds with what you're putting out there will appear for you. What you're putting out there includes your thoughts, your feelings, the elements you are most grounded in, and your intentions. (The

---

35. Matthews and Matthews, *Encyclopaedia of Celtic Wisdom*, 65, 234.

36. Zell-Ravenheart, *Grimoire for the Apprentice Wizard*, 328–29.

exceptions are requests for defense and for healing. In these cases, you may receive a dragon who is strong in elements where you are weak.)

I have worked with dragon calling for many years. Between working in the domestic violence field and doing lots of spiritual work, I've felt the need to set up protective boundaries around my home. Anytime that I call my warding dragon, I see her snake around the house, the ground rumbling. I sometimes leave out offerings of flowers or fruit. She doesn't need them—it just increases our bond.

I have called dragons for others as well. About ten years ago, one of my friends who knew about my dragon calling work asked me to call a dragon for her property. Several of her neighbors, all single womxyn who worked outside the home, had been burglarized during work hours. My friend was the only one in the neighborhood who had not yet been burglarized, and she was living in fear that she would be next on the hit list. We called a dragon, and she was not burglarized. She and her dragon still have a relationship; she leaves shiny trinkets around her garden each year as a "thank you" to her dragon.

Last year, that same friend asked me to call a dragon for one of her friends who was motorbiking across the Australian outback. Her friend wanted protection for herself, and she was also worried about hitting kangaroos with her bike. I called her a dragon, and her trip across the outback was safe and successful.

If any of this sounds cool to you, then you may want to try calling a dragon for yourself. The following meditation can help you do just that! I believe the work deepens your relationship to your local land, so it's beneficial in many ways. And you may make a strong bond with a dragon that really improves your life! As with all magick, give yourself time to practice. Try calling a dragon more than once if it doesn't work out the first time. If you're not getting the results you desire, try working in a different location, whether that is around your own home, at a cool nature preserve, or at a local cave. Whatever you feel called to do tends to be correct as long as you always respect the law and the land.

The following meditation can be done indoors or out. Before beginning the meditation, think about the questions you'd like to ask a dragon and what favors you might like to ask for.

DRAGON CALLING MEDITATION

In your meditative space, settle into a relaxed position. Take a few deep, grounding breaths.

Visualize a spiritual flame that creates a circle around your space. The color is up to you. Know that this flame will protect your meditative space and only allow correct spiritual energies to enter.

Spend a few moments focusing on your quest: your goal and your needs. When you feel ready, say, "I am calling out to ask for the friendly partnership and help of a dragon who will work with me on my quest. Blessed be."

Prepare to see, hear, smell, and otherwise sense your dragon. What does your dragon look like? Does it make sound or have a specific smell? How does your dragon's presence feel? Does your dragon have a name? Does your dragon have a gender, no gender, or more than one gender? What element(s) does your dragon seem centered in? Earth, air, fire, water, spirit? Does your dragon have wings? Gills? Webbed feet? Is your dragon snakelike? Does your dragon breathe fire?

What powers does your dragon have? Some may be visible, like flying or breathing fire. Ask your dragon what powers they possess.

Tell your dragon what you believe your quest is. How will your dragon work with you to fulfill your quest? Does your dragon have a message to give you about how you should proceed in your own work toward this goal?

Ask your dragon how you should continue to call and connect with them. Are there colors you should wear? Are there songs you could play or sing? A bell you might ring? Also ask your dragon if they like to receive little offering gifts of food, song, or service.

Spend as much time as you like with your dragon. You may learn about where they like to hang out, how other humans work with them, what worries your dragon has about the state of the world or spiritual matters, or what your dragon is happy about or proud of.

When you feel ready to leave this meditation, say goodbye and thank your dragon. Note how they take their leave. Do they fly away? Leap into an ocean? Or have they taken up residence under your bed?

As you leave the meditative state, take more centering breaths and open up the meditative space by visualizing the colored flames of your circle fading into a smoke that returns to the spiritual source. Know that this smoke will carry

the energy of your work into the spiritual source to be manifested for your bene-
fit. Say, "I give thanks for the presence of this dragon and for all the assistance I
know I will receive in succeeding at my quest. Blessed be."

Spend some time journaling about your dragon, your experiences in the meditation, and how you plan to follow up on your quest. Since you may be new to working with dragons (or working with them in this way), I've included some additional journaling questions that you may want to tackle now or after later interactions with your dragon.

JOURNAL PROMPT

Do you believe in literal dragons? Or do you think they are an aspect of the deep self? Are they forces of the elements and nature? Are they all of this and more? What do you think you can learn from dragons in your rituals and meditations?

• • • • • • •

Now that we've covered tapping into your physical and spiritual self, let's discuss the issues you might be passionate about. The goal of activism is often to make small changes while impacting social fabric as a whole. For instance, we don't just want to end one act of discrimination—we want to end discriminatory thinking. Let's take a look at the ultimate act of peaceful protest: voting.

Voting Is One Mother of a Privilege

No matter what form of activism is important to you, you can achieve it more effectively if you're engaged in local politics. Whether you're passionate about reproductive rights, wage equality, school districts, animal welfare, roads and infrastructure, social security, or something else, there is probably a political component.

Womxyn having the right to vote is still a relatively new phenomenon: the US Constitution's nineteenth amendment celebrated its one-hundredth anniversary in 2020. Our great-grandmothers fought hard for this right, but now womxyn have had the right to vote for a few generations, and those of us who were born with it have gotten a little complacent. I get it. The vote was a huge deal for our great grandmas, our grandmas, and maybe our moms. To some of us, though, it might seem like nothing but a hassle. Whenever you are tempted to not bother voting, you might want to think about all the aspects of life that are impacted by a ballot:

- Do you like having worker rights such as overtime? Do you think there should be a minimum wage? Vote.

- Do you think moms (and dads) should get maternity/paternity leave from work? Vote.

- How do you feel about nondiscrimination laws regarding where you can work, where you can live, or how far you can progress in your education? Vote.

- Do you want to be able to retire with safety and dignity after a lifetime of paying taxes and otherwise contributing to your society? Vote.

- Do you like having legal access to condoms and other contraceptives? Vote.

- How do you feel about abortion? Either way, you gotta vote.

- Do you think domestic abuse should be illegal? Vote.

- Do you think people should be able to buy assault rifles? Decided by votes.

- Do you want your state to fix the potholes on the highway, already? Vote.

- Do you wish they'd run a commuter train line into town or increase the bus routes? Vote.

The list goes on and on. Your vote influences the outcome on these issues. And you have the power to elect local, state, and national politicians who are on the same page as you. With your votes and your guidance, politicians push society in one direction or another.

Well, heck… Great-grandma was onto something! Show up on election day and know what vote you want to cast when you get there. Goddess knows we'd better be part of an informed electorate or "the man" just might legislate us back to the Middle Ages!

If you're not sure what side of an issue you fall on, there are nonpartisan voting support sites available. In the United States, one to check out is the League of Women Voters. A quick web search should connect you with whatever you need; there is a ton of civic information online. There are also plenty of volunteer opportunities so you can encourage other womxyn to exercise their nineteenth amendment as well.

Tips for Informed Voting

- Study up on candidates running for election. Keep your eyes peeled for local events where representatives or other activists are discussing an issue.
- If you feel overwhelmed by all the issues on a ballot, focus on one issue that is of interest to you and become a local expert.
- Vet your sources of information. Sample your research from more than one place. Get as close to firsthand info as you can. Listen to people whose ethics you trust.
- Take notes on your votes! Sometimes the wording on a ballot can be sneaky. For instance, sometimes a "Yes" vote means "Yes, ban this." Plan ahead.
- Encourage your friends and family to vote. Help out by offering to give them a ride to policy panels, voter registration, and the polls, if you can.
- Don't underestimate the magick of the web. Host a party at your place and have friends or family listen to an educational talk online. Registering to vote can happen online as well.

Now that you're informed and activated, the following blessing will help you use your craft to make the most of your vote.

TRUE NORTH BLESSING TO HELP YOU CAST YOUR VOTE

On the morning before you go to the polls, consider having a cup of sage tea. This herb helps bring in spiritual clarity and mental focus. If the voting process stresses you out, try calming chamomile tea. Whatever your beverage, repeat the following mantra at least three times while you sip:

"Let my compass point true north. Guide my feet as I step forth. Give me peace and clarity. My votes will keep me safe and free."

For extra protection (and to cut all the crap), bring an obsidian gemstone with you to the polls.

• • • • • • •

Whether you agree with someone's political views or not, you can use mothering energy to wish peace on yourself and all of your fellow beings.

WORLD PEACE SPELL FOR OUR PLANET

This spell is one way to focus on maternal, protective, and loving energy in order to make the world a lovelier place. As you send out peace, you also receive it according to the laws of the craft. Therefore, this is a nice ritual to conduct for your own well-being. It empowers you and helps put you at ease.

IDEAL TIME: The waxing moon, the full moon, or a Monday.

PREPARATION AND ITEMS TO GATHER:
- Prepare a meditation space. The spell work section involves quiet meditation while sitting or lying down. You may wish to place your altar on a side table near your bed or favorite chair, for example. You could also set cozy meditation cushions next to your altar. Consider whether you would like relaxation amplifiers like meditative music, candles, aromatherapy, etc.
- Color correspondences for your altar like green, brown, and the colors of your favorite flowers will draw in healing earth energies. Blue is a healing energy and mirrors the appearance of our lovely planet.
- It may be fun to have a globe on or near your altar. A toy bouncy ball that looks like a globe would also be fine; it's just there to help with your visualization. I have a little Yule tree ornament of a globe that I use. Magazine images of Earth would work too.
- A smudge stick and matches or a lighter. If you prefer a smokeless option, mix a potpourri of healing herbs.

- If you'd like to incorporate gemstones, labradorite or lepidolite are good options.
- If you'd like to incorporate flowers, sunflowers would be right at home. Adding flowers to your altar for this ritual is a great idea.

CIRCLE UP: If you are able to, I recommend casting the circle with a smudge stick. These bundles of ritual herbs can be purchased at many metaphysical shops and even at some health food stores. This bundle of herbs incorporates all five sacred elements that are represented by the pentacle: the plants that formed the herbs contain earth and water energy, the burning end of the smudge contains the fire element, and the smoke rising skyward contains both air and spiritual energies. There are many types of herbs commonly used in smudge sticks. They might include mugwort, sage, cedar, or lavender. No matter what you choose, it will get the job done.

If you can't burn smudge in your environment, try making a potpourri out of the same types of purifying herbs. Sage, cedar, sweetgrass, mint, and rosemary are some optimal ingredients. Crush the herbs to increase their scent just before the ritual. When you circle up, take a deep whiff and use the energy of the herbs to help you cast a protective circle.

SPELL WORK: Sit in your chosen meditation spot and get comfortable, taking a few centering breaths. Allow yourself to just sit for the first few minutes. Be aware of your own body and how it feels to live inside it. Give thanks that your body takes care of you.

Visualize the planet earth. If you have a globe present, you can gaze at it or hold it. Take some time to enjoy the beauty of Earth's atmosphere and its features. Allow a blue-green light imbued with spiritual healing to envelope the entire globe. Know that this light, sent from the spiritual source, is realigning the energies of the entire planet to be peaceful and correct. What does "peace" mean for you?

Next, visualize the country that you live in. Allow the healing light to envelope it. How would your society change after spiritual energy corrected and recalibrated it for peace? Affirm that this work is indeed being done.

Visualize your life, workplace, family, and home. Repeat the process of imbuing your vision with the healing light. As you accept the gift of healing and realignment from this process, meditate on what positive changes it may bring. How will peaceful energies change your relationships, communication, and self-image?

When you feel ready, allow your consciousness to settle back into your body in your meditative space. Do the usual grounding activities like wiggling your fingers, stretching, and taking some deep breaths.

CLOSE UP SHOP: Use your smudge (or potpourri) to clear the space, affirming that the smoke (or scent) that drifts away from your circle is carrying your spell to the spiritual source in order to be manifested.

• • • • • • •

Earth, our own mother, provides all the mothering imaginable. She is nurturing, protective, and life-giving. Due to the natural consequences of our actions, she is also a disciplinarian. Mostly, however, she is always there for us. The following outdoor meditation gives you some tools to build your practice connecting with her.

TIME TO PUT DOWN ROOTS MEDITATION

This is a great meditation to help you root yourself in healing earth energy. It is meant to be doable on the fly and is ideal for time spent out in nature. Go for a walk on your lunch break or chill out in your own backyard. Don't let any lack of access to those types of places deter you; while being outside is lovely, this meditation can also be performed indoors (including at your desk during a quick break at work). This journey is a journey of the mind, so you can cast your roots into the earth from anywhere. All you need is an appropriate place to meditate. Whether indoors or out, choose a place that is quiet and comfy. Sit or lie down in such a way that you feel your bottom fully settled into a supportive surface.

IDEAL TIME: Anytime you are stressed, sad, lonely, mad, confused, or otherwise discombobulated. It is also good for when you feel conflicted about an important decision.

Preparation and Items to Gather:

- We're going to be working with roses in this meditation. If you can have roses nearby—wild, cut, dried, or as an essential oil—it may enhance your experience.

- If you'd like to incorporate gemstones, I recommend hematite or jasper (worn as jewelry or placed in your pocket).

- Optional: Your outdoor magick craft bag (see chapter 1).

Circle Up: Visualize a hedge of wild roses growing up around you in a protective circle. Affirm that you are part of this rose colony, rooted into Mother Earth and protected on all sides.

Spell Work: Settle into your seat and feel where your body meets all that supports it. Breathe in through your nose and out through your mouth.

With each breath, visualize your own roots stretching down into the earth below where you sit. These energetic roots may be brown, orange, red, or another color. Even if you are in a high-rise apartment, your roots easily reach deep down into the earth.

As your roots go down through the layers of earth, what do you see around them? Other roots, worms, or insects? Groundwater? Stones? If you see symbolic visions, let them happen. Think about your connection to the earth that sustains you and all other life. Feel your heart and blood syncing up with the cycles of the earth and its waters. Affirm this by saying, "I am one with the goddess and all of her life on this earth."

Now is your opportunity to sync up with Mother Earth. She supports you. She connects you. She made you. She is you. Allow yourself to feel this synchronicity by saying, "My heart beats with your heart. My heart flows with your flow. I trust you. I trust me. I am okay." How does this connection feel to you? Does it bring up emotions?

Now that you're strongly and consciously rooted to Mother Earth energy, release anything you'd like to be rid of. This might include fleeting experiences or hurt, anger, confusion, or embarrassment. Release deep baggage like past life trauma or childhood trauma. The deeper the wound, the more times it may take to actively purge it. Yet, you will probably see some positive changes immediately. Be patient and kind with yourself. You're not "fixing" yourself; you are just using all that energetic crap to fertilize the spiritual source. Mother Earth will make good use of it.

When you have finished releasing, say something like, "I release all that doesn't serve me. What does me no good can be recycled by the spiritual source. I give it as a gift. May I be gifted in return with joy, abundance, love, and peace."

Leaving your roots anchored in the earth, let your consciousness return to where your body sits. Visualize a beautiful rose plant growing out of your belly, heart, shoulders, and head. What color are the roses? How numerous and sharp are your thorns? How broad are your leaves? What scent are your rose petals? Give thanks for the beauty of your flowers. Honor the protectiveness of your thorns. Feel sunlight and oxygen soaking into your leaves. Enjoy your connection to the natural powers of air and earth. Know that they are always present for you. They always connect you to the goddess, both within and without.

Allow the rose plant to withdraw back into your body. Affirm that the beauty of your roses is always present in your head and heart energy centers. Allow your roots to return to your root chakra from the depths of the earth. Affirm that if you ground yourself in the earth energy of the goddess, she will always be there to calm your fears and reconnect you to her wisdom.

Open your eyes and wiggle your fingers and toes.

CLOSE UP SHOP: Watch the protective circle of roses withdraw back into the earth. Affirm that these flowers are carrying the energy of your ritual back to the spiritual source.

This isn't the type of work that is a one-and-done. Be prepared to repeat as needed, and allow the meditation to become a freestyle technique that makes sense to you. I used the rose plant due to its strong feminine energy and its healing, loving properties, but you can use any type of plant. Using an herbal-healing book as a guide, explore which plants have the medicine your body and spirit need.

Quick Tips for Environmental Health

Most of us are aware that the health of the planet is directly tied to our own physical health. Pollution, pandemics, and the availability of resources are a few of the connected issues. It's an important time for people everywhere to consider climate change and environmental wellness as serious concerns. Incorporate Mother Earth's loving energy in your daily life.

- Get into the habit of using reusable shopping bags, water bottles, and other convenience items like sandwich baggies or straws. Be patient with yourself as you develop the routine. It can take some time to remember, but it gets easier with practice.

- Reduce your animal product intake. Recent climate studies have suggested beef is the biggest culprit in terms of water and carbon footprints, but they all add up.[37]

- For the green version of a gold star, join a co-op, find a farmers market, or strive to buy local. Purchasing local produce supports your farming neighbors and reduces the water and carbon costs of food transport.

- Gasoline has a huge water footprint in addition to the impact of fossil fuels.[38] Walk, bus, bike, or carpool when it's realistic to do so. When it comes to cycling, it is often an option to put your bike on a bus storage rack in order to reduce your pedaling distance. Local cycling groups can be sources of friendship and can also give helpful tips.

- Take advantage of rebates and energy-efficiency grants to replace energy-vampire household appliances with greener versions. Programs that support increased household efficiency can help, and you'll end up saving money on your utilities in the long run.

- Landscape your property in a way that doesn't require much watering. To be more water-efficient regarding yard work and gardening, consider recycling rainwater.

- Consider "adopting" the natural area where you take your meditation walks. Bring some garbage bags and protective gloves and pick up trash.

- As for your own impact on any areas where you do spiritual work, it's best to follow the adage "Leave nothing but footprints." Be prepared

---

37. Ranganathan and Waite, "Sustainable Diets."

38. Food and Agriculture Organization of the United Nations, *Livestock's Long Shadow*; Ridoutt et al., "Meat Consumption and Water Scarcity."

to carry out anything you carry in. Only leave biodegradable spiritual offerings that will not harm wildlife.

- Magickal folks have developed various ways to send healing energy to nature. Research the types of spiritual work you might like to do outdoors. Options include water purification rituals, sound therapy using drums or crystal bowls, the use of sacred sculptures, and medicine wheels or stone circles to perform a type of "acupuncture" on the land. Do your research before jumping into any spiritual work.

The following meditation will help you feel your spiritual connection with the natural world around you if you are new to doing spiritual work outdoors (or for the benefit of the ecosystem).

MOTHER NATURE MEDITATION WALK

Before you begin this meditation, pick a spot to connect with Mother Nature. This will vary based on your locale. It may be a park, a beach, a nature trail, or your own backyard. It would be ideal if you found a nearby spot you could visit repeatedly; this can become a long-term relationship where you learn about the seasons and the moods of the natural world around you.

IDEAL TIME: Anytime you want to get in touch with nature.

PREPARATION AND ITEMS TO GATHER:
- Decide whether you will sit, lie down, or remain standing for your meditation. If you are going to sit, you may want to bring a small blanket or cushion.

- Only carry the personal belongings you need. Refer to chapter 1 for ideas on creating a craft bag for outdoor spiritual work. At the very least, basic supplies include water, sunscreen, bug repellent, and a GPS program or old-fashioned compass. If possible, lock your money and other essentials in the car (or leave them at home). This will help you focus more fully on your work.

- When considering the dangers of human civilization, make sure someone knows your itinerary and when you plan to return. Have a plan for checking in and a plan for what happens if you don't.

CIRCLE UP: Begin your meditative practice as you journey toward your meditation spot. I like to use a technique that I call third eye scanning. Picture yourself as a lighthouse with a spotlight that scans all around you in a big, bright circle. What is around you on all sides will be periodically illuminated. When using this technique, you are simply opening your intuition (often thought to reside in your third eye) in order to take "scans" of the energetic features all around you.

When you practice third eye scanning in nature, you may pick up what many call *elemental energies*. Elemental energies are the spiritual vibrations of natural life, including things like plants, stones, wind, and water. You may also see wild animals and, if you're a believer, elemental spirits. Human beings throughout history have told stories and passed on their own beliefs about diverse beings that are of a more elemental vibration than humankind. The most common examples are beings like gnomes, elves, fairies, dragons, and the like. If you're open to seeking out these enchanted creatures, you never know what your third eye scans might reveal!

No matter what you're open to or who you run into, a third eye scan during your walk toward your meditation spot will deepen your spiritual connection to this area. With practice, you can scan without pausing. At first, however, you may wish to stop periodically, close your eyes, and reach out with your psychic awareness. Take this time to use your other senses as well. What do you smell? What do you hear? How does the air taste?

Once you reach your meditation spot, use the elemental energy around you to purify a sacred space. If it's a sunny day, picture the sunlight casting protective light around you. If it's windy, use the breeze. If it's stormy, visualize the rain or snow casting a circle of water. In any case, say, "I affirm that my circle is cast by these elements in order to heal and protect me. Blessed be."

SPELL WORK: A simple way to place yourself into a meditative state is to let all of your senses experience what it is like to be part of the environment.

Pick a prominent aspect that's around you. It might be water, a tree, a flower, the clouds, the grass, a boulder, or something you feel particularly drawn to. Find a way to experience that aspect; it may be the sound of water, the solidity of rock, the song of birds, or the breeze rustling tree branches. If possible, close your eyes. Focus on this cue and feel yourself becoming part of the environment. What if you were a tree here? A flower? A lake or a stone? How is the sun important to you? The rain? The clean air? What is your role in creating this environment? Spend as much time as you like integrating yourself into this environment and asking yourself questions.

Next, ask questions to better understand the challenges in this environment. What role do humans have? Is the lake filled with trash? Are the tree branches snagging plastic shopping bags? Is the water too polluted to drink? Are there hazards to the wildlife? Whatever the challenges are to the environment, how might you and other people seek to fix them? Could you pick up trash or stop using plastic shopping bags? Think about air pollution and water pollution caused by sewage and other industries. What spiritual work might you do to help the energies of this place? Can you do this work? Would you need help or guidance? If so, where might you find help?

Before you leave the meditative state, send some healing energy to this place. It's like making a wish or saying a prayer—you are giving the gift of some of your own energy for the spirit of this place to use. Remember that energy follows thought: all you have to do is think about making this gift and it is done.

When you are ready, gently allow yourself to separate from the natural elements you've been working with and fully occupy your own body. Breathe and move your limbs to ease yourself through this process.

CLOSE UP SHOP: Give thanks to this place, do any cleanup you need or want to do, and head home. If you're game, try doing some more third eye scanning on your way out. It may be interesting to see how your experience of the area has changed.

chapter eight

(WITCH)CRAFTY CREATIVITY

Your first hint that I'm a hella creative person was probably this book. Yet it may surprise you to know that I believe that you are hella creative too. Creativity is more than the ability to make a film, put on an art exhibit, or publish a book. At its core, creativity is the expression of the wonderful human instinct to contribute and communicate. Even if you are writing in a private journal, you are expressing this need because you are communicating with yourself.

Creativity also allows you to learn. It helps you find and celebrate the authentic glories of self. You can even use creativity to measure change in yourself. A good practice of creativity helps you tap into what you really want; sometimes your deepest desires appear from a subconscious level (or a spiritual one) long before you are aware of them in your waking mind.

Let's Get Creative

Obviously, this isn't a creativity book. It's a magickal one. But remember, there is a ton of creativity in the craft. Even though a book like this suggests spells and things for you to try, you are designing your altars and many elements of your practice on your own. All of this is creative! And the more you get into it, the more power and individuality you bring to your casting.

Building your creative practices will increase the power of your manifestations. This may sound similar to what I said about a strong sexual practice. This isn't a coincidence—the two are very connected. Like sex, your creativity is a major source of deep and intimate fuel. The more you integrate it into your daily life, the more you can use the craft to get what you really want. I don't think it's a coincidence that Amy Jo Goddard (a sexuality advocate and therapist) and SARK (a creativity mentor and maven) both call their respective fields "the juice" of life.[39]

I think I replaced my sexuality with creativity for quite a while due to my history of childhood sexual trauma. This isn't a bad thing. But if you think you may be doing the same thing, take it from me—you can have both. Why choose between sex and creativity? That's like choosing between chocolate and ice cream.

There is no "right" way to be creative. I've dabbled in lots of different creative pursuits over the years: expressive art, music, scrapbooking, drawing, taking photos. My outlet of choice is writing, whether that is in my journal or as a columnist for *SageWoman* magazine or another periodical. I've even written poetry!

Poetry is what I am the most insecure about. I've had some poems published, but even those never quite sat right with me. Nevertheless, I persisted. Creativity is about communication. You aren't required to share your creativity with the world, but sometimes that's what you need to push yourself a little. For instance, here's an old poem of mine that I think is fun and has a spinstress vibe:

Scrying: A Poem
Scrying
is to seek the future by reading the flight of birds.
Never in the motherland did it involve taking bird guts in the hand.
This was the pursuit of priests
who envied her seasons of bleeding and
would sneak out to play with mother's toys.
Boys will be boys, expressing the need to penetrate

---

39. Goddard, *Woman on Fire*, 193; SARK, *Eat Mangoes Naked*, 11.

be visceral, eviscerate, and dominate the fates
who sit spinning in the basement
peering over horn-rimmed glasses
at the comings and goings of great men
like Byron and Aristotle, then sigh and
snuff them out like guttered candles.
These doting aunts will give kisses
and old ribbon candy from a bottomless
dish but will not be run around the block
by men in black no matter how they cant
in dead languages just because they can and
then try to Divine by tormenting living things.

I took this poem to poetry society meetings and even to an open-mic night! Poetry is not my first choice when it comes to expressing myself, but I pushed myself out of my comfort zone. Originally, I got into poetry because I thought experimenting with language would sharpen up my prose. I think it has, and I had some fun in the process.

This is what creativity is all about! There's the comfortable stuff that you always rely on. Then there are the scary first tries; this stuff reminds you that you're alive. Sometimes you leave your comfort zone and find your new favorite thing. Again, it's a lot like sex!

You will probably find a good balance of fun and fear in your own creative journey. Take your time and do what feels right. This chapter offers spells, rituals, meditations, and resources to allow your inner creativity to come out and play. Right off the bat is a spell to help you tap into your creative spark.

QUICK SPELL TO IGNITE YOUR CREATIVE CORE

This is one of the super simple spells I encourage you to use out in nature, in the parking lot at the craft store, or anywhere inspiration is required and requested.

IDEAL TIME: Anytime you feel the call of your creativity.

PREPARATION AND ITEMS TO GATHER:
- A (gem)stone. Some options are amber, clear quartz, or a stone you found in nature that really appeals to your creative side.

CIRCLE UP: Get into a comfortable position and take a few deep, centering breaths. Visualize a white light around you as you hold your stone against the center of your forehead, where your third eye chakra is located.

SPELL WORK: Say, "I welcome in the energies of my deepest creativity. I welcome participation for all energies and powers that love me unconditionally. Help me to express my gifts." (If this doesn't appeal to you, feel free to make up your own creative thing!)

Spend some time thinking about the creative project(s) you would like to do. Follow your train of thought wherever it goes; this is the time for brainstorming! If you are doing this spell prior to attending a class or buying some supplies, think about how that experience will help you meet these creative goals.

CLOSE UP SHOP: Pocket your stone and get going on that project! Have fun.

Rites for Creativity

Since love and creativity are basically the same thing, it's helpful to remember that the ritual correspondences for love will also work for creative ventures. This is especially true in the sense that it takes a certain level of self-esteem to allow oneself to create. Here are some ways to embrace creativity in your daily life:

- Add your creativity goals and samples of your work to your personal power altar.
- Use love-boosting essential oils and herbs like bergamot, rose, vanilla, cinnamon, and amber to stimulate creativity. Burn them. Wear them. Bathe in them. Dab them on a love letter and mail it to yourself.
- Create personal deadlines. Creative productivity is like other forms of exercise; it's a discipline that you can improve at with effort.

- Explore local resources for honing your creative crafts. Many states have a poetry society, independent film association, arts council, community theater troupe, or musical group that take new members. If there is a community radio station near you, these rely on volunteers. If you're willing to put in the hours, they will train you to run studio equipment, host shows, and more. There are lots of ways to follow your interests without investing a ton of cash.

- Reject notions of artistic or writer's block. Do the work. If you hit a wall in one aspect of your project, go ahead and do something else. Multitasking is often very effective for creative people. Don't force yourself to finish one thing before moving on to another; go where inspiration moves you.

- The colors orange, yellow, and gold symbolize success. They also raise energetic vibrations of positivity and creativity. Keep these colors around you. Wear them. Incorporate them into your art. Boost your positive and creative vibes by using citrus essential oil on your pressure points or in a diffuser. Eating citrus also helps. I find citrus especially helpful during dark or cold seasons of the year.

- Collect fun items to build your creativity altar and to use in creativity rituals. I bought an old, broken Hermes typewriter and turned it into an altar piece. Hermes, if you haven't met him yet, is a Greek god associated with knowledge, messages, and other types of communication. I also have my paternal great-grandpa's quill pen on my altar; I don't use it to write, but I like having it around. Once, I even used it as a wand for casting a creativity spell!

Up next is a full ritual that gives you a chance to build your creativity altar. The goddess Brigid will help you out as you plan or reignite a hot creative idea.

BRIGID'S FLAME: SPELL FOR CREATIVE SPARKS

Have you ever seen a picture or statue of the Celtic goddess Brigid where it looks like her hair is on fire? This alarming hairstyle actually symbolizes the sacred flame of creativity that anoints Brigid's brow. As such, she is a kickass muse for a spinstress looking to create art, writing, a social movement, or another lovely gift for our world.

IDEAL TIME: Anytime you feel the call of your creativity.

PREPARATION AND ITEMS TO GATHER:
- Your creativity altar. Choose whatever colors, stones, and other goodies appeal to you!
- A white candle.
- Lavender essential oil.

CIRCLE UP: Take a few deep, centering breaths. Visualize a golden light of protection and inspiration around your sacred space. If you like, call upon Brigid as the keeper of the creative flame.

SPELL WORK: Anoint your candle with lavender essential oil. As you do so, think about your creative goal(s). As you light the candle, say, "I dedicate my creative flame to (describe your goal or project). Whenever I need focus or encouragement, I know that I can return to this flame."

CLOSE UP SHOP: Once the candle has been dedicated, you may burn it at any time. Replace it is needed until your goal is met. Leave the altar up and continue this work for as long as is needed. You may want to add new items to the altar or, if you start feeling stuck, redo it completely.

• • • • • • •

Sometimes, the creativity that you need is finding time to do magick! This mix-and-match spell menu gives you optimal chances to do a quick spell in a pinch.

MULTIPURPOSE BIRTHDAY CANDLE SPELL

Amid a busy schedule of caregiving, working, creativity, and activism it can be hard to find the time for personal practices. When I want to do a spell but don't have a lot of time to spare, I like to work with birthday candles. Any will do, though I get sustainable ones from a local health food store that are a tiny bit larger than the common varieties. Either way, a box of birthday candles gives you lots of color correspondences to match different types of spells. Don't leave the burning candles unattended. This is one of the reasons it works great to use such tiny tapers: the burn time is short.

To easily burn a birthday candle, you can stick it in a dish of salt or sand. Another option would be to stick it into an actual cake or muffin and then leave the confection out as an offering to the divine. (Yes, okay. You can take a few bites.) This may sound like thinking outside the (cake mix) box, but it's not a new notion. It's possible that birthday candles originate from an ancient Greek practice like this, when cakes laden with little torches (known as *amphiphontes*) were left out for the goddess Hecate.[40] If you leave food out for the local critters to enjoy in her name, make sure it contains no harmful ingredients; chocolate and raisins, for instance, are toxic to dogs and should be avoided.

In addition to deciding how to handle your birthday candle, think about other ways to boost your power. Working on the optimal day of the week and during the best moon phase are options, though it's not essential. Anointing candles with an appropriate ritual oil is a common technique. I'll suggest a few options, but you can check an almanac or even buy a book about candle craft if you plan to work this way a lot.

I'm offering a general spell and some ideas for homing in on some common goals. It's just a starting point for you to work from; your correspondences will vary according to your purpose. Here are some common ideas:

LOVE

- A pink, red, or white candle.
- Rose quartz, amethyst, lepidolite, garnet, or emerald gemstones.
- Rose absolute, amber, or synthetic musk essential oil.

MONEY

- A green, purple, or white candle.
- Lodestone, emerald, or citrine gemstones.
- Cedar, frankincense, or sandalwood essential oil.

---

40. d'Este and Rankine, *Hekate Liminal Rites*.

PROTECTION

- A purple, blue, or white candle.
- Jet, hematite, clear quartz, shungite, or emerald gemstones.
- Myrrh, cedar, or sage essential oil.

HEALING

- A green, pink, or white candle.
- Clear quartz, jade, shungite, or bloodstone gemstones.
- Sage, lavender, or eucalyptus essential oil.

GENERAL SUCCESS

- A yellow, orange, or purple candle.
- Clear quartz, jasper, labradorite, citrine, or agate gemstones.
- Frankincense, cedar, or grapefruit essential oil.

IDEAL TIME: Check out my suggestions about moon phases and days of the week in chapter 1.

Almanacs can give you additional ideas, including planetary phases and holidays from around the world.

PREPARATION AND ITEMS TO GATHER:

- A birthday candle of your choice.
- Matches or a lighter.
- A dish of salt or sand (or a confection) to support your burning candle.
- Essential oil for anointing candles.
- An altar cloth in the color of your choosing.
- Gemstones, incense, or music to match your ritual purpose.
- Optional: It's always a good idea to have water nearby when you burn candles.

CIRCLE UP: Visualize a clear energy (or the color of your choice) encircling your sacred space. Affirm that it is letting only correct and positive energies into contact with you and your spell. Get into a comfortable meditative position and take some centering breaths. Have your music going if you've chosen some. Take some time to focus on your goal before you light the candle; it won't burn for very long, so you want to be ready from the jump.

SPELL WORK: As you light the candle, say, "As quickly as this candle burns, so shall my purpose be achieved. With harm to none and for the good of all, so shall it be." Personalize this affirmation as desired.

As the candle burns, meditate on your goal. Use positive affirmation techniques to manifest your goal. Think with gratitude about what you already have that will support you in achieving your goal. Affirm that the goal you seek is already manifesting in your life. Visualize yourself having reached your goal. Raise the feelings you will have when you have achieved success and bask in them. Ask for guidance in achieving your goal in the best possible way and with harm to none.

Birthday candles usually take a few minutes to burn out. Continue your meditation until the candle has burned down to the point of extinguishing itself. (If the candle splutters and begins to scorch the base where you have it anchored, blow it out or douse it with water.)As the smoke dissipates, visualize your spell going into the spiritual source in order to manifest your desire.

Affirm that your manifestation has been achieved by saying, "So it is, and so shall it be. I give thanks that my magick is achieved."

CLOSE UP SHOP: Visualize the energetic shield you created dissipating back into the spiritual source. Affirm that your spell will manifest and have a positive effect on the world.

• • • • • • •

Coming up with all these great ritual ideas can be thirsty work. Hydrate magick style with this creativity-boosting brew.

⌂REATIVI-TEA

Make a cup of tea by steeping herbs like rosemary, mugwort, thyme, yarrow, or mint. These herbs can be mixed with a base tea like green or black. You could go with loose tea or bags, depending on your preferences and supplies.

Add a slice of lemon or some dried orange peel to boost your sense of creative empowerment.

Once you have poured a cup, say the following blessing over it while it cools:

"Mother Earth, infuse this brew with your power of creativity. Bless me with the inspiration to take correct action and the support that I need to bring my ideas to bloom. Like yours, may my creativity bring joy and sustenance to myself and others. Blessed be."

Switch out your blends occasionally in order to keep inspiration fresh.

• • • • • • •

The next spell (or menu of spells) require some creativity because you choose your own design; it's like going to one of those ice cream bars where you order your own mix-ins. Have fun!

ROSIE'S RIVETING RITUAL FOR DIY GOALS

If you're interested in do-it-yourself (DIY) projects, this ritual can help you bring a little enchantment into your work. Whether you are looking to redecorate your space or rewire your entertainment system, this little ritual will bless your work and the outcome by helping you to construct and dedicate an altar specifically for your project.

If you're working to reclaim your personal space, the cumulative task can sometimes seem overwhelming. Focus on a little bit at a time! If you aren't able to make changes throughout your entire home, concentrate on the spaces that belong to you. In shared areas like a kitchen or living room, try to negotiate some private spaces like a personal cupboard, refrigerator shelf, or reading area. If you're overwhelmed by clutter, pick one manageable area to reclaim first. Ideally, this is a place where you spend a lot of time; a living room or bedroom might be the prime candidate. If you have to break the task down even further, pick one area in the room that you often gaze at and tidy that space first. Seeing this change will calm you down and inspire you.

When doing home improvement work, things often don't go quite according to plan. You need to be creative, flexible, intuitive, and practical. Return to your altar whenever you need a boost.

IDEAL TIME: The moon phase you use depends on the type of work you are doing. If you're cleaning out your attic or similar, you may want to work with the dissipating energies of a waning moon. If you are creating or bringing in something new, use the waxing moon. Sundays also correspond.

PREPARATION AND ITEMS TO GATHER:

- Make an altar somewhere in your home that will bless this endeavor until it is completely done. If your DIY goal is extensive, it may take some time. Altars can be tucked away in a cupboard or built on a windowsill; they don't have to take up a large space.

- Place some images or tools that represent your project on your altar. If you're cleaning, a broom (preferably a ritual besom) could be present. If you are doing repairs (or hiring them out), put a hammer on the altar. Think symbolically and creatively to bring the correct energies in.

- If you have a tarot card deck, put the Three of Pentacles on your altar. This card symbolizes construction, repair, and other sorts of creative manifestation. If you don't have a tarot deck, print out a picture of this card. Placing three coins on your altar also embodies this energy.

- Some sort of purification tool, like an herbal smudge or salt water.

- Optional: Bring a pretty geranium into the house if you wish to correspond with the cleansing energy of new beginnings. Geraniums are toxic to dogs and cats; if you have furry friends, you may wish to print some images of geraniums instead.

CIRCLE UP: Waft smudge smoke all around the area where you are creating your altar. If you'd prefer not to work with smoke, sprinkle salt water for the same cleansing effect.

SPELL WORK: Place your hands over the top of the Three of Pentacles card. Say, "I ask for the correct spiritual forces to be present and at work in my DIY project. I know that I am being helped and that the outcome will be exactly as I desire. May I be inspired to find the right plans, the right supplies, and the right help to aid in this task. May the work be solid and long-lasting, and may the outcome be exactly as I desire. I give thanks for this assistance. With harm to none and for the good of all, so shall it be."

CLOSE UP SHOP: Use your smudge or salt again and visualize the energy of your sacred space dissipating. Affirm that as the energy returns to the spiritual source, your spell will be manifest in every correct way.

Repeat some version of this ritual as needed while your project is ongoing. Consider adding new items as focal points or offerings when you need to regroup or strategize about a change in your plans.

• • • • • • •

Next up, let's explore one of my favorite creative outlets: writing.

Sacred Stories

Storytelling via fiction, poetry, or music forms the canon of sacred storytelling. Whenever you talk about gods and goddesses in your religion, this is sacred storytelling. An entertaining story is an effective way to express and even spread beliefs; tall tales, poems, and songs are easier to remember than theological discourse. Some stories last centuries longer than the religions that created them. This type of storytelling is (and should be!) a modern art.

Sacred story has deep meaning encoded within an entertaining package. All religious stories are—at their core—stories. They would not have survived if people had not found them interesting. Think of all the cultural traditions and religious information that would have been lost forever if not for the arts! Folk songs, fairy tales, and nursery rhymes are just a few examples.

Authoring Your Own Sacred Stories

Many people assume that sacred stories are documents of the past. It's a common notion that works written by our ancestors are too divinely inspired to be redacted or set aside. This can leave us feeling trapped by sacred tomes that reflect cultural practices society has moved beyond.

I believe that the sacred stories of the past are no different than the sacred stories of today. Ancient stories were written by inspired human beings. We can and should learn from the wisdom of our ancestors, but that doesn't mean we can't write, dance, or sing stories of our own! Prose, dance, poetry, film, and song are all great methods of storytelling.

Storytelling is as crucial in modern times as it was in the past. This is true for individuals and cultural groups. Telling your personal sacred story is reflective. It helps you clarify your own beliefs. And if you share your sacred story with others, you help them to engage in their own process.

Try writing your own sacred stories. These are the stories that inform your life and convey your beliefs to yourself and maybe even others. Your sacred stories could be totally fictional. They could be autobiographical segments of your own life story and lessons. They could even be revisions of religious stories you were raised with.

It can be especially helpful to author your own sacred stories if you feel you are underrepresented (or unrepresented) in the tales you hear. Don't worry if what you are creating doesn't feel like your ultimate truth right away; stories evolve over time. In fact, I believe that storytelling itself is a vehicle for personal as well as social transformation. Here are some ideas to jump-start your writing:

- Keep a journal of ideas, story lines, and verses.
- Pick a story that has always spoken "truth" to you or that you have always been drawn to. Prepare to write your own version! Read more than one version of your chosen story. Research the meanings of the character names, the historical context, and the deeper spiritual meanings. As you do this research, take note of your own thoughts. When you're researching, what you disagree with is just as important as what resonates. Rewrite the sacred story to better reflect your beliefs.
- Write a story that represents your beliefs, religion, relationships with other creatures, or the world around you.
- Take a workshop or class on a storytelling format that you want to work with. You might find writing workshops offered at bookstores or through adult education programs.
- Does a Neopagan group near you have a Bardic (storytelling) circle? If not, you could try starting one.
- Have some fun. Don't pressure yourself to share your work. If you feel ready to share, start with someone you trust. You have just as much right to speak as anyone else!

Music and Sacred Sound

Another very common—and very cool—form of creative expression is music. Drumming, singing, chanting, songwriting, and crystal bowls are just a few ways musical spinstresses can get down. Have you ever noticed that music can help you relax, meditate, celebrate, grieve, work out, make out, and more? You're not wrong.

In the introduction, I mentioned that I am ordained as a priestess under the care of the Iseum Musicum in Bangor, Maine, founded by composer, musician, and priestess Kay Gardner. Kay was also a pioneer in the research of sacred sound as a source of spiritual enlightenment and all types of healing.[41] I got to work directly with Kay for a while after college before she crossed to the other side in 2002. This section will include some of the things I learned from Kay as well as my own research about the many uses of sacred sound.

While hymns and chants enhance worship and an appropriate playlist boosts our manifestations, the power of sound is much vaster than all this. Pythagoras, an ancient master of the occult and a mathematical genius, taught that musical notes grant access to energetic vibrations that are the key to spiritual advancement and ultimate enlightenment. Pythagoras is credited with creating the musical scale still in common use today.[42]

Magickal Music Correspondences

In modern concepts of sacred sound, major keys are associated with magickal correspondences and healing systems. Making use of a singing bowl or similar instrument tuned to a specific pitch is thought to enhance certain healing and manifestation energies. For instance, the heart source corresponds to cardiac issues, emotion, love, fertility, and deities like Venus or Freya. The musical pitch thought to correspond to these energies is the key of F. Other musical correspondences as I have learned them include:

- A: Psychic work, divination
- B: Reincarnation, karma, enlightenment

---

41. See Gardner, *Sounding the Inner Landscape* to learn more about her work.
42. Sethares, *Tuning, Timbre, Spectrum, Scale*, 163.

- **C:** Grounding, home, sex
- **D:** Protection of self and others
- **E:** Self-esteem, success
- **G:** Communication, wisdom, learning[43]

Working with Sacred Sound

You can work with sacred sound using a technique called a sound bath. A sound bath is simple and intuitive. It's great for healing work because it doesn't have to be planned out in advance. This is great for group work, so give it a shot with your spinstress tribe.

To participate in a sound bath, one or more people (the more the merrier!) hum, chant, or sing a sort of spell or prayer that is being sent directly to the spirit of the recipient. The person in need might stand or sit in the center of the group while everyone else sends their musical offering toward them. It may sound chaotic until you try it, but every sound bath I have ever seen or joined in has been beautiful and unique. They are so powerful.

Other techniques for working with sound include:

- Playing a singing bowl that is attuned with the type of energy you want to raise
- Chanting a mantra; look up different sound mantras or write your own
- Using chimes, bells, gongs, or rattles to raise energy for a circle
- Singing a song while holding hands, marching, or dancing
- Listening to musical arrangements that evoke the type of energy you want to work with and project (most people already do this, often without even realizing it)

Journal Prompt

How are music and sound important to you? In what ways do you currently work with music and sound? How might you add more sacred sound into your spiritual routines?

---

43. Kay Gardner, *Music As Medicine: The Art & Science of Healing with Sound*, Sounds True, Incorporated, February 1, 1998, audio cassette, unabridged.

part three
CRONE: PURPOSE

This aspect of the goddess calls us to name and claim our expertise. Leadership, longevity, and experience are positive traits for womxyn. Womxyn of any age can work with crone energy. You rock the powers of the crone when you speak up and ask for the promotion that your company was about to give someone you trained not too long ago, or when you mentor younger generations by offering workshops and classes or write a book. The crone invites us to reintroduce honoring our elders in a largely ageist mainstream.

You embody crone energy when you practice spiritualism or divination techniques that ground you in your inner voice and help you choose your path. Crone energy also includes weaving connections to the land of spirit by challenging your fears about death and rebirth. This section's rituals, recipes, activities, and meditations will help you with all this and more—pointy hats completely optional.

The message of the crone is: "Remember purpose."
Claim your expertise and be a leader for
the future generations of sisters.

In my years spent traversing the globe in a womxyn's body, I have done all sorts of things to try and gain wisdom and a sense of my own power. In both cases, I think it all had to do with needing to feel safe and to boost my self-esteem. I have traveled the globe visiting sacred sites, touched Stonehenge, crawled through the birthing chambers of ancient underground temples, wedged myself into underground caves, and witnessed spiders as big as my hand. I've climbed mountains and crossed raging rivers and been taught to fight with sticks. (Well, they *tried* to teach me to fight using sticks. It turns out my best technique for self-defense is my caustic vocabulary.)

No, I wasn't an Indiana Jones wannabe. I was just a girl who didn't feel like enough; I was trying to feel like *more*. More intelligent, more experienced, more spiritual, and sometimes more tough. All of this comes down to a thing that many Pagans and witches call *sovereignty*. The term literally means "royalty" or "monarchy." It's obviously got some patriarchal and imperialist tones, so a lot of womxyn reject it. Still, the meaning underneath is as serious as anything gets. It's about the right and ability to call your own shots. It's about running your own life. It's about taking your own power. Sovereignty is often associated with the crone phase of life because of the confidence and life experiences older womxyn have. That's fine. Older ladies deserve that respect!

The sovereign goddesses associated with the crone phase are usually triune and represent every age and stage of womxyn's lives, yet they are often seen as old. This might be because their history and occult observances are ancient, but they're so much more than "old"—they're badass. Sovereign goddesses are comfortable with their power. Mess with these womxyn at your own peril. But they weren't exclusively a source of terror; they enforced justice and led nations with their power. Their bitchy side was reserved for those who committed injustices or treated the goddess herself with disrespect. We're going to work on the idea of power in this part of the book. Sovereignty, whether you care for that particular term or not, is about *being* power, not taking power, wanting power, or even having power.

You don't have to fear the crone phases, babies. These wicked womxyn have learned enough of the rules to know when to break them. Wise womxyn run the world and smash any glass ceilings that get in their way.

Goddesses with Crone Energy

Many goddesses we think of as the crone have a triune identity. This isn't a surprise when you think about it: the crone contains the experience of the maiden and mother within her.

- **Cerridwen:** This Welsh goddess was brewing a potion in her cauldron and hired a young man to tend it. He ended up splashing the potion on his hand and instinctively licked the burn. In the process, he took in the powers of the cauldron, which threw Cerridwen into a murderous rage. Cerridwen and the young wizard who would later become Taliesin (Merlin) began a shape-shifting chase. When he changed into a songbird, she changed into a hawk. When he changed into a rabbit, she turned into a hunting dog. You get the picture. The boy ended up as a single piece of grain and Cerridwen as the hen who gobbled him up. Once inside her belly, he became a child and was reborn to Cerridwen as Taliesin, meaning "radiant brow." Cerridwen captured the attention of modern witches, particularly in Wicca, who often relate to her as the goddess. Her powers include herb craft, shape-shifting, and other transformations. As the crone goddess, she and her cauldron represent the cycles of death and rebirth.

- **Hecate:** In modern times, Hecate is mostly seen in her crone role and as a deity with powers over the realm of the dead. Hecate was a guardian within the underworld; she carried a flaming torch and helped souls negotiate their journeys between death and rebirth. Hecate's power to determine the fate of souls gave her a whole lot of pull. In the story of Persephone's abduction by Hades, it was Hecate who brokered the treaty that allowed Persephone to move between the lands of the dead and the living. Hecate was known to hang out at triple crossroads with her undead hounds, accepting offerings like honey and garlic. A jill-of-all-trades, she had shape-shifting powers like Cerridwen. It seems many goddesses associated with life, death, and reincarnation expressed their knowledge and skill by changing their form more often than Beyoncé changes her bustier!

- **Morrighan:** Here we have another badass, shape-shifting, powerful triple goddess that is often pigeonholed as a crone by modern witches and wizards. This Irish goddess has the same range of phases and powers as the other dark ladies mentioned here. Associated with sex and death, Morrighan often shape-shifted into forms like the cow, the crow, the eel, and the wolf. And because she was associated with death and rebirth, she was thought to haunt battlefields and to grant victory in wars. A powerful goddess with the power to make or break kings, it's no wonder her name means "phantom queen."

- **Kali:** From the outside, the Hindu goddess Kali looks like some sort of terrifying monster whose devotees worship her in cemeteries. But people worship her in maudlin places in order to remind themselves that this life is impermanent, yet the soul lives on. Kali's role in death is only the tip of the iceberg. She is looked to for justice and protection. Whenever images show Kali ripping up someone, it invariably turns out to be a demon. How's that for a badass role model?[44]

---

44. Monaghan, *Encyclopedia of Goddesses and Heroines*.

chapter nine

MAGICKAL SELF-DEFENSE

With all the cultural baggage flying at womxyn every day, we need self-defense. It isn't about being aggressive; it's more about owning your boundaries—and, if needed, defending them. You don't have to take kickboxing lessons to defend your space (unless you want to). A lot of this comes from within. Energy work that helps you name and claim your limits is often enough to clearly project that you won't take any shit. It won't avoid every need for direct communication, but it will help.

The following bag of tricks includes crafty self-defense tools like wards and sigils. We'll also look at defining ethical positions so you know exactly where you want to draw your lines in order to be true to yourself. And if a dish of salt isn't quite doing the trick, we'll even talk about how to call dragons. Yes, that's a thing. Ready? Enjoy.

Building and Working with Sigils

Maybe you became interested in magick after reading fantasy books or watching fantasy films. Certainly, people also encounter witchy symbols in the horror genre as well. At any rate, the power that magickal men and womxyn have worked throughout the ages is very real. While some media is more respectful and accurate than others, it's all just the tip of the iceberg.

In just about every film I've ever seen on magick, at some point the womxyn produces a really cool-looking ritual symbol or two. It may appear in a spell book or on an arcane scroll. It may be drawn on the ground, in front of the hearth, or even written in blood. For good or evil, these are always badass-looking symbols. In real craft, these powerful symbols are called *sigils*.

I'm sure you've heard the saying "A picture is worth a thousand words." That's the idea behind sigils. What they do is take your intention and boil it down from a string of words and thoughts and complexities into something very concrete. You cut your ideas down into a few letters or numbers, design them into a symbol, and use it in your spell work to enhance and quickly transmit your focus.

There are many ways to design sigils, but in this chapter I'm going to give you an example of how I tend to work with them. Sometimes I research and try someone else's techniques, but for the most part, I like to keep my sigil magick functional and simple.

Design a Sigil

You can use sigils for fun, profit, love, or kicking someone's ass. Seriously, you know I don't advocate offensive spells (often called *hexing*), but getting your claws out is sometimes needed to defend your boundaries or physical safety. In this spirit, I offer the following example.

Say you broke up with someone, but they just won't leave you alone. In addition to using your direct communication skills and, if needed, a personal safety plan that you design with friends and/or professionals, you want to add a little boost. You could use the following sentence as a starting point. It's a concise version of what you want, but a little verbose: "Jo Schmo, leave me alone!" or whatever. Feel free to cuss Jo's ass. It's your sigil.

When you have the first sentence, you start boiling it down in your cauldron of verbal magick. List the letters in the sentence, omitting any letters that are repeated in the sentence. So, in Jo's case, you have JSCHVN left.

Next, you would design a symbol that looks good to you and incorporates all of these letters. This can be as elaborate as you like. I'm not an elaborate type of artist, so I simply arrange the letters in a way that looks good to me. Once you get started, you'll find that some letters overlay: an "n" can be built right into an "h" and so forth. Just play with it until you like the effect. As I said, there are systems for converting these letters into numbers and boiling your symbol down even more. You can look into this if it sounds interesting to you; I like to work with the letters. Either way, your design is created using your base ingredients (letters or numbers). What you have at the end of this process is your sigil. It is the boiled down, crystallized form of your original statement.

Before you put your sigil to use, you will first want to empower it with a small blessing, similar to the way you would empower an oil, tea, or other tool that you made. It's like putting gas in your lawn mower before you try to start it! You can write your blessing or just wing it. Here's an example:

"By all the powers of the spiritual source and the elements of creation, and with the correct guidance of the divine intelligence, I empower this sigil. Where it is set it cannot be stopped from working my will. Let it be fixed, set, and done, with harm to none."

Looking at this sigil and understanding where it came from—it came from inside yourself!—you have a focal point that is sharper and more powerful during a meditation. That's the idea, anyhow. Rather than chanting a sentence over and over, you can simply stare at your sigil while you raise energy, then release it into the spiritual source.

At the end of your spell, or if you find that you no longer need this sigil around, you can release it into the spiritual source by burning it, burying it, or otherwise erasing the image. You can also say a little spell like: "I thank this sigil for working my will. May your powers now resolve and dissolve. Return now to Source with my blessing and thanks. So be it."

You can use sigils in many ways, including:

- Draw sigils on paper and carry them in a spell bag, place them on the altar, or simply tuck them in your pocket.

- Draw them on a surface like a mirror or wall to provide invisible protection. You can use oil or just your finger to draw the sigil.

- Paint sigils on a stone or something similar and make them a permanent feature in your ritual work. This is a great option if the sigils represent a goal you want to stay anchored in for a long time.

- Use them in sex spells (alone or with a partner) as a focal point while raising sexual energy for a goal. Back in chapter 5, I mentioned that sigils are a great way to simplify your intent and hold your focus while raising and directing sexy magickal energy.

- Use a piece of driftwood to draw sigils on the beach and then let the waves carry your wishes into the realm of manifestation.

- Put a healing sigil into a get well card for a friend who has asked you for healing prayers and energy.

- Chalk them on the pavement (provided it's allowed where that pavement exists).

- Use them in group work. Each group member can participate by creating a sigil. Note that you should never use a sigil in secret when in a circle with others; that's just proper etiquette. Everyone in the circle should know what they are helping raise energy for.

That's about it from me, though there are lots of other sources and magickal systems that can teach you more about sigils if you're interested. With your wicked sigil practice, you can build symbols to empower all the spells in this book and more! Now we're moving on to a field related to sigils: warding. In fact, you may want to use sigils while constructing these enchanted security systems.

Warding and Protection

Warding is a practice of defensive magick in which a witch or wizard turns some sort of object into an energetic battery that powers an enchanted security system. Wards serve as a trigger to remind our subconscious minds to keep our psychic defenses up. They also serve as a sort of psychic security system that repels incorrect (or otherwise unwanted) energies. Once an object becomes a ward, it should be treated respectfully by everyone, including you.

BASIC BOBBLE WARDING SPELL

It's best to start simple when creating wards. Just play with the practice by starting with a gemstone, a natural stone from your yard or a special outdoor spot, or perhaps a piece of your jewelry.

IDEAL TIME: The new moon.

PREPARATION AND ITEMS TO GATHER:

- If you are building an altar for your warding work, good color schemes might include black, red, or purple.
- You will need the object you intend to ward and a dish of earth. Make sure you choose a dish that is large enough to hold the warding object and the earth. For earth, you could use a bit from your yard or garden or you could use potting soil. Graveyard dirt is an excellent addition to a defensive altar (more about this in chapter 10). Whenever you collect earth for use in magick, leave an offering. If leaving a food offering, it should be something environmentally friendly that is of use to the creatures of that place. I feel that an offering of labor, such as cleaning up trash, is often more useful and therefore more pleasing to spirits of place.
- A pentacle is a powerful symbol of earth and protection. Set an altar pentacle in or under the dish of earth. Bonus points if you use a dish with a pentacle design on it!
- If you'd like to incorporate herbs, try tobacco leaf, sage, cloves, mugwort, or garlic braids.
- If you'd like to incorporate gemstones, add jet, obsidian, shungite, tiger's eye, emerald, or hematite.
- Optional: Add protective sigils or an equal-armed cross. The equal-armed cross creates balancing and supportive energies. It's important to note that an equal-armed cross is not the same as a crucifix.

CIRCLE UP: Visualize a purple pentacle surrounding your sacred space. Say, "This space is protected."

SPELL WORK: Use the index finger of your right hand to draw a pentacle in the air directly over your warding object. If you prefer, you can draw an equal-armed cross instead. As you do so, affirm in your mind that this symbol is helping you remove incorrect energies from the item.

Once the warding item is cleansed, recharge it by connecting it to the earth's energy. Place the warding object into the dish of earth. Visualize energetic roots of earth energy growing up into the aura of your object. Say, "I charge this object with the power of the earth. By the earth element, may it remain defensive and strong. I affirm that this object will enhance the protective energies of the space around it. With harm to none and for the good of all, so shall it be."

CLOSE UP SHOP: Visualize the purple pentacle dissolving into the earth, grounding your energies.

Carry your ward with you or leave it in an area that makes you feel secure—near your front door, on the bedside table, or wherever. You could also leave it on a permanent altar if you want to keep doing defensive magick during a time when life circumstances are making you feel vulnerable.

Recharge your ward by repeating this ritual whenever you feel it is needed (or at least every six months). If you decide to stop using a ward, do a final ritual in which you allow the magickal roots to recede back into the earth element and thank the ward for its service.

• • • • • • •

Wards can be general, or they can be created for special purposes. Up next is one example of a warding spell for a more specific purpose.

Dealing with a Stalker

There are few things as scary as a stalker. While some of these creepers can be coworkers or casual acquaintances, it's far more likely that womxyn will be stalked by an ex-partner. In any case, there are some non-magickal steps you can take to enhance your safety when dealing with a stalker, including:

- Make a safety plan with at least one friend or family member. If you're going to be out and about, make sure someone you trust knows about your plans, where you are going, and when you'll be home.
- Consider telling the appropriate people at your workplace about the situation.

- Keep a calendar where you document every incident of stalking that you are aware of. Keeping documentation helps you establish a pattern over time.

- Meet with your local domestic violence program. These agencies deal with stalkers all the time. They can help you make your safety plan and talk to you about your legal options.

- Ask trusted neighbors to keep an eye on your property and give them the information they need (who is bothering you, what kind of vehicle they drive, if you have a restraining order, and whatever else you think they need to know) to report any shady activities, whether you are home or not.

- Consider installing outdoor cameras to capture evidence of a stalker around your home. Motion-capture wildlife cameras marketed to hunters are affordable and do the job.

- Make use of this book's Basic Bobble Warding Spell. Turn items like your security camera, your doormat, or your mailbox into enchanted defenses.

Now that we've covered basic safety in the day-to-day world, let's work in a little craft.

ANTI-STALKER WARDING SPELL

This spell is for protecting your home. For protecting your office space or your vehicle, I suggest using the Basic Bobble Warding Spell and putting talismans in those other spaces (or simply carrying one with you at all times).

IDEAL TIME: The waning moon, the new moon, or a Saturday.

PREPARATION AND ITEMS TO GATHER:

- I recommend you walk your property before beginning the spell. You will want to have the details and contours of the property as it is right now fresh in your mind's eye. If you can't walk the entire property, just do as much as makes sense.

- Choose a protective symbol. Some typical choices are the pentacle, the Eye of Horus, the ankh, or an equal-armed cross. Choose whatever symbol you feel will draw in your spiritual supports and make you feel safe. A family crest or even a simple heart are options if they pack the most meaning for you.

- If you set up an altar, utilize the protective powers of white (which repels energies), red, or blue. Whether you use an altar or not, set up your sacred space in a part of your home where you feel safe and comfortable.

- If you'd like to incorporate gemstones, jet, shungite, and moonstone are good options.

- If you'd like to incorporate scent, mint and sage correspond.

CIRCLE UP: Chant your name in whatever musical tone feels right to you. Musical vibrations are both healing and protective. Chanting your own name will strengthen your aura and make your magick stronger. It will also protect you.

SPELL WORK: Settle into your sacred space and get comfortable. You will be entering a light, meditative space in order to create a powerful energetic ward over your property. When you feel ready, close your eyes.

As you sit and relax, count down into an alpha state from ten to one: ten, nine, eight, seven, six, five, four, three, two, one. In your mind's eye, visualize the room you are in. Then allow your perspective to rise above your home so you can see the whole property as if from a bird's-eye view. From this position, visualize your protective symbol appearing over your entire property in a bright, golden light. Affirm that this light is directly from the highest spiritual vibrations and will work to repel all harm. As many times as feels right (ideally, in multiples of three), chant, "By the power of three times three, my ward remains to protect me." Once you feel

like your ward is up and running strong, thank the
spiritual powers for aiding you in this work.

Allow your mind's eye to return to your home and into the space where you sit. Count one, two, three, four, five, six, seven, eight, nine, and ten. Wiggle your toes and fingers. Turn your head gently side to side. When you feel ready, open your eyes.

CLOSE UP SHOP: Either chant your own name again or chant the "Om" tone as you visualize the sacred circle dissipating. Affirm that this energy will join that of your ward and continue to protect you. End with, "So mote it be."

This ward is meant to be powered by the elements and does not need regular recharging.

After your ritual, ground yourself by having a snack and/or some water.

• • • • • • •

Okay, we're gathering a large arsenal of spiritual protections. Next, let's work on magickal powders.

Making and Using Defensive Powders

Classic powders used in defensive (or offensive) spells often contain caustic ingredients like dried peppers of varying heats. These "hot-foot" powders are effective, but they pack too many potential unintended consequences for my taste; you don't want kids, neighbors, or critters bearing the brunt of your defenses.

For me, the power of defensive craft is in your spiritual intent. It's true that strong ingredients can help you create strong thoughts and, therefore, strong enchantments. For that reason, I do sometimes use sulfur powder or salt. Bear in mind that salt will kill plants in your yard, however. It must be used and disposed of carefully. But when dealing with a particularly noxious spiritual entity (living or not), I prefer items that link my own mind to spiritual potency; items like consecrated earth, oil, and water.

Powders are most effective if the person using them tweaks the recipe a bit in response to the situation at hand. Listen to your personal intuition. To make your own powder from scratch, start with a base ingredient such as earth, sand, or salt. Add other protective ingredients like:

- Bay leaves
- Benzoin
- Bergamot
- Black chalk
- Brick dust
- Carpentry nails (especially coffin nails, which are sometimes used as symbols to "seal" a spell)
- Charcoal dust
- Cloves
- Consecrated earth
- Corvid feathers (crow, raven, jay, magpie)
- Dragon's blood resin
- Garlic powder
- Hawthorn berries
- Holy water
- Iron filings
- Nettle
- Onion powder
- Pure tobacco
- Rosemary
- Sage
- Styrax resin
- Sulfur
- Your urine (this is a very old-school ingredient; use it if you dare)

Some of these probably give you the shivers, which is 100 percent the point. This type of craft tends to be linked to an earth element or spirit element source so that it becomes a battery that never wears down.

"BACK OFF!" POWDER FOR PERSONAL SPACE

This is a small batch of powder that you could keep in a cloth satchel under your car seat or in your purse. You could also fill a saltshaker with it and keep it on your desk or nightstand. It is meant to be carried on your person or sprinkled around the boundaries of your property. Do not throw it at people!

PREPARATION AND ITEMS TO GATHER:
- Dried sage.
- Bergamot tea leaves.
- Dried rose petals.
- Anointed oil of any type.
- Benzoin powder.
- Consecrated earth or earth from around your home.

SPELL WORK: Crumble a pinch of each herb with your fingers and combine them. Then stir in the benzoin powder, oil, and earth. While holding your hands over the dish of powder, say, "I call upon the powers of spirit and earth to empower this spell. Where I place this powder, let it be my stronghold. Let it serve as my anchor to my powers. I affirm that I am protected. I know that my boundaries will hold strong. With harm to none and for the good of all, as I will, so shall it be."

Place the powder in whatever container you plan to use and you're good to go!

MACHA'S "DON'T MESS WITH ME" POWDER

Macha is an Irish battle goddess and is commonly seen as an aspect of the triple goddess, the Morrigan. Her name means "crow." She is a badass who is often associated with both offensive and defensive combat. Consecrate your powder in her name and let the crows help keep an eye on you. Nobody will mess with you, period.

PREPARATION AND ITEMS TO GATHER:

- Consecrated earth.
- Iron filings scraped off the bottom of a cast iron pan or the edge of a nail.
- Activated charcoal powder.
- A corvid feather, found outside or online.
- A small stone.

SPELL WORK: Mix together pinches of consecrated earth, iron filings, and activated charcoal powder. Dust the feather by lightly dragging it through this powder and say, "I entreat the great goddess Macha to watch over this place. May her eye be upon it, warning me of danger. May her powers be ever-present, warding off all who mean harm. Let no one of ill will be able to bear her presence or remain in this place."

Leave the feather near your home, weighing it down with a stone. You can also pour a line of the powder across the end of your driveway or across the bottom of your household doors. Feed your friendly neighborhood corvids as thanks for their help.

• • • • • • •

If you're familiar with air travel, you know that airplane emergency safety guidelines instruct you to put on your own oxygen mask before helping others. In a very practical sense (and especially in a low-oxygen environment), you aren't going to be strong and healthy enough to take care of your loved ones if you aren't taking care of yourself.

The same idea applies to psychic self-care. Many of us already know that you need to get enough sleep, drink enough water, and eat an optimal diet in order to keep yourself going. But did you know that your energetic self needs a maintenance routine of its own?

Psychic Self-Care

There is plenty of wear-and-tear on your energetic self out there in the daily world. One of the big sources of psychic pollution are the people around you (even if you adore them). People are energetic beings, but not everyone recognizes that. Those who don't tend to their energetic business may unintentionally project destructive vibes into their environment. People feeling depleted and down may even draw upon the auras of those around them like dry plants sucking up water. This is called being a psychic vampire, though it's usually unintentional and less sinister than the term implies.

It's crucial to protect your energetic self. You can do this in public, at home, or at work. Even if you work in an office where you have very limited personal space, there are some down-low defenses you can use to keep your psychic fences mended. A few simple ideas for protecting yourself include:

- Drink bergamot tea. Bergamot tea is a powerful energy cleanser. As you drink it, visualize the power of the plant infusing you with spiritual purification. When the tea is cool, you can even dip your fingers in it and sprinkle a barrier around your physical space.

- Use salt. Salt serves as a protective barrier from negative ions in the environment, including incorrect energies or unhelpful spirits. It's usually not ideal to pour a salt circle around yourself, so a solution would be to find a cool saltshaker that you can set out. You could use a nostalgic saltshaker (perhaps from your grandma's kitchen for an ancestral boost) or buy a new saltshaker for this purpose. Toss some dried rosemary or cloves in with the salt for extra protection. While you fill the shaker, affirm that you are filling it with powerful spiritual protection.

- Draw a sigil or write a protective spell and keep it nearby. If you're doing this at work, try hiding it behind a framed photo on your desk. Make sure the art or photo in the frame makes you feel happy and safe.

- Wear a protective amulet. Consider an amulet of a pentacle or one with a defensive stone like kyanite, hematite, or emerald.

- Place a warding spell on an innocuous object. If you'd like to bring a ward to work, for example, choose an object that looks at home in your professional space. You may want to pick an object that holds some sort of personal meaning, like a statue or carving of your power animal, but this isn't a requirement—you could ward your stapler if you'd like!

These tips will help you keep your psychic oxygen mask firmly in place. But psychic self-care isn't just about protecting your physical self; it's also about how you speak to yourself and others. I want to check in on the power of words. You've probably heard the saying "Sticks and stones may break my bones, but words can never hurt me." However, in the craft, we acknowledge the power of what we think and say.

Witchcraft, Bitchcraft, and the Power of Words

We've all heard the puns, right? "Life's a witch," "bitchcraft," and so on. To the mainstream, *witch* is a curse word in more ways than one. As far as I can tell, words like *witch* and *bitch* are a lot like *spinster* in their use by patriarchal culture: they function to try and control the behavior of womxyn.

Both men and womxyn use *bitch* and *witch* in this way. People have even started calling men "bitch," rather like telling boys not to throw, run, or cry "like a girl." This serves as an insult, but being feminine is not shameful. It's interesting that "bitch" has become such a derogatory term. Several powerful ancient goddesses—particularly crones—were associated with dogs and wolves and, as such, were referred to as "bitches" by devotees as a term of respect and not derision.

There are plenty of negative connotations with the term *witch* as well. Most of us have grown up with ideas that witches are ugly, mutated hags who do vaguely evil things (even if we're never clearly told what those bad deeds might be). In some parts of the world, womxyn are still sometimes jailed or killed for being "witches" if they fail to obey strict patriarchal social norms. While *witch hunt* has become a carelessly used term, it refers to deadly business. Untold numbers of womxyn have lost their lives over the centuries due to extrajudicial and superstitious attacks. Like bitch, the word witch was not always derogatory, especially if you look into the word's etymology. Rather, it connoted holiness and power. Sensing a pattern, spinstress?

The spinstress path is about being thoughtful and empowered weavers of reality. As such, I call on my fellow womxyn to be thoughtful about the power of these words.

JOURNAL PROMPT

Write about your own history with words like witch and bitch. You may want to add in others, like spinster or hag or similar. Have you experienced them as shameful words? Have you used them as such yourself? Have you heard them used as terms of empowerment? If so, how was that done? Did it work, or did it have unintended consequences? How do you plan to use words like these in the future? Do you plan to use them at all? How might you respond when those around you use them in disempowering ways?

• • • • • • •

A great thing about the craft is that you can find enchantment in common daily practices. Make them more powerful with a little spell casting and you're golden! Religious practices don't have to be loaded with formal ritual or guided by austere clerics.

For instance, here's a spell to help you wash that bad energy right out of your home and, at the same time, make your floors spic and span. No matter what you need to cleanse out of your space, a vervain wash is great.

VERVAIN FLOOR WASH FOR RECLAIMING PERSONAL SPACE

Once you have done some good work creating and defending your boundaries (and maybe throwing some problems to the curb), it's literally time to clean house. The badass spinstress herb vervain is ready to lend a hand.

I think very highly of vervain. Sometimes known as "the witches' herb," there's not much it can't help you accomplish. Christians used it to clean the altars in the holy land during medieval times; at the same time, Druids were using it for initiations. It's good for love spells, protection, initiation, banishment, and drawing in abundance of all types.[45] Out with the bad, in with the good!

This water blend should be okay to add to most cleansers for their recommended surfaces, but use your best judgment. You can add the blend to a spray bottle and spritz around the room if you don't want to do a full mop.

---

45. Rosean, *Encyclopedia of Magickal Ingredients*, 283–84.

IDEAL TIME: When you just finished a major transition in life—or when your floors are dirty.

PREPARATION AND ITEMS TO GATHER:
- Your mopping supplies. Use whatever cleanser you like, but an unscented and/or eco-friendly brand will create the best vibrations.
- Vervain tea (about four tea bags) or a handful of fresh-cut vervain flowers with leaves.

CIRCLE UP: Fill a teakettle or water boiler and wait for the water to boil, then pour the hot water into a teacup and steep the tea bags or herbs. While the tea is steeping, hold your hands over your teacup and say a blessing like: "I charge this brew with the powers of protection and cleansing. I harness the wisdom and power with which the divine intelligence has imbued vervain. Blessed be."

SPELL WORK: Fill your mop bucket with tap water. Then pick up your teacup, remove the tea bags or herbs, and pour your tea straight into the mop bucket. Mop as you normally would. If you really feel the need for a strong cleansing, pray or chant while you mop. You could say something like "Remove all incorrect energies. Let only the good remain." Or you could say something very simple, like "Fresh start. Fresh start. Fresh start."

CLOSE UP SHOP: After you've finished mopping the floor, dispose of the mop water in your usual way.

· · · · · · ·

No book about witchy craft could fail to mention the sacred broomstick. I'm sure you're well aware of the iconic image of the witch on her flying broomstick. It's true that witches and wizards often use brooms in ritual. Unfortunately, no one I'm aware of is using them for air travel.

The broomstick is well documented as a tool of medieval witches. The humble broom was observed on the hearths of every female and, during the witch hunt persecutions, brooms were castigated as the instrument witches would enchant in order to fly to covert meetings with the devil.

In real magickal practices, the broom has been defined as a different sort of vehicle. Some of you may have a *besom*, a special broom used only for magick. Like the wand, the besom is a tool of air used to cast the circle. In this way, the ritual broom does indeed transport us from one place to another. With it, we move from our normal reality into our sacred space that is sometimes called a "world between worlds."

The following ritual puts the broom to good use.

A MAGICK BROOM SWEEPS CLEAN: RITUAL FOR CLEANSING

Just as a regular broom is handy for knocking the dust bunnies and cobwebs out of your life, the besom can be used to cleanse energies. Use this ritual when you need to clear out a stale or negative energy pattern.

You can do this ritual to clean a literal space in your home or office. You can also use it to cleanse your spirit or life path of certain energies, such as the end of a relationship, a new diet or exercise regimen, a job change, and more.

IDEAL TIME: The waning moon or a Sunday.

PREPARATION AND ITEMS TO GATHER:
- A broom. There is nothing wrong with using a household broom. It might be fun, however, to dedicate a ritual broom (besom) if you haven't yet.
- If you want to turbo-charge your cleansing, bundles of cleansing herbs like sage, mugwort, cedar, or lavender can be burned. If you prefer, you can buy or make room sprays infused with these herbs (usually in a base liquid like witch hazel).

CIRCLE UP: Use your broom like a wand to point at and define the sacred space. If you have enough room, you can literally sweep the boundary around your space. Visualize this space being filled with pure golden light. Say, "The circle is cast. Blessed be."

SPELL WORK: Use your broom to sweep just above the floor as you walk around your ritual space. Say, "With this broom I clear the path before my feet. I affirm that my new endeavors will be successful and always in service to my highest good. With harm to none and for the good of all, so shall it be."

Go around the circle again. This time hold the broom up and sweep above your head as if you were removing cobwebs from the ceiling. Say, "I clear the channels for all good ideas and spiritual assistance. I affirm that the positive changes I seek to make will be supported by correct and positive energy. Let all energetic influences and thought patterns that no longer serve me be swept away and not return. With harm to none and for the good of all, so shall it be."

Spend some time inside this freshly cleansed sacred space. Visualize yourself successful and happy as your desired changes are manifest. Affirm this reality by saying, "I give thanks that it is so. Blessed be."

CLOSE UP SHOP: Sweep or otherwise use your broom to indicate the sacred circle again, this time visualizing the golden light you have cast being returned to its spiritual source. Say, "The circle is open. Blessed be."

chapter ten

THE SPIRIT REALM AND ARCANE WISDOM

This is the stuff that got many of us interested in magick or witchcraft in the first place: foggy cemeteries, black cats, Ouija boards, fortune-telling, and Gothic teas. Have I got your attention? The crone zone is filled with this spooky, cobwebby goodness. Get out your badass pointy hat and follow me.

First up, let's set the mood with some spooky and magickal scents.

DARK ONE MUSKY INCENSE RECIPE

This incense evokes the protection and psychic awareness often needed to work with crone energies. Burn it by sprinkling it a pinch at a time over incense charcoal in a fireproof dish.

PREPARATION AND ITEMS TO GATHER:
- 1 tablespoon benzoin.
- 1 tablespoon ground frankincense resin.
- 1 teaspoon dried lavender buds.
- 1 teaspoon dried pine needles.

- 5–10 drops of cypress essential oil.

- 3–5 drops synthetic musk oil of your choice.

- Optional: A pinch of graveyard dirt.

SPELL WORK: Grind the dried ingredients together using a mortar and pestle, found in occult shops or at mainstream stores in the kitchen supplies section. Once the dry items are well crushed and mixed together, stir in the cypress oil and musk oil. Add graveyard dirt if you are using it.

Consecrate this incense by saying, "I call upon the goddesses, grandmothers, and guides who are willing to support and protect me. Thank you for the blessings of your power and wisdom. Bless me as I aspire to be what you are. Blessed be."

Store leftover incense in a plastic bag or in a repurposed vitamin bottle. One awesome crone that I know uses her old prescription medicine bottles for saving incense and incense ingredients.

• • • • • • •

When I think about the crone phase of the goddess, I definitely think about all things dark and mysterious. When working with the dark moon, this energetic detox spell is one way to take advantage of the powerful energy.

DARK GODDESS DETOX SPELL

Often we emphasize the waxing and new moon cycles in magick; we tend to think a lot about what we would like to call into our lives. At the same time, the waning and dark phases of the moon are kickass for removing obstacles to those goals. You can think of this as a time for energetic detox. A strong energetic field, detoxed of obstacles, can manifest powerful effects.

IDEAL TIME: The waning or dark moon.

PREPARATION AND ITEMS TO GATHER:
- A black candle.

- Unscented anointing oil (or something woody like pine or cypress).

- If you set up a full altar, use the color black heavily. You're going for a simple, dark, receptive energy that matches this moon cycle and your goal.
- If you'd like to incorporate gemstones, clear quartz and selenite correspond.

CIRCLE UP: Put a clear crystal egg of energy around yourself and your sacred space. Say, "I affirm I am protected by the dark goddess and dark moon energies as I undertake this detoxifying work. Blessed be."

SPELL WORK: Anoint your black candle. Stare at the lit candle and visualize the black wax pulling any excess or incorrect energies out of you. Thank the candle for burning these away.

Say, "I cast aside all thoughtforms, energies, and patterns that get between me and my goals. I offer all that does not serve me for the correct spiritual forces to repurpose. Thank you for your help and wisdom. So shall it be."

Spend some time affirming your goals. Call in everything that you wish to have in order to replace the detoxed energies.

CLOSE UP SHOP: Allow the crystal egg to dissolve back into the elements. It will take the energy you expelled and use it for something beneficial. Say, "I thank you that this work is finished. Blessed be."

Repeat as needed during a waning moon.

• • • • • • •

Few creatures are as linked to magick as the cat. Particularly the black cat!

Magickal Creatures 101: The Kickass Cat

Unlike our unicorns and dragons from earlier chapters, the cat is a critter that virtually all of us have seen up close. In fact, many of us have one or more of them lounging around the house. Does this make kitties less powerful than the fantastic beasts of myth and legend? I say no way! Perhaps it means their power is even more formidable. Cats rule the roost wherever they go, and they have done so throughout the ages.

In Egypt, the spellbinding cat was and is revered. Feral cats that populate that nation still largely have the run of the place and are loved on wherever they choose to be; they are rather like the sacred cows of India in that way. Their power goes back to ancient times, when they were inextricably linked to a central domestic goddess, Bastet. Even then, cats were connected closely to goddesses and the womxyn who worshiped them.[46]

Bastet, sharing forms with the domestic cat, had provenance over home, family, and love. Her sister, Sekhmet, however, was a real wildcat. Literally. This lion-headed goddess was invoked for retribution and offensive and defensive battle. In one apocalyptic story that's like a Goth take on the biblical flood, Sekhmet decided no humans were worth saving and was well on her way to eating every last one. The other gods drugged her with blood-colored beer to keep her from finishing us off. For that reason, she's sometimes referenced as the mother of vampires. Sekhmet was definitely a more high-octane feline, yet the two sisters had more in common than not. It's helpful to think of them as two sides of the same kitty coin.

Associations between the cat and the female continued across the map. For example, cats were sacred to Artemis in Greece, Diana in Rome, and Freya in Scandinavia. From Egypt to Greece to Rome to all the ports of call on the globe's trade routes, cats sailed forth as indispensable crew members on untold ships. They were considered lucky and prized for their prowess at rodent control.

Unfortunately for kitties, their close link to womxyn in general—and witches in particular—has led to persecution of felines wherever a culture exhibits violent misogyny. Black cats (and sometimes black dogs) have been mythologized as familiars to demons and devils. In modern times, many cultures that still fear witches also abuse cats, especially black cats. Even in societies that think they are past such prejudices, animal shelters report that black cats are the least likely to be adopted.[47]

During the witch hunts of the Dark Ages, cats were nearly exterminated in certain areas. Though I can't back up this theory, I've heard it suggested that the spread of the Black Plague was partly due to the eradication of cats. Without cats to control the rodent population, plague rats abounded. If that theory is true, it makes an argument for the concept of instant karma. It also

---

46. Guiley, *Encyclopedia of Witches and Witchcraft*, 48–49.

47. Workman and Hoffman, "An Evaluation of the Role the Internet Site Petfinder Plays in Cat Adoptions."

suggests that the way we treat one another, human and nonhuman, has an impact on all of us sooner or later.

If you have a kitty in your life, you're probably already aware that cats are very comfortable around spiritual energies. Many seem to be drawn to spiritual energy. You'll know right away if your cats have an interest in magick or in spiritual healing; they tend to pop up in the middle of any spiritual work you try to do, even if they'd been sound asleep in another part of the house when you got started! Some kitties will be a very mellow presence, snuggling up on or near you the way they might claim a warm windowsill. Others have more of a high priest/priestess quality and will be very bossy about your rituals. This type especially likes to redesign your altar, particularly by making room on it for themselves. If you're going to accept their help and allow them in the room during your work, you may as well accept this and let them be in charge.

If your kitties like to work with you in your sacred spaces, you will want to alter your setup. For example:

- Avoid lit candles, incense, or oil burners. Use LED candles or an electric aromatherapy diffuser to achieve some of the same results.
- Keep the altar minimalist and always leave room for your kitty. Avoid any breakable items like statues or cups.
- Place a cozy catnip mat on the altar instead of (or over) your usual covering of choice.
- Offer a treat after the spiritual work to thank your familiar for the help.

When you're working with an animal familiar in your craft, you need to treat them with particular honor. This applies to the individual critters you may share a home with, but also to the broader species. You get special gifts from an animal familiar, and you create a better flow of correct energies when you engage in reciprocity. In other words, treat others the way you'd want to be treated.

You will learn lots about your craft, the world, and yourself from relating to a familiar. For instance, cats are often thought to teach us lessons about independence, self-assuredness, and the skill of keeping your bad-assery under wraps until you choose to deploy it.

If you're drawn to cat magick but you can't share your home with the real thing, there are plenty of other ways you can honor and connect to kitties. Here are a few ideas:

- Study the habits of felines and the issues they face in the modern world. For domestic cats, the primary concern they need help with tends to be overpopulation and large colonies of feral (stray) cats. With wild felines like tigers, the issues tend to be ones of habitat conservation or poaching. In both cases, cat populations struggle when they find themselves competing with human populations for room and resources.

- Donate funds to charities that support domestic or wild types of cats. Research these charities in advance to make sure your donation is well spent.

- Contribute bake-sale items, silent-auction items, or other types of resources to support local cat charities.

- Volunteer time to work with cats via local charities or activism projects. You could spend time socializing (petting and grooming) the cats, cleaning crates out, etc. Some activism involves running stray cat colonies by building and maintaining outside houses and distributing food. Many of these groups practice "trap, spay/neuter, and release" activism to slow down the population growth of feral cat colonies.

- Share information by blogging, writing news editorials, or posting online about cats, cat charities, and what folks can do to help.

In these and other ways, you should be in good position to reap the reward of a sacred feline relationship.

• • • • • • •

Ready to continue the journey? Let's do it in a labyrinthine path. Seriously, I want to talk about the magick of the maze.

The Power of a Labyrinth

You experienced the labyrinth in your spinstress journey to meet the fates. The labyrinth is a common tool for people of many faiths. It's believed that walking a labyrinth with your body—or even just with your mind—is a powerful meditative practice.

A labyrinth symbolizes the path within and encourages the seeker to contemplate spiritual matters by tapping into the authentic self. The authentic self may be understood as your core truth as well as the part of your soul that deeply connects you to divine wisdom. Using a labyrinth can help you connect to your deep subconscious, slow down and learn to walk mindfully, incorporate body movement into a practice of meditation or prayer, and focus and lengthen the time you can easily spend in meditative practices.

The labyrinth is a well-known symbol of one's inner journey.[48] Though some choose to stay within the realm of the personal consciousness, many see this journey as spiritual. For most witches and wizards, there is no difference between the two. According to the common occultist belief that "energy follows thought," the consciousness is a great link to your spiritual self.

Though you can still find a walking labyrinth in some religious spaces (some churches and monasteries have featured large paths of labyrinths so their members could engage in a full-body meditative process) and even some public parks, many folks find it beneficial to use a finger labyrinth as a meditative or ritual tool. A finger labyrinth is usually about the size of a coaster and contains a grooved labyrinth that can be traced with one digit. They are often made of wood, metal, or ceramic and can be purchased or built from scratch. If you don't want to spend money on a finger labyrinth, print a simple finger labyrinth off the web or create your own by gluing down a tactile substance such as glitter or yarn.

Hecate Finger Labyrinth Spell

In the ancient world, the goddess Hecate was believed to hold the wisdom of the labyrinth. Remember, Hecate was the one in Greek myth who found and liberated Persephone from the underworld. As the torch-bearing goddess who would guide souls between realms, Hecate was and is both feared and revered as a deity with the power to give a soul an easy journey or a rough ride.[49]

---

48. Artress, *Walking a Sacred Path*, 96.

49. d'Este and Rankine, *Hekate Liminal Rites*.

You can do this work without connecting it to any deity, or even to any spirituality. Yet, I have chosen to honor Hecate as one of our badass crones as well as a patroness of the spinstress craft.

IDEAL TIME: Hecate is strongly associated with the new or dark moon. This is also a good time for solitary and internal work.

PREPARATION AND ITEMS TO GATHER:

- Cypress is sacred to Hecate. Make a quick oil to anoint candles or yourself when working with Hecate. Simply use a base oil like olive or almond and mix in a few drops of cypress essential oil until it smells the way you want it to. If you use a quarter cup of base oil, you will probably want between five and ten drops of cypress.

- Have some mint or dandelion tea to honor Hecate and to prep for psychic (intuitive) work.

- Black items correspond to this work. Black is the receptive color that draws wisdom to you. Like the phase of the dark moon or the blackness you experience when you close your eyes, it symbolizes the journey into the subconscious as well as the spirit world.

- Get your hands (especially your fingers) onto a tabletop labyrinth or explore a walking labyrinth in your community. If neither of these options works for you, remember that magick comes through the focus of your mind. You can do the work by visualizing yourself walking through a labyrinth if it's what makes the most sense for you.

- Prepare a question to focus on as you journey deep into your core of spiritual guidance and personal wisdom. If no specific questions are springing to mind, you can use something general like "What do I need to know right now for my own highest good?"

- While there is a lot to be said for silence in this journey, a playlist is always an option. Something acoustic and soothing is probably best.

- Have your journal at the ready to record what you learn. As with guided meditations, it's best to write down your impressions immediately. Writing before closing up shop and leaving your ritual space is best.

CIRCLE UP: If you have developed a cue for anchoring yourself in your inner strength (like rubbing your temples or placing a hand on your heart), use that cue now. You may want to ring a bell to signal the beginning of your journey. If you are using a playlist, start it up.

Visualize a blue circle of energy forming your sacred working space. Blue is a color of communication and spiritual essence. Affirm, "The circle is cast. Blessed be."

SPELL WORK: Take some deep, grounding breaths and focus on your question. When you feel ready, say, "Wise Hecate, great queen of the dead and mistress of the maze, I ask you to bless my journey into the inner world of mind and of soul."

Begin the journey of the labyrinth. Whether you are using a finger maze, a walking maze, or a visualization, don't rush.

As you work your way to the center of your labyrinth, be patient. If you hit a wall, work your way back. Thank the spiritual powers you relate to for helping you learn each lesson. It is good to affirm that you can always retrace your steps. You can always begin again.

As you go, note any messages you feel you are receiving from spirit or from within. These could appear as visions, memories, or song lyrics. If you are outdoors, pay attention to the creatures who may appear. Absorb the information for later; don't pressure yourself to understand meanings right away.

Every once in a while (especially if you feel yourself losing focus), recite your chosen question. You could also repeat your request for Hecate's guidance and blessing.

At some point, it's likely that you will reach the center of the maze. This is a great opportunity to be still and meditate for as long as seems right to you. Many labyrinths have a floral or a star-patterned design at their center. This is to symbolize divine wisdom and pure spiritual access. Contemplate what this means to you. Are you communing with your inner self? An ancestor? An angel, deity, or other guide?

Repeat your chosen question and allow yourself to get at least some of the answer. If you still feel stumped, affirm that you will receive an answer that you will readily understand within the next forty-eight hours.

When you feel you're ready to leave the center of the labyrinth, say, "I give thanks to spirit and to myself that I have this access to deep wisdom at any time I wish. Blessed be."

As you return to the exterior of your labyrinth, continue to be patient and open to spiritual information. You are still on the journey; reaching the center of the labyrinth doesn't mean you're done. It's very possible that you will receive the most important tidbit of information as you work your way out of the maze.

Once you have left the labyrinth, say, "I thank and bless you, Hecate, for your guidance and wisdom."

Remember to take the time you need to journal about your impressions before you close up shop.

CLOSE UP SHOP: If you used a bell or a personal cue at the beginning of this journey, use it again now. Visualize your circle of blue light dissipating. Affirm that it is returning to the spirit source as you say, "The circle is open. Blessed be."

If you used a tabletop labyrinth, wrap it in a special cloth and store it in a safe place.

Repeat the labyrinth journey as often as you like to aid in your meditative practice and to help you make life's big decisions.

• • • • • • •

The maze is deeply associated with the journey of a soul between the realms of life and death. Therefore, this is a good place to segue into our work with the realm of the dead. While a lot of this has to do with divination and the spirit realm, it's best to get right to the chase and deal with our own demise.

After all, it's fear of mortality that is often beneath fascination with the dead. Instead of holding a séance or hanging out in a cemetery, there are practical things you can do to take control of your own final plans. It can bring a lot of peace of mind for you, and often for your loved ones as well.

Don't Fear the Reaper:
Tips for Planning the Ultimate Transition

Many find it morbid to think about their own demise. They may think that planning for death is some sort of jinx, inviting their time to come too soon. Even checking the box about organ donation on a driver's license form seems like a bad omen to some folks. Of course, you don't exist in isolation. Even if you are comfortable with this topic, your friends and family may not be. It can be hard to talk about your final wishes or to ask your loved ones about theirs.

Spinstress womxyn empower ourselves in every aspect of life. This includes the end of it. While we often think of this type of planning when a person grows older, it is also the activity of the wise of any age. As much as we don't like to acknowledge it, we know that people of any age may unexpectedly die or become incapacitated.

Making final plans for yourself ensures that you'll always have input for the big decisions that matter to you most. These big decisions can range from who gets your fab shoe collection to where your pets or children would live if you died while they still needed care.

Making your own final arrangements is a kind act toward your loved ones as well. The fewer decisions they need to make when you pass, the more space they have to manage their own natural feelings of loss, grief, or stress. You can alleviate any financial burden on those you leave behind by purchasing insurance, considering certain kinds of trusts, and even prepaying for your own funeral or burial. These plans might include the following:

- What your preferences would be if you were incapacitated. For instance, if there was a choice between artificial life support or not, what you would want and to what extent. Also, who in your life would be entrusted with having your back should this ever occur.
- Who would care for your kids, pets, or other dependents, such as elderly parents.
- Whether any or all of your assets would go to a charitable institution.
- Details about what you would like done with your remains, such as cremation versus burial, embalmment versus a "green" burial, etc.

- Purchasing an urn, grave marker, burial plot, or the like in advance. When you buy a cemetery plot, you get a deed like you would for any other piece of real estate. Cemeteries all have their own rules about the use of their plots. Often multiple family members can share one grave and one marker in the case of cremation. Make sure the rules of any cemetery you consider align with your priorities. For instance, is it important to you that your loved ones be able to put flowers or other offerings near you? If so, make sure this is allowed.

- Preplanning or purchasing an entire funeral service. Many local funeral parlors have these options. Are you afraid your loved ones will be too sad to throw you the kickass wake of your dreams? Preplan the whole thing. You can manage every aspect of your final service if you want to. You can even write your own obituary or eulogy! Though it would help to get feedback from your friends and family, they may find you taking the initiative of your final wishes to be a great relief.

- Consulting with loved ones before leaving them items, especially things like your home or your pets.

Like sitting down with a certified accountant for retirement planning or the college funds for your kids, it's best to hire an estate attorney to help with these final plans. Some of these arrangements can be complicated, and you want to make sure your final plans will work out. Rules about finances, burial, and other similar matters will vary widely depending on where you live. Planning for pets can be especially tricky since they are usually seen as property under the law. As shocking as it may seem, pets might be dealt with more like a dining room set than a fur baby if nothing is arranged in advance.

You will also want to get feedback from your loved ones at some point during this process. Let them know that you have made these sorts of plans. How people react to this varies widely. It should be helpful to let them know that you are not assuming the worst will happen; making these plans is meant to get that hard stuff out of the way and to make things easier for those you care about. You may find that your friends and family will feel more open to sharing their own final plans and preferences once you initiate this conversation.

Once you have your final plans made, they will only need to be reviewed and updated occasionally. If you know your loved ones will be taken care of whenever your time may come and that your final wishes will be looked after, you don't have to fear the reaper.

Returning to the spirit realm in ritual and in magick, I want to discuss a rather uncommon topic. I'm going to talk about using consecrated earth (graveyard dirt) in your craft.

Ancestor Magick: Working with Consecrated Earth

You may think spell ingredients like graveyard dirt are offensive tools of the dark arts, but collecting consecrated earth from the grave of an ancestor is actually very much in keeping with earth-based religions. Earth-based religious traditions don't tend to stigmatize death; there are rich and varied traditions of revering—and even communing with—the deceased.

Everyone has a different level of comfort with this subject. If you are uncomfortable working with graveyard dirt, I always consider it an optional ingredient. Personally, I think it's important to collect your own consecrated earth if you're going to use it at all. Working with the ancestors is sacred; as such, you should be using consecrated earth from the plot of a close friend or relative who you feel would agree to the idea of it. I'm uncomfortable buying this type of ingredient from an occult shop when I can't vouch for where it came from.

In New England we have a long tradition of tending to the graves of our ancestors every year on Memorial Day. People scrub gravestones clean, pull weeds, or put plantings or flags next to headstones. School children are often encouraged to clean the memorial stones of long-dead veterans as a sign of respect and as an act of civic pride. It's during this time that I tend to take a small amount of graveyard dirt from the plots of my own relatives. It's just a matter of keeping a small trowel of earth after putting in some fresh flowers. I use the ingredient so sparingly that I only need to do this every few years.

Earth collected from consecrated ground is very special and should only be used for thoughtful and important rituals. A dish or container of graveyard dirt at the center of the altar can help you call in your ancestors and spirit guides. A small amount of this type of earth in a protection powder will go a long way for protecting you from threats, both of the spirit and of the flesh.

RITUAL TO GATHER GRAVEYARD DIRT

If you already have a tradition of tending the family graves, you might like to use this spell and collect some consecrated earth for your practices. If the tradition sounds nice to you, it's not too late to begin! Just check the rules of every cemetery you plan to visit. They are often available online. Some cemeteries allow fresh plants; others do not.

If you don't live near your family graves or if you don't have relationships with your ancestors that make this activity seem okay, you can also consider getting consecrated earth from another type of site. The memorials of friends are also an option. Go with your intuition—and with what you know about the personality of the deceased. Ask spirit where you should go and what you should do.

No matter what, always be respectful, and never do damage to any type of sacred site. The amount of earth you take from any source should not chop up or damage the soil.

IDEAL TIME: The new or dark moon, since it's sacred to underworld guides like Hecate. Mondays, associated with the moon and psychic work, are also appropriate.

PREPARATION AND ITEMS TO GATHER:
- A garden trowel, a small pouch or box to hold the earth, and anything you plan to use to enrich the gravesite like a planting or memorial wreath, etc. (Remember to check cemetery rules in advance.)
- If you are going to be planting something, remember to bring some fresh water along.
- If you are going to clean the grave marker, gather those materials as well.
- Optional: If you wear a pentacle for grounding or protection, you'll want to wear it here.
- Optional: A moonstone in your pocket will give you an extra boost.

CIRCLE UP: Sit near your loved one's grave with your feet and/or fingers touching the soil. Take some deep, grounding breaths and visualize a circle of positive spiritual energy around you and the resting place. Affirm that only correct and positive energies can be present within this space. Greet the body and spirit of the deceased and thank them for letting you visit their grave.

SPELL WORK: Say, "With reverence for your memory and with honor to all my ancestors, I ask that you allow me to take home a small measure of this consecrated earth. When I work with it, I will honor you and continually seek your guidance."

Take a moment and use your intuition to decide whether your request is granted. If you feel something "off" when you ask the question, and if that sensation is beyond your discomfort at trying something new, you can decide not to take anything. Whether you take soil or not, make sure to say thank you.

If you feel you have the green light to take some soil, carefully remove some with your trowel. It may be easier to work close to the gravestone or at the base of any plantings. Of course, if you are putting a plant in, you can take some dirt as part of this process.

Place a small amount of dirt in your pouch or other container. When you are done, make sure you have repacked the soil and turf and left the site in pristine condition.

CLOSE UP SHOP: Visualize the positive energy you have cast around the space being grounded near the grave. The sacred ground and your ancestors can use this offering of positive energy in any way they choose.

Do any other work (like cleaning the gravestone, watering plants, or whatever else) before packing up and leaving.

SUPPLIES FOR CLEANING GRAVES

It's best to use just plain water when cleaning gravestones. Other tools for cleaning graves include:

- A newly purchased spray bottle (or one that has never contained chemicals)
- Toothbrushes with bristles of different firmness
- Wooden chopsticks

The toothbrushes and chopsticks are for carefully cleaning the grooves around images and lettering on the gravestone. If the stone has significant chipping or cracking, you may not want to clean it.

· · · · · · ·

When you have a group of kindred spirits to work with, having a day of mourning is a wonderful and healing thing to do. In our fast-paced world, taking time to honor the dead is a lost art.

Mourning

Most cultures have at least one day set aside for remembering and honoring the dead. The Christian holiday All Souls' Day, the Pagan holiday Samhain, and the Mexican holiday Día de los Muertos (Day of the Dead) are a few examples.

The concept of mourning is not meant to be morbid. Mourning is taking the time to remember and to love those who have passed. It may still be sad, but it is not sadness for sadness' sake. When done in an organized and spiritual way, mourning is the type of grief that facilitates healing.

For me, brewing up herbal tea seems to match the emotional quality of mourning. The herbs can evoke relaxation, healing, and psychic ability. The act of steeping tea itself slows me down to a more spiritually beneficent tempo. Brewing loose-leaf tea also gives you the option to play around with tasseomancy, which is old-school tea leaf divination.

Mourning Tea Party with Loved Ones

Host a mourning tea party to engage in activities that honor those who have passed. Encourage each participant to bring a dish to share that celebrates their beloved departed. For instance, they could bring their dad's favorite cookies or grandma's recipe for apple pie. These foods will evoke the fond memories they will be encouraged to share. They could also bring favorite tea blends of the departed. Certain herbs might help facilitate the proper theme.

ETERNI-TEA

Brew a base tea (simple black tea works) and add in any of these herbs:

- Chamomile: Relieves stress and grief
- Mint: Protective; stimulates dreams
- Bergamot: Protective; spiritual
- Mugwort: Promotes psychic attunement
- Thistle: Protective; healing

As you let the tea steep, say, "I empower this tea to heal our hearts and sharpen our senses. May we feel the presence of those we have loved and learn from their wisdom."

As you drink your mourning tea, begin a group activity. For example:

- Work on a collective scrapbook. Invite participants to bring a few photos of their beloved dead. Have a scrapbook and appropriate materials ready so each person can make at least one or two pages. Make it a tradition to build your group's book every year.
- Ask friends and family to share memories of their beloved dead out loud. Poetry, song, and other artforms should be encouraged so that folks can share in the ways that are most meaningful to them.
- If any members are familiar with a form of divination or spirit communication, have a little "psychic fair." You could also pool your resources and hire a reputable medium from your community.
- Music improves any party and is also soothing during periods of mourning. Plan a playlist in advance or host local musicians if you can.

RITUAL TO REMEMBER THE BELOVED DEAD

This ritual is perfect as a centerpiece to your mourner's tea, but it can also be performed on its own. If you are doing this ritual as part of a gathering, decide in advance whether it should be done at the beginning (allowing for food and celebration after) or at the end (a somber remembrance). Though not necessarily painful, this ritual is always emotionally powerful.

IDEAL TIME: Samhain or a Monday.

PREPARATION AND ITEMS TO GATHER:
- Create an altar with contributions from each participant. Encourage everyone to bring at least one item that commemorates their beloved dead. Items may include photos, personal items, or less intimate symbols. Those honored might include cultural heroes, historical figures, pets, friends, or family. Some wish to honor the victims of certain crimes, even if they didn't know the victim personally.
- When mourning, most think of the color black, but other colors can help achieve different goals. Consider gold or light blue for healing, red for rebirth, or white for spirit.
- If you'd like to incorporate gemstones, labradorite and quartz crystal are both powerful spiritual stones.
- If you'd like to incorporate herbs, burning sage and mugwort can raise the spiritual vibrations of the sacred space. Frankincense resin can also be burned to open the heart chakra.
- If you'd like to incorporate music, it should be acoustic, healing, and quiet. Lyrical music may throw off the internal experience of participants. If people wish to play other types of music that represent their loved ones, it should be done at another time.

CIRCLE UP: If you are burning herbs like sage or mugwort, use the smoke to define the sacred circle around your altar and your group. If you aren't burning herbs, designate one group member who will walk clockwise around the outer edge of the group while sweeping a circle with a besom or drawing a circle using a wand. When the group member returns to their spot in the circle, say, "The circle is cast. We are between the worlds. Blessed be."

SPELL WORK: Starting anywhere in the circle and moving clockwise, give each member a chance to say what they brought for the altar and who it honors. Ask the group member if they have anything they want to share about their beloved dead; they have the option to pass.

After everyone has had a chance to speak, a designated group member says, "We affirm that our beloved dead are with us between the worlds. We are grateful for this opportunity to speak to them once again. We also know that we can share our thoughts with them at any time."

CLOSE UP SHOP: The person who cast the circle retraces their steps in reverse (counterclockwise) with besom/wand or smoke as before. When the group member returns to their spot in the circle, say, "The circle is open, yet unbroken. Blessed be."

• • • • • • •

You may think that all you have to do to care for your soul is keep on breathing, but there is a lot more to it than that.

Soul Repair

In modern terms, soul repair has to do with processing and healing deep forms of trauma. Most of us have heard about trauma. You may be familiar with the term post-traumatic stress disorder (PTSD). It is commonly associated with veterans or sexual assault survivors, but PTSD is something that anyone who has experienced trauma can develop. Trauma may be individual or collective, historical or contemporary. Hate crimes like racism, sexism, and heterosexism cause trauma. Terrorist attacks and pandemics cause trauma. Wars and family violence cause trauma. *Vicarious trauma* is the term for trauma one takes on after witnessing a friend or loved one be hurt. When you think about all the ways you might encounter trauma, it's no wonder most of us could benefit from a little healing work.

The frequency, severity, and duration of trauma have an impact on how you heal. The personal resources you have available—shelter, income, a support system, your beliefs, and the other aspects of life that help you recover from hardships—also impact your healing. Depending on how the type of trauma interacts with your personal situation and resources, you may have a hard time healing all of your wounds. Trauma that you may need a little extra help dealing with can cause many symptoms. These include, but are not limited to, the following:

- Anxiety
- Chemical dependency on alcohol or other drugs
- Chronic headaches
- Compulsive eating or other eating disorders
- Depression
- Fatigue
- Feeling isolated
- Gambling, compulsive shopping, etc.
- Insomnia
- Low self-esteem
- Reckless sexual activity
- Self-harm
- Suicidal thoughts

Unresolved trauma isn't just about your physical body. Some of this wounding occurs on a spiritual level. Negative energetic patterns get caught inside you and repeat over and over. This can cause negative experiences to manifest repeatedly in your life since energy follows thought. These scars on the soul, like scratches on a vinyl record, create an interruption in correct messages and patterns. When the wounds are bad enough, they can even effectively tear off chunks of your spirit, depriving you of wholeness. That's the idea behind the shamanic concept of soul retrieval, at any rate.

If you've experienced wounding that you believe has left marks on your soul or your spiritual life, this ritual is for you. If trauma symptoms continue to affect you, I encourage you to explore therapy in addition to your spiritual work. Cognitive behavioral therapy (CBT) is a popular choice; CBT helps people replace negative thought patterns and coping behaviors with better ones.[50]

---

50. Bowers, *Everything Guide to Cognitive Behavioral Therapy*.

THE SPINSTRESS GUIDE TO CARE AND REPAIR OF THE SOUL

Part of the spell work here includes the concept of forgiving those who have wounded you in the past, including yourself. Forgiveness can be a loaded concept; some people who experience trauma are browbeaten to forgive before they are ready, or they are asked to forgive in unfair or inauthentic ways.

Forgiveness does not mean that those who wounded you are excused from accountability. With that being said, forgiveness is more for you and your healing. When you forgive, you are letting go of the burdens your wounds have left you with. If you prefer, think of it as *releasing* rather than *forgiving*. You are releasing yourself as much as—or more than—you are releasing another. You want to be released from their influence for the remainder of this life. If you believe in living more than once, you are also cutting this karmic cord for the future. As angry as you may be, if you forgive (release) them now, you won't end up dancing the same nasty tango with them in some future life.

IDEAL TIME: The waning moon or a Sunday.

PREPARATION AND ITEMS TO GATHER:
- A dish of earth. This dish can be a chalice from your altar, a plate from your cupboard, or a family heirloom—whatever makes sense to you and helps you sync up with the energy of this work. Gather your soil from the outdoors. Adding a pinch of consecrated earth is optional if it makes sense to you.

- Water in a cup or chalice. You will be drinking from it, so make sure the water and the chalice are clean.

- Make sure you have a comfy place to sit and meditate for a bit during the spell work. If you decide to listen to music, I recommend choosing songs that represent positive aspects of your childhood or other times when you felt happy and strong.

- If you burn a candle, pick one in a color that soothes you. Green or pink are common choices. White can always be used if you want to keep the altar neutral and clean.

- If you want to incorporate gemstones, amber is a good stone for love and for changing energetic patterns. This makes it a great stone to work with in this spell. Lepidolite is for changing emotional patterns.
- If you want to incorporate incense, try frankincense or copal.

CIRCLE UP: Visualize an equal-armed cross that is linked on four sides by the four elemental directions (earth, air, fire, and water). There is a circle around the exterior of this cross as well. This pattern gives balance and solid grounding to your sacred space. Affirm this by saying, "This circle is cast with perfect balance and anchored by the elemental powers. I give thanks that only correct energies and forces are welcomed here. Blessed be."

SPELL WORK: Settle into a comfortable position. Take the dish of earth between your two hands, holding it in your lap or near your chest. Look into the rich darkness of this earth element and visualize every trauma that you want to release being sent into the dish like fertilizer. Bad memories, negative thought patterns, and cruel actions taken against you or committed by you may be included. Take your time doing this. You may enter a meditative state as you visualize. When you feel finished, say, "I commit these items to the keeping of Mother Earth. I know she will recycle them and put even the negative energy into a new and positive use. Blessed be."

Set down the dish of earth and hold the chalice of water between your hands. Bless the water by saying, "I ask the spiritual source to imbue this water with all the energies and qualities that I need in order to heal my spirit. By your power and your grace, I call back the totality of my soul. As I drink, I take all that was lost to me back into myself once again. I give thanks for your blessing and your healing. What was once lost to me will never be severed again. Blessed be."

Drink from the cup. As you do so, know you are taking in the healing that you need. The energy you are consuming is restoring any lost or wounded aspects of your soul.

Affirm that this healing is permanent and give thanks. Welcome back what was lost to you and assure your soul that you will always love it and care for it. If you have ever self-harmed in action, thought, or word, commit to ceasing those habits and beliefs.

CLOSE UP SHOP: Visualize your cross and circle dissipating back into the spiritual source. Say, "I give thanks that my work is fixed, set, and done. I affirm that the energies of this circle are returning to their source elements and continuing to manifest my magick there. Blessed be."

After your ritual work is complete, take the soil and remaining water outside to place in nature or let it go in another way that feels right to you.

JOURNAL PROMPT

Record your spell work experience. What did you release and what did you call back? When addressing past trauma, what was it like to forgive others and forgive yourself? Did anything come up that you weren't expecting? Keep journaling for a week or more as you integrate the changes brought about by this healing.

Be patient with yourself; healing is taking place. If you don't feel like your self-esteem is improving, try revisiting exercises like Mirror, Mirror Self-Esteem Glamour in chapter 3 or the Writing a Love Letter (to Yourself) in chapter 4.

• • • • • • •

Part of the work of the crone is completing the circuit between this life and other lives. One tool that has long been used for this is communicating with spirit. Sometimes this type of communication is performed directly by mediums. Other methods for spirit communication involve tools like tarot, runes, scrying mirrors and balls, pendulums, or spirit boards.

If you're looking for a form of divination that allows a bit more distance between yourself and spirit, look into oracle cards. Oracle cards are a symbolic system of illustrated cards that can be used for divination. You can even make your own oracle cards to reflect your spinstress craft.

Make Your Own Spinstress Oracle Cards

While many of us are familiar with the images of the Rider-Waite-Smith tarot deck (or have seen it used), there are tons of other ways to do divination with cards. By working with other types of symbols in oracle cards, you may have a more personal connection to your messages. If you love traditional tarot and know it inside and out, you may want to stick with that system. In my experience, making some simple oracle cards can be empowering and fun. It could even be a family activity! In the past, I have put symbols on wooden eggs and held a witchy Easter (Ostara) egg hunt. Have fun and be creative!

You can personalize your own oracle card system. I suggest starting with a thirteen-card spinstress set. You don't have to do thirteen, but hey, it's a witchy number. Draw your card images or make a collage using magazines, almanacs, or calendar clippings. Since you are making these cards yourself, I don't think you need to put verbal explanations on the cards, but you can if you like. You can make your cards out of paper, scrapbook paper, or cardstock. If you decide to use the collage technique, I'd recommend using cardstock; this is a heavier paper, so gluing items to it won't make it wear through.

Spinstress Card Symbols

These are some starter ideas for your spinstress oracle cards. This would be a fun group activity to do with your family or a womxyn's group. Use these ideas or start from scratch! Don't worry too much about how detailed the cards are—what matters most is that you enjoy your cards and that they are meaningful to you.

- **Black Cat:** Claim your independence. Know your limits and set boundaries. Kitty got claws.
- **Witch Hat:** Raise your cone of power. Do some magick to meet your goals.
- **Teacup:** Relax. Sit and let things steep a while.
- **Rose:** Get outside and connect with the beauty of nature. Stop and smell the roses if you've got them.
- **Heart:** Make some time to pamper yourself, including in the bedroom. Maybe you should whip out those consecrated sex toys.
- **Mirror:** Do some affirmations, stat! Mirrors are a tool to unlock the power within.
- **Broom:** Get out of the house. Walk around the block, stroll through the mall, or plan a vacation.
- **Spiderweb:** Connect with your tribe, in person or online.

- **High-Heeled Shoe:** Glam it up. Do whatever you need to do to make yourself feel gorgeous.
- **Apple:** Eat something healthy to nourish your body. If you think you need to, plan some dietary changes.
- **Candle:** Spend some time in prayer or meditation.
- **Book:** Let your inner bookworm come out to play. Read whatever floats your boat.
- **Artist Palette:** Embrace your creativity in whatever way feels right for you.

Reading Your Oracle Cards

Some folks like to picture a protective circle around themselves before doing divination. Others say a little blessing. If you'd like, say, "I affirm that these cards will speak to me of true and good things" before pulling your cards.

When I use my oracle cards, I ask a question and then draw one card at a time. For a simple reading, I lay out three cards to represent the past, present, and short-term future of the question.

For more complex types of card readings, I recommend researching tarot card spreads. But remember, you made these cards. Feel empowered to use them intuitively!

chapter eleven

POWER, EXPERTISE, AND LEADERSHIP

In this chapter I'm going to ask you to take a look at your personal feelings about power and leadership, which might be combined into the notion of sovereignty. There is an idea in American culture that power has a limited supply and that we all have to grab what we can, even if it's to the detriment of everyone else. Sometimes this feeling is mandated by patriarchal systems when things like minority quotas are instituted; a business might have a quota that states that a specific number of staff members must be womxyn or people of color, etc.

It's important to remember that everyone has power, even if it doesn't feel that way all the time. You are powerful—yes, you! When we look at power in this chapter, I'll encourage you to keep thinking about where your power resides. Is it part of you, or do you feel like it is a prize that you have to win from another source? I will help you reclaim your power.

If people dared to try a new approach to life, it could lead to a world where power is healing and leadership is a shared endeavor. Having worked in the violence prevention field for twenty years, I have come to believe that these types of paradigm shifts are probably our only shot at ending abuse of power. So, take a power nap and get ready to talk about this complex topic.

Handling Power

As you already know, I have worked for twenty years as an advocate in the domestic violence prevention field. It's one of the main reasons I felt called to craft the spinstress path and this book. My work has shown me how twisted power has become.

Almost every human nowadays has a bent idea about power. It's an "us versus them," "mission accomplished" kind of mindset. Men and womxyn are taught to approach power in totally different ways, and power imbalances play out accordingly.

Those of us working in the domestic violence and sexual assault prevention world consider violence to be "power and control" or, more recently, "coercive control." Because of the patriarchy and different socialization of the genders, male privilege has always been considered a part of this problem. Most violent offenders are men who have unhealthy ideas about power; they have developed dangerous tactics to express power.

In the seventies and eighties, womxyn who were working to end domestic violence identified these tactics in an educational tool that came to be known as the power and control wheel. They identified tactics of coercive power that included economic coercion, threats and intimidation, and geographic or social isolation.[51]

In an attempt to create a different model of holding and using power, womxyn came up with consensus models. Some were developed based on the governing systems of earth-centered and often matrilineal indigenous cultures. When I entered the domestic violence prevention field, the groups I was part of were operating with consensus models of decision-making. My temple and my employer were using the same system: the Peace and Power model, based on the work of Peggy Chinn.[52] This system and others like it have similar tenets. I'm oversimplifying, but they include things like:

- Commitment by each group member to fully participate in decision-making and leadership

---

51. See https://www.theduluthmodel.org/wheels/faqs-about-the-wheels/ for more information.
52. See Chinn, *Peace and Power*.

- Consensus decision-making (versus executive decisions or majority votes)
- Check-in and check-out processes through which all group members are asked to be accountable for what they are bringing into the meeting (their mood, other commitments, things still troubling them from a past meeting, etc.) as well as how the meeting's process worked for them (one strength and one challenge)
- Process monitors who, during meetings, keep an eye on things like talking over another, body language, and intentional or unintentional silencing of a person or demographic
- A conflict-mediation process to manage issues that come up between individuals or factions of the group

Sounds like a lot, right? The truth is, coming up with different styles of handling power can be exhausting and tricky. It's so much easier to revert to a more traditional style where a few leaders rise to the top and end up calling all the shots. Both womxyn and men are socialized into these types of power imbalances, and people can't shake that tendency without some very hard work. Egos and biases come into rooms of collective decision-making and sometimes derail them completely.

For instance, the coalition that I work for eventually dropped the Peace and Power model and went to a board of directors style of governance. A board of directors approach still shares decision-making, but it is not representative of everyone doing the work. Our group arrived at this decision because the time, energy, and occasional chaos that came with a truly diverse and consensual process didn't keep the same time frame as other big businesses.

Changes in how you think about or use power are not easy or quick, even when you have good intentions. This is especially true if you are trying to make these changes with diverse groups of people.

The Physical and Energetic Body

Each area of the body (physical and energetic) holds different pieces of your puzzle. In this section, I am going to talk about how you can use your body's energy centers, also known as chakras, to interact with your power on all levels.

About Chakras

We're going to use the chakra system that I learned while studying Usui Reiki to move through the body and think about internal power. All matter is made of energy, and this is ours. The chakras are:

- **Root Chakra:** This chakra is located at the base of the spine and grounds you in the environment and to the earth.

- **Sacral Chakra:** The sacral chakra encompasses the groin and sex and sexuality. It is a powerful "seat" of your authentic self.

- **Solar Plexus Chakra:** Located near your belly button, this is where your "gut feelings" about yourself and others reside. These are strong beliefs or intuitions, both positive and negative, and are often deeper (and more stubborn to change) than ideas that occur in the intellectual mind.

- **Heart Chakra:** This chakra is exactly what you would expect. It is located in your chest and is an area of love for self, the world, and all others.

- **Throat Chakra:** The throat chakra houses communication and has everything you need to communicate effectively. If your throat chakra isn't fully open, it can hold repressed feelings and ideas.

- **Third Eye Chakra:** This chakra is in the center of your forehead, between your eyes. It is an energy center for intuition, psychic and spiritual input, and inspiration.

- **Crown Chakra:** This chakra is at the top of your head where a crown would be. It extends out of your body and into the spirit realm. The crown chakra has to do with spiritual connection and your higher self or "over soul," including moral guidance.

In the following body scan exercise, you will ask the same two questions about each chakra and then listen to your body's feedback. I want to give you the opportunity to think about these questions before you begin. The questions are: What about my ___ chakra makes me feel powerful? What do I need, if anything, to make my ___ chakra stronger?

Once you start thinking about ways to engage your chakras, the list could seem endless. A few ideas to get you started are:

- Taking a class
- Teaching a class
- Exercising
- Getting bodywork (massage, mani-pedi, Reiki, etc.)
- Having a talk with a friend or loved one
- Doing something you enjoy
- Screaming into a pillow
- Creating art or writing
- Dancing
- Meditating
- Religious practice
- Divination
- Spending time in nature
- Focusing on meaningful work

Sometimes the "fix" will be a bit more complicated, like working with household members to carve out some sacrosanct "me time" for yourself. It could even mean ending certain relationships or affiliations (groups, jobs) if your body scan indicates these commitments are a serious enough problem. Use this opportunity to check in with yourself about what really makes you feel powerful. This can help you prioritize things so you aren't putting off the important stuff. Your body scan can tell you which direction to head in and what you are lacking in your life.

PEACE AND POWER BODY SCAN

This body scan is a great way to check in with your own sense of power. Since an individual's relationship to power is so complex and ever changing, you may want to do this body scan several times as a kind of check-in with yourself.

IDEAL TIME: Anytime you want to check in with yourself about your power. For example, someone might be pushing your boundaries, you are starting a new relationship, or you need to decide what to do. There's never a bad time to check in with yourself.

PREPARATION AND ITEMS TO GATHER:

- You only need yourself and a meditative space. This is a simple meditation that would ideally be performed outside if you can find a good spot.

- If you want to incorporate gemstones, hold a grounding stone like hematite or lepidolite.

- You may want your journal and writing utensils nearby.

CIRCLE UP: Connect to earth through your feet, even if you are inside. Feel the ground underneath you. Do a quick invocation of the elements by chanting, "Earth, air, fire, water, spirit" a few times.

SPELL WORK: Settle into a cozy position, making sure nobody is going to bother you. You may want to sit on the ground with crossed legs. Lying flat on your back is an option; so is sitting on a bench or chair with your feet firmly planted on the ground. Just make sure you are touching the ground somehow.

Close your eyes and focus your attention on your lower body, from your thighs down to your feet. Your energetic roots are connecting to the world around you. What color are your roots? Are they thick or thin? Long or short? Do they hum with any sound?

Ask yourself, "What about my root chakra makes me feel powerful?" Take some time to think of your answer.

Then ask, "What do I need, if anything, to make my root chakra stronger?" and think about this. A talk with a trusted friend? Bodywork? A good shout?

Next, focus on your sacral chakra. How vibrant is your power in this area? Are you comfortable relating to your sexual body? What energetic colors do you see around this area? Are they vibrant and happy or sludgy and stuck? Are parts of your sexual body frustrated? Silenced? Pissed off? Check in. Even if you work on your sexual practices and feel pretty good about this area of your body and life, you may find things that surprise you.

Ask yourself, "What about my sacral chakra makes me feel powerful?" Take some time to think of your answer.

Then ask, "What do I need, if anything, to make my sacral chakra stronger?" and spend some time thinking.

When you're ready, focus your attention on your belly or "gut" area. How does it feel? What energetic colors do you see? Do you feel satisfaction? Humor? Anger? Maybe pain? There's no correct answer. You're just getting to know your energetic power landscape.

Ask, "What about my solar plexus chakra makes me feel powerful?"

"What do I need, if anything, to make my solar plexus chakra stronger?"

Next, focus on your heart chakra. It may take a few passes to evaluate how you feel in your heart area. What colors do you see? What temperature do you feel? Do you hear a vibrational tone or any other sound? The heart chakra has a lot of societal expectation heaped on it. Don't be afraid to disagree with what you think you "should" see or feel there. This is how you learn.

Ask, "What about my heart chakra makes me feel powerful?"

"What do I need, if anything, to make my heart chakra stronger?"

Focus your attention on your throat chakra. What do you need to say to be in your power? You might find you have a few layers of communication to reevaluate. Perhaps you want to tackle only one priority and commit to returning to your throat chakra periodically.

Ask, "What about my throat chakra makes me feel powerful?"

"What do I need, if anything, to make my throat chakra stronger?"

Shift your attention to your third eye chakra. Do you feel inspired? Do you listen to your intuition? Are you able to express your beliefs? Are you receiving and sending what feels authentic to you?

Ask, "What about my third eye chakra makes me feel powerful?"

"What do I need, if anything, to make my third eye chakra stronger?"

Finally, focus on your crown chakra. This energy center allows you to connect with everything else. If you feel inauthentic about the spiritual or religious path you are on (especially if you are conforming to other people's beliefs or expectations instead of your own), you might have a lot to work through. Your crown chakra should be a massive source of personal power.

Ask, "What about my crown chakra makes me feel powerful?"

"What do I need, if anything, to make my crown chakra stronger?"

Now allow your attention to focus on your whole body and all seven chakras at once. Then wiggle your fingers and toes, turn your head from side to side, and open your eyes.

CLOSE UP SHOP: Chant "Earth, air, fire, water, spirit" as you did when you cast the circle. Visualize all seven chakras in perfect alignment.

After you've finished your body scan, I recommend journaling about which chakras felt strongest and which areas need work. How are you going to commit to strengthening your weak spots?

Repeat this exercise as needed.

• • • • • • •

Next up, let's take a look at the cultural baggage you may have to check at the gate in order to get comfortable with your own sovereignty. It's well worth the effort.

Claiming Your Power

Even if you strive to be an independent womxyn, there is a lot of cultural baggage around owning your expertise. Generations of womxyn have been taught to be "polite" (that generally means quiet) in their homes, classrooms, and offices. Even where there is some room to show leadership, there are likely guardrails, especially when it comes to disagreeing with—or having to show leadership over—men.

No matter how far you've come on the path to your own power, it never hurts to have a little encouragement. The following tips, tools, and ritual will help you push through the tangle of societal baggage, guilt, and self-doubt while you learn to see yourself as a leader.

Crone Energy Tips and Tools

In partnership with my awesome mother, Mary Jane, here are some tips to help embrace crone energies with joy and hope rather than angst or regret.

- Live close to the earth. You can do this even if you live in a city. Eat the most pure and healthful grains, veggies, and fruits you can get.

- Remember that any mistake you have made or any difficulty you have faced helps you learn, grow, and advance.
- Keep an open mind. Be tolerant of belief systems different from your own.
- Use your power wisely, with harm to none.
- Master prosperity and manifestation craft so that your needs will always be met.
- Watch for signs in nature. Collect items like feathers, acorns, leaves, pine cones, or rocks. Look for cloud formations; they will tell you their secrets.
- Treat other animals with the respect and attention they deserve. They are on a spiritual journey just like the rest of us.
- Do not ignore your womxyn's intuition or gut feelings. They are almost never wrong.
- Celebrate the freedoms of every age. When one door closes, another will open.
- Do not fear death. It is only another transition on the soul's journey.

NAME YOUR POWER CRONING RITUAL

Like spinster, *crone* is a good word to reclaim on this adventure. While those who want to hold womxyn down have shamed and stigmatized us with words, a spinstress knows she has the power to pull apart and reweave reality.

One thing that can empower us in the crone aspect is the support of our peers. Therefore, this ritual is designed as a group celebration. Like the Queening Ritual in chapter 6, this is a milestone ritual. These occur in many religious communities, especially regarding youth becoming adults (confirmations, quinceañeras, and Bat or Bar Mitzvahs are some examples). But it's good to celebrate milestones of other ages as well. Since the spinstress tradition honors the wisdom of the crone, we want to have a major party when we become one!

IDEAL TIME: The new moon or a Wednesday.

PREPARATION AND ITEMS TO GATHER:

- A cauldron to represent the crone goddess.

- A table or a cloth spread on the floor to accommodate all of the ritual items. You may want to use purple as a prominent color since it is associated with royalty and sovereignty.

- A besom.

- A smudge stick for each womxyn being honored. While sage or cedar are common ingredients for a smudge, mugwort is great for crone energy and is becoming more widely available. You could also make your own smudge sticks by harvesting your own herbs, drying them, and then wrapping them with twine. If you can't use flames or smoke in your chosen location, consider using a bell to cleanse each person's energy field with musical vibration.

- Musical accompaniment that matches the energy of the group. You could drum, sing, or put on a playlist.

CIRCLE UP: Have the attendees form a circle. Designate someone to sweep clockwise around the outside boundary of the circle using a besom. At the same time, have someone read the following invocation:

"Welcome north, power of earth, flesh and bone. We call upon you to empower our bodies.

"Welcome east, power of air, the breath in our lungs. We call upon you to empower our voices.

"Welcome south, power of fire, the warmth of the sun. We call upon you to empower our passion.

"Welcome west, power of water, oceans of the world. We call upon you to empower our compassion.

"Welcome center, power of spirit. We call upon you to empower our souls."

SPELL WORK: Ask each new crone to come forth one by one. Each crone should say their magickal name, which might be different from their given name. Ask each crone to say what quality she would like to bring forth in her own life as she claims this new phase of life. After she has finished speaking, give the crone a smudge stick as a gift and ask her to return to her place in the circle.

CLOSE UP SHOP: Have the same attendee as earlier sweep the besom counterclockwise to open the circle. While she does this, have another attendee say:

"Farewell west, power of water. Thank you for expanding our compassion.

"Farewell south, power of fire. Thank you for enhancing our passion.

"Farewell east, power of air. Thank you for strengthening our voices.

"Farewell north, power of earth. Thank you for blessing our bodies.

"Farewell center, power of spirit. Thank you for being at one with our souls."

After this ritual, you may want to have a potluck or some tea. Plan whatever follow-up feels the most fun for you and your guests. Enjoy!

Wise Rites for Grounding

One of the many gifts of the crone is knowing when and how to center and focus. Magickal folks often call this grounding or anchoring. This is the art of checking in with your body and emotions, and often with Mother Earth. It may be helpful to come up with a personal cue that reminds you to ground yourself in your inner power; perhaps you cross your fingers or lay your palm on your chest near your heart chakra. Accompany your cue with a mantra like "I am connected to source," "I am blessed," "I can get what I need," or "I am safe."

You may think of grounding as mindfulness, but you are checking in with your body too, not only your mind. While you are developing your grounding practice, you may find it helpful to add new things to your daily routine. Find activities that help you connect to your personal strength and joy. For example:

- Take a hike. Walking in nature can really connect you to your root chakra. In some Buddhist practices, meditative walks are a core element of mindful practice. Find a walking pace that is contemplative rather than a pace focused on speed.

- Pick up a stone from a field or pond and hold it in your left hand. Feel yourself drawing the heavy, solid energy of the stone into your own aura as you say, "I ground myself to the energy of this land. Blessed be." Toss the stone back to its ecosystem and visualize your excess, unfocused, or negative energy leaving with it.

- Have a picnic on a beach or in another natural setting that you're drawn to.
- Sit on the floor (inside) or the ground (outside) and meditate through stillness. You don't have to do anything fancy. Just sit.
- Find a form of physical movement that makes you feel at home in your body: yoga, dancing, swimming, walking, cycling, hooping, or whatever draws you. Enjoy this movement with a buddy if you're able.
- Chill out and listen to a playlist that anchors in the energy you want to achieve. Swap playlists with a friend in order to find some new tunes and tap into a slightly different feel.

BE A TREE: QUICK GROUNDING EXERCISE

This is an exercise you can do in line at the grocery store or during a tense meeting at work. Give it a little practice and you'll get really good at it.

Visualize yourself as a tree. In your mind's eye, let your own roots go deep into the ground. Anchor yourself in the healing energies there. The earth has been there for millions of years and will be there long after you are gone. It is way bigger than your problems and dramas. Ground yourself in the earth and connect with that stabilizing energy.

When you feel you no longer need to be so grounded, simply use your thoughts to pull your roots back up. Having been grounded for a while may give you an extra charge.

JOURNAL PROMPT

Make a list of the ways you ground yourself in your inner power. Also write about the grounding experiences you have had and any nuggets of wisdom you acquired through your process.

• • • • • • •

The grounding techniques we just covered can be helpful when you feel overwhelmed, off-center, or a little scared. But sometimes a fear is bigger and has to be worked on with a little more intention.

Let's unpack the difference between healthy and unhealthy fear. Yes, there is a such a thing as healthy fear. Healthy fear is there to save you from harm; it burns bad experiences into your neurons so that you aren't doomed to repeat them. Healthy fear weighs valid risks and plans for them. Healthy fear releases its grip on you and allows for a calculated risk once safe plans have been constructed. We wouldn't survive as individuals—or even as a species—without healthy fears. Healthy fear helps protect both body and soul.

The problem is that protective fear can become addictive. Instead of helping you avoid harm, it may instead cause you to miss new opportunities. In this case, your fears turn from a protective shield into a cage. Instead of a reasonable warning, unhealthy fear becomes a negative feedback loop. The "what if" of unhealthy fear can keep you from trying for a promotion, a career change, or new love.

Do you see the difference? Healthy fear is a talisman of protection. Unhealthy fear is a millstone around your neck. Over time, one can turn into the other.

Unhealthy fears that started out as healthy fears could probably be rehabilitated; you may need to see a therapist or a trusted faith leader to help figure this out. But truly unhealthy fears need to be released. Assess your fears; which of your fears are unhealthy? Which of your fears are limiting you?

STONE'S THROW SPELL TO RELEASE A LIMITING FEAR

This spell is great because it can be done on the fly; I've done it impromptu on a nature walk. Dealing with your fears has a kind of "rinse and repeat" factor to it. You may find yourself having to do it more than once. I have also found that analyzing one fear leads to another, so don't be surprised if you end up using three or four stones to excise multiple codependent fears.

If you do this spell inside, you might like to do it at your personal power altar. Working with your fears there should help you connect to and ground in your authentic self.

IDEAL TIME: The new moon, the waning moon, or a Tuesday.

PREPARATION AND ITEMS TO GATHER:

- Go outside and find a stone. It could be in a field, forest, or stream. It could even be cut gravel on the side of the highway. Before you grab it, use your intuition to ask and sense whether the stone's energy is willing to work with you on releasing your fear. If you have a positive feeling, go ahead and pick it up.

CIRCLE UP: Quickly visualize an energetic barrier like a crystal egg going up around you. Know that the energy of this crystalline thoughtform is imbued with the correct energies and forces to protect you and to make sure your spell works for the highest possible good. A simple circling technique like this will work for you whether you are at your altar or out in nature.

SPELL WORK: Hold the stone in your hand and think about the unhealthy fear you want to release. Say, "I thank this fear for trying to protect me. I acknowledge the ways it has served me in the past."

Speak about your specific fear. You may find that you wish to keep part of your caution while releasing what is limiting. For example, you may wish to keep the caution that leads you to take it slow when starting a new relationship, yet you wish to release the fear that every prospective partner just wants to take advantage of you.

When you feel ready, move on by saying, "I am ready to release this fear. May it return to nature and be recycled into something else productive and good. With harm to none and for the good of all, so shall it be."

If you are out in nature, toss the stone into a stream or set it in a field. Do whatever feels right in that moment. If you found a connected fear that you'd like to address, grab another stone and keep going!

If you have done the spell inside at your altar, take your stone(s) outside and "release" it as soon as you are able.

CLOSE UP SHOP: This happens informally, especially if you are walking out in nature. Just give thanks to your inner spinstress and to the powers of nature for helping you with this work.

If you need to repeat this spell several times to address the same fear, don't feel like you've failed. Some fears are present in your life for years—maybe even lifetimes. It's natural that fears will recur and need to be addressed in layers.

Dealing with fear is complex, so journaling about this spell work and what came to the surface for you is an excellent idea.

· · · · · · ·

The following tea will give you one more way to celebrate your true self and your bravery.

VERI-TEA

This latte recipe will give you the courage to speak your truth. Use rooibos tea for decaf and a nice orange glow. If you want a caffeine boost, use black tea.

PREPARATION AND ITEMS TO GATHER:

- ¼ cup canned pumpkin.
- 2 teaspoons pumpkin pie spice.
- A pinch of salt (⅛ teaspoon or so).
- 1 tablespoon brown sugar.
- 2 teaspoons of loose tea (or two tea bags).
- ¼ teaspoon of vanilla extract.

Place all the above items in a cotton tea bag or a piece of cheesecloth.

- 1 cup water.
- 1 cup milk (any kind, dairy or plant).
- Maple syrup, pumpkin coffee syrup, or other sweetener to taste.

Put the water, milk, and vanilla in a saucepan and bring to a boil. Reduce to a simmer and keep a close eye on it as you add the cotton tea bag or cheese-cloth wrapping.

Turn off the heat and steep for fifteen minutes. Discard the bag of flavorings and pour your latte. Makes two small cups or one large one.

SPELL WORK: As the tea is simmering or steeping, say, "May this tea be infused with the power and self-love that I need in order to speak my own truth. Blessed be."

Kick Ass and Take Names

Communicating what you truly think or need can be tricky. Direct communication is a skill that usually has be developed and learned through experience; it's not something taught in a classroom. Direct communication can improve—and perhaps even save—some important relationships. Rather than spending time on misunderstandings or passive-aggressiveness, you can learn to get and receive what you want from others. At the very least, you learn a bit quicker when a relationship simply can't or won't ever meet your needs.

Working in fields where feminism and grassroots organizing have been prominent, I've been lucky enough to receive institutional training on direct and nonviolent communication. Some of the foundational principles include:

- Speaking for yourself only, often through "I" statements like "I feel that was unfair," "I need some help with this," or "I wish we could go scent-free in our buildings"

- Questioning to clarify before you jump to conclusions, like asking, "How did you decide to do it that way?" or "What did you mean by that?"

- Practicing ethical (also called nonviolent) communication by speaking directly to a person you feel in conflict with rather than gossiping or complaining elsewhere

- Being open to both giving and receiving constructive feedback, even when it feels hard. This often includes being checked on your privileges based on race, gender, or other factors

- Forgiving yourself when you don't have perfect direct and ethical communication skills and realizing that it's a learning process

When you make a personal decision to practice this type of communication, it can be a bit daunting. Like many other lifestyle changes, your attempts may confuse or even upset the people in your life. For instance, it can be very difficult to break out of the practice of gossiping. Gossiping is often seen as a trusting or bonding activity within families or with coworkers. If you decide that you no longer want to practice this ultimately unethical communication style, it can make your peers defensive. It can be tricky to thread this needle, but it's not impossible. It may help to let the people in your life know what you've learned about direct and ethical communication. Use your "I" statements to tell them something like, "This is something that I think might help me, and it's something I'm going to try."

Up next is a tarot spell to add some craft to your communication.

TAROT SPELL FOR DIRECT COMMUNICATION

Using tarot cards can enhance your focus. Not only do many folks love and collect tarot decks, but the symbolism of these cards is loaded with power. Think about the masses of power gathered in these symbols after so many decades of accumulated collective energy. The spell work utilizes symbolism from Rider-Waite-Smith-style tarot cards.

Please note that you don't need to purchase a tarot deck to do this spell if you don't intend to use them at any other time. You can easily find images of the cards used in this spell online.

IDEAL TIME: The waxing moon, the full moon, or a Wednesday.

PREPARATION AND ITEMS TO GATHER:
- Five tarot cards: the Chariot, Judgement, the Six of Wands, the Eight of Wands, and a significator. A significator is a card meant to represent you within your spell or reading. An obvious choice for a spinstress's significator is the High Priestess, but feel free to pick another card that calls to you.
- If you'd like to incorporate gemstones, I suggest using garnet, opal, or carnelian.
- If you'd like to incorporate herbs, try cinnamon, clove, cedar, or tonka bean.

CIRCLE UP: Visualize an equal-armed cross in light blue, a color associated with communication. Say, "I cast this protective space as a place of power where my desires will be manifest. With harm to none and for the good of all, so shall it be."

SPELL WORK: Arrange your five cards in the shape of an equal-armed cross. Your significator goes at the center. To its left, place the Eight of Wands. To its right, place the Six of Wands. Above your significator, place the Chariot. Below, place Judgement.

Place your hand on the Eight of Wands. This is a card of movement and new information. Say, "I affirm that I am opening myself up to new skills of direct communication."

Next, touch the Chariot. This is another movement card. It is associated with progress and personal growth. Say, "As I open myself to these new skills, I ask for opportunities in my life that will guide my progress in a positive way."

Touch the Judgement card. This is a card for clearing out the old and making way for something better. Say, "As I move onto this path of direct communication, make my way clear with those around me. Help me make these changes in a way that supports my community."

Finally, place your hand on the Six of Wands. This is a card of victory. Say, "I affirm that my new habit will be successful and serve my highest good."

CLOSE UP SHOP: Visualize the blue equal-armed cross again and allow it to dissipate as you say, "I release this sacred space and affirm that the energies of this circle will go back into the spiritual source in order to manifest my will. With harm to none and for the good of all, blessed be."

JOURNAL PROMPT

Write down some practice "I" statements that you will use to handle some of your recurring communication challenges. If you think there are people in your life who will push back when you make certain changes, practice ways you will tell them why it's important to you.

Claiming Your Expertise

The crone aspect of a womxyn's identity is often overlooked. A crone is some-one with a wealth of experience, but the crone's wisdom has largely gone by the wayside. Womxyn of any age can embrace the crone's powers, just as womxyn of every age contain the maiden. In modern times, the crone's expertise is just as often expressed in a professional setting as it is on the home front.

Womxyn are still perceived as pushy or narcissistic if we claim power and status at work. For example, coworkers may come to resent you if you put yourself forward for promotions. Through a tactic that social justice activists call *horizontal hostility*, womxyn and other marginalized groups are encouraged to compete for limited advancement opportunities amongst themselves rather than competing directly with white, cisgender, heterosexual men. For all these reasons and more, you may have found yourself sitting back and watching newer, less-experienced coworkers pass you by to get advancements you didn't think you should grab. Have you been supervised by a string of less-experienced staff, perhaps even someone you initially trained? This is a very common experience for professional womxyn.

Do some journaling about your professional life. What do you love about your job? Or what do you wish you got paid to do? Think about your professional goals. Do you need a promotion? A lateral move? A total career change? Then write about tangible steps you may need to take in order to manifest these goals. Some examples are:

- Talk to your supervisor about opportunities for advancement.
- Attend conferences or symposiums for your workplace. This is a chance to beef up your personnel file, and workplaces often pay for travel and lodging.
- Explore an entirely new degree, whether you sign up for classes at a technical college or decide to pursue a graduate degree.
- Look into grants, scholarships, and loans that will fund further education. Investigate the possibility of a workplace scholarship or work with your boss to develop a schedule that allows you to go back to school.
- Take a class to boost specific skills. Your workplace may even pay for it!

The more tangible goals you have in mind, the clearer your manifestations will be.

FRUITS OF YOUR LABOR ADVANCEMENT SPELL

This ritual will help you honor your own expertise and open yourself up to opportunities for advancement. Affirm that this ritual will help you let go of emotions like fear or guilt that so often keep womxyn from asking for their due at work.

IDEAL TIME: The waxing moon, the full moon, or a Sunday.

PREPARATION AND ITEMS TO GATHER:
- Put a fresh sunflower in a vase near where you do your work to call in positive, sunny energies.
- Have a fragrant cup of lemon verbena tea (or a citrus drink of your choice) before or after you meditate. Citrus evokes the powers of the sun.
- If you'd like to incorporate gemstones, consider lodestone, amazonite, emerald, and gold. Jade will improve your sense of self-worth. Tiger's eye will make you bold.

CIRCLE UP: A pentacle is a popular sigil not only for protection but also for abundance. Visualize a green pentacle that is sparkling with gold. This pentacle creates a sacred circle around you and your meditative space. Say, "I affirm that this space is protected, and is drawing in all the optimal energy to manifest my goals. With harm to none and for the good of all, blessed be."

SPELL WORK: Get into a comfortable meditative position and take several focusing, centering breaths.

Visualize your energetic roots growing down into the ground like those of a strong tree. Let your roots find the earth beneath you no matter where you are. Your roots travel with the power of your mind and anchor you in the earth element.

Once your roots are anchored in the earth, feel yourself transforming into a strong and healthy tree. Do you recognize the type? What sort of leaves do you have? How does it feel to be contained within a strong trunk, with roots well anchored in Mother Earth? How does it feel when sunlight or rain interact with your leaves? Remember that you can do this sort of meditation at any time, grounding yourself in the soothing power of earth.

Say, "*My roots are strong and I have great reach. I am grounded, powerful, and wise. The fruits of my labor are important for me and for the world around me.*"

Think about the changes you want in your career. It could involve an advancement opportunity at your current job or perhaps a new one.

Think about the traits and wisdom that you bring to your professional life. Visualize the gifts that you bring to your workplace as the fruits that grow on your tree. Depending on the tree, these might resemble acorns or cones rather than berries or apples. Either way, the fruits of a tree are what feed their ecosystem. As the fruits decompose into the ground or are eaten, their seeds are carried into the world to create even more productivity. Realize that your labors in your profession are the same; they support your own life and the lives of many others.

Say, "*The fruits of my labor are important to those around me. They are a gift that I am willing and able to share. I affirm that my gifts have great value to myself and to others. I am paid and appreciated accordingly.*"

Take a few minutes to feel what it's like to be well paid and well appreciated. Draw this energy into your life. Enjoy the feeling. If you feel any fear or guilt, acknowledge it and put it aside. As many times as is needed, repeat, "*I affirm that my gifts have great value to myself and to others. I am paid and appreciated accordingly.*"

When you feel ready to end the meditation, visualize your tree-self transforming back into your marvelous normal state. Allow your energetic roots to pull back up from the earth element and into your body.

Wiggle your fingers and toes, turn your head from side to side, and open your eyes.

CLOSE UP SHOP: Allow the green, sparkly pentacle surrounding your sacred space to dissipate as you say, "I affirm that the energy of this circle will continue to manifest my goals as it returns to its source. For the good of all and with harm to none, blessed be."

This would be a great time to enjoy a cup of tea. You could stick with lemon or switch to a relaxing mint blend. Rub some diluted mint essential oil on your wrists and temples; minty hand lotion or similar products will also work. Whenever you need to, repeat the affirmation that you deserve a promotion in your professional life. Carry that inspiring energy with you as you work toward your goals.

CONCLUSION

Over the course of this book, we've explored the ways that you share commonalities with crafty womxyn everywhere and of every age. This book inspired and guided you to:

- Create altars, rituals, crafts, spells, and blessings that enhance your sense of personal power. Perhaps you've even chosen a magickal name!

- Deepen your sexuality, enhance your sex life, combat body shame, claim your worth, and heal your sexual wounds. You are worth being loved, and only worthy lovers need apply!

- Claim the role of the mother whether you are raising children or not. Your spinstress tools can help you rock your mama power when it comes to birthing art and activism or saving the planet

- Embrace the shadowy realms of the crone when it comes to divination, honoring the beloved dead, claiming your own expertise, and releasing limiting fears

- Work with magick and meditation to defend and care for yourself when it comes to energy vampires, stalkers, and insomnia. You have practiced personal health advocacy, direct communication, and more

- Use guided meditation as well as rituals and journaling to receive ongoing education or inspiration from the spiritual source

Remember that you can cycle through these chapters and these phases in any order, again and again. On the spinstress path, age doesn't determine which goddess phase you should be vibing with.

We are all part of the whole, and the whole (the great mother) is always a part of us. Even though this particular book was meant to empower womxyn, the goddess's blessings hold true for men, boys, and nonbinary folks too. Cool, right?

As you move forward and design a spinstress path that is all your own, remember that you can connect with strong womxyn in person or in meditation work at any time.

TAKING FATE IN YOUR HANDS: A GUIDED MEDITATION

Do you remember the fates meditation from the preface? The following meditation returns to the fates' cave and tapestry. If you need a refresher of this magickal space and the work we've already done here, refer back to the preface.

This meditation is designed to help you think about the ways you might participate in the spinstress community, spiritually and socially. What special gifts do you bring?

IDEAL TIME: The full moon or a Sunday.

PREPARATION AND ITEMS TO GATHER:
- Form an altar by gathering up some of your fave spinstress items: gemstones, incense blends, a cup of tea, love letters to yourself, or whatever you resonate with most.
- In addition to your favorite items, items that correspond to this meditation include emerald, sandalwood essential oil or incense, and a multicolored altar cloth.
- Your journal and your fave writing utensil.
- You might want to use one of your favorite playlists. If using music, pick something that seems to resonate with the mood and goals of the meditation.

By the time you're ready to begin, your altar should be a buffet of memories from your work throughout these pages. Congratulate yourself for committing to the work and the fun!

During the meditation you will be invited to impart some of your own wisdom to a new initiate on the spinstress path. Before beginning, take some time to write in your journal about what you have learned on this journey and what tips you would give womxyn just starting out. Have your journal at the ready within the magickal circle.

CIRCLE UP: Visualize a multicolored circle of light creating your sacred circle. It should look like you are being hugged by a rainbow. Say, "I give thanks that all the colors and all the vibrations of the spiritual source are here to protect me from incorrect energies and forces. I know that my experience of this guided meditation will be enjoyable and for my own highest good. Blessed be."

SPELL WORK: Get comfy, start your playlist (if you've chosen one), and take some deep, grounding breaths.

Allow the darkness behind your closed eyelids to give way to a swirling pattern of colors. Yellow, red, blue, and green are splashed with flashes of light. You may see visions as you merge deeper into the spiritual power that forms the tapestry of the fates. What do you see?

Gradually, this swirl of color and visions solidifies, and you see the giant loom of the fates. This magickal tapestry that unites everyone with the spiritual source is what swirls and blinks with colors, energies, and visions.

As you face the tapestry, you realize that you are holding the weaving tools. Your two sisters stand beside you. You are embodied as one of the three fates within the spinstress cave of initiation!

Who do you embody: maiden, mother, or crone? Remember, womxyn contain all the elements and stages of the goddess. But today, you are embodying one stage in particular. Without judgment, notice which one. Are you surprised? It may be a phase of life you have not yet had in terms of chronological years. Whichever fate you have stepped in for, there is a reason.

You begin to weave with your two sisters as the pungent herbal smoke of the cave swirls around you. In moments when the smoke thins, you see a line of new spinstress initiates waiting for their turn to approach you. Do you remember what it was like to be one of them? As you once took your turn facing the loom and asking for the blessing and guidance of the fates, now you will guide a new group of womxyn.

As you watch, one of the new initiates approaches from across the expanse of the sacred cave. She blinks into the mysterious smoke, looking both excited and scared. Once she draws close enough, she looks up at the three of you and at the tapestry with awe.

The three fates offer her the same wisdom that you were given in your introductory meditation. The maiden says, "Remember playfulness." The mother advises, "Remember passion." The crone urges, "Remember purpose."

Once these core messages are given, you share your wisdom with this new initiate. Think back to the journaling you did prior to this meditation, but also feel free to share the inspiration of the moment. What do you want your spinstress sisters to know as they enter this process of honoring themselves and other womxyn?

Once you have shared your wisdom, the initiate makes her way out of the cave. As she leaves, you look up at the tapestry. How has it changed in response to her visit? How does it change for you now?

As you stare into the multicolored images spread over the loom, you enter them. Once again, you dissolve into the multiple colors swirling behind your closed eyelids. You know that you are returning to your body and your normal waking state.

With your eyes still closed, begin to wiggle your fingers and toes. Take a few deep breaths. Feel fresh oxygen entering your body. When you feel ready, open your eyes.

CLOSE UP SHOP: Enjoy the rainbow circle for a few moments before allowing it to fade away. Say, "I affirm that the energy from my sacred circle has returned to the spiritual source in order to manifest every blessing for me, according to my highest good. Blessed be."

JOURNAL PROMPT

How did it feel to be a mentor in the spinstress cave? If you added any words of wisdom to the new initiate that you hadn't planned in advance, document them now.

· · · · · · ·

Our journey together is almost at an end, you wonderful womxyn. As I thought about how to end this book, I thought about a tale that represents the endless quest that is a spiritual life: the tale of the Holy Grail.

The Holy Grail of the Spinstress Path

For those of you who don't know, the Holy Grail is the sacred resurrection cup that Jesus supposedly drank out of at the Last Supper, and it was used to collect his blood during the crucifixion; many quests were conducted to find this cup afterward, but none were successful. In the twelfth century, French author Chrétien de Troyes popularized the tales of King Arthur and his knights questing for the Holy Grail. He died before he finished his project, but lots of others came along to build the legend. The quest to locate the Holy Grail still fascinates people today; it has been the focus of numerous books, movies, and television shows. I think this is because the Grail symbolizes great things like magick, healing, the spirit world, and hope. It is therefore a sacred story and, while popularized by medieval Christians, it has become popular to many others, including Neopagan and secular audiences.

You may be wondering what the Holy Grail has to do with spinstress craft and why it's here, at the end of the book. After much deliberation, I really do think the Holy Grail belongs in this book's conclusion. The Holy Grail is, after all, the never-ending story. This makes it the perfect metaphor for your never-ending journey on the spinstress path.

So, what's today's Holy Grail for men, womxyn, nonbinary folks, the earth, all her creatures, and the other interconnected spirit realms? I like to ask the big questions. The spinstress path suggests this answer: The Holy Grail might be a world where people don't have to defend their gender, pronouns, size, race, religion, or any of that. The Holy Grail might be a world where we've moved past all that. No way we're doing that without the divine feminine, in this world or the next.

☙CAMELOT'S HOLY GRAIL MANIFESTATION SPELL

This spell will help you manifest the best parts of the Holy Grail legend in your daily life.

IDEAL TIME: The full moon or a Sunday.

PREPARATION AND ITEMS TO GATHER:

- A white candle and matches or a lighter. If you don't want to work with fire, you can use a white LED candle.

- A chalice. This could simply be a nice cup or something more fancy—your choice!

- Your favorite beverage. You will be taking a few sips of it during the spell work. You could choose milk, water, juice, wine, etc. Make sure you have extra to pour out as an offering.

- Optional: A Holy Grail–themed altar to inspire your visualizations could be fun. Ideas include a collection of chalices, medieval-themed items, images, clippings, and so on.

CIRCLE UP: You are going to cast your sacred space in the image of Camelot, King Arthur's castle. Camelot was meant to be a place of equality, beauty, and spiritual ideals. What does a realm of equality, beauty, and idealization look like to you? Picture your own version of Camelot—a medieval castle, perhaps with Camelot's strong fortress walls—surrounding you. Say, "I create the energies of Camelot for my sacred space. Blessed be."

SPELL WORK: Light your candle, then fill your chalice with your favorite beverage and hold it between your hands.

Look in the chalice and begin to speak aloud all of the good things that you wish for people around the world. For example: "Love, justice, equality, fairness, opportunities, a fair deal, to feel beautiful, to feel safe, to have what they need," etc. Keep going until you feel you have run out of ideas. All of these positive energies have imbued your drink, making it a Holy Grail.

Say, "I take in the energies of this sacred cup." Take a drink. Leave enough liquid in the cup for an offering later or, if you prefer, drink the entirety of the first cup and prepare a second for the offering.

CLOSE UP SHOP: Visualize the Camelot of your imagination dissipating back into the spirit realm. Say, "I give thanks for this vision of a sacred and just land. May it be manifest here on earth. Blessed be."

After your ritual, remember to take your chalice and pour an offering into a plant, a pond, the grass, or wherever makes sense for you. Be mindful that your beverage will not cause harm wherever you place it. As you leave your offering, say, "I pour out this essence of the Holy Grail. May it work to manifest the energies of Camelot here on earth. Blessed be."

Where Do We Go from Here?

Good womxyn, we have reached the end of this part of the journey. I hope to see you on the web or perhaps during one of my meditative visits to the spinstress caves. All written works must end, but the rest of the story still lies ahead and belongs to all of us.

May you find this book to be a starting point for an exciting and empowering journey of your own. Always remember: You are enough.

Merry meet, merry part, and merry meet again.

RECOMMENDED READING

Allen, Lasara Firefox. *Jailbreaking the Goddess: A Radical Revisioning of Feminist Spirituality*. Woodbury, MN: Llewellyn Publications, 2016.

Ashwood, Brigid. *The Earth Child's Handbook: Crafts and Inspiration for the Spiritual Child*. Books 1 and 2. Self-published, 2012.

Auryn, Mat. *Psychic Witch: A Metaphysical Guide to Meditation, Magick & Manifestation*. Woodbury, MN: Llewellyn Publications, 2020.

Badonsky, Jill. *The Nine Modern Day Muses (and a Bodyguard): 10 Guides to Creative Inspiration for Artists, Poets, Lovers, and Other Mortals Wanting to Live a Dazzling Existence*. New York: Gotham Books, 2003.

Baker, Jes. *Things No One Will Tell Fat Girls: A Handbook for Unapologetic Living*. Berkeley, CA: Seal Press, 2015.

Cabot, Laurie, Penny Cabot, and Christopher Penczak. *Laurie Cabot's Book of Shadows*. Salem, NH: Copper Cauldron Publishing, 2015.

Castellano, Deborah. *Glamour Magic: The Witchcraft Revolution to Get What You Want*. Woodbury, MN: Llewellyn Publications, 2017.

Chase, Elle. *Curvy Girl Sex: 101 Body-Positive Positions to Empower Your Sex Life*. Beverly, MA: Quarto Publishing Group, 2017.

Gallagher, Ann-Marie. *The Wicca Bible: The Definitive Guide to Magic and the Craft*. New York: Sterling Publishing, 2005.

Grossman, Pam. *Waking the Witch: Reflections on Women, Magic, and Power*. New York: Gallery Books, 2019.

Hoffman, Mary. *The Great Big Book of Families*. New York: Dial Books, 2011.

Johnston, Hannah E. *Children of the Green: Raising Our Kids in Pagan Traditions*. New Alresford, UK: Moon Books, 2014.

Maisel, Eric. *Fearless Creating: A Step-by-Step Guide to Starting and Completing Your Work of Art*. New York: Jeremy P. Tarcher/Putnam, 1995.

McMeekin, Gail. *The 12 Secrets of Highly Creative Women: A Portable Mentor*. San Francisco: Conari Press, 2000.

Newman, Felice. *The Whole Lesbian Sex Book: A Passionate Guide for All of Us*. San Francisco: Cleis Press, 2004.

Newman, Lesléa. *Heather Has Two Mommies*. Somerville, MA: Candlewick Press, 2015.

O'Reilly, Jessica, and Marla Renee Stewart. *The Ultimate Guide to Seduction & Foreplay: Techniques and Strategies for Mind-Blowing Sex*. Hoboken, NJ: Cleis Press, 2020.

Penczak, Christopher. *Spirit Allies: Meet Your Team from the Other Side*. San Francisco: Red Wheel/Weiser, 2002.

———. *The Witch's Heart: The Magick of Perfect Love & Perfect Trust*. Woodbury, MN: Llewellyn Publications, 2011.

———. *The Witch's Shield: Protection Magick and Psychic Self-Defense*. Woodbury, MN: Llewellyn Publications, 2004.

RavenWolf, Silver. *Halloween!: Customs, Recipes, and Spells*. Woodbury, MN: Llewellyn Publications, 2011.

SARK. *Living Juicy: Daily Morsels for Your Creative Soul*. Toronto: Celestial Arts, 1994.

Savage, Candace. *Witch: The Wild Ride from Wicked to Wicca*. Vancouver: Greystone Books, 2001.

Starhawk, Diane Baker, and Anne Hill. *Circle Round: Raising Children in Goddess Traditions*. New York: Bantam Books, 2000.

Stein, Diane, ed. *The Goddess Celebrates: An Anthology of Women's Rituals*. Toronto: Crossing Press, 1991.

Strings, Sabrina. *Fearing the Black Body: The Racial Origins of Fat Phobia*. New York: New York University Press, 2019.

Subramanian, Sunny, and Chrystle Fiedler. *The Compassionate Chick's Guide to DIY Beauty*. Toronto: Robert Rose, 2016.

Taylor, Sonya Renee. *The Body Is Not an Apology: The Power of Radical Self-Love*. Oakland, CA: Berrett-Koehler Publishers, 2018.

Ventimiglia, Mark. *The Wiccan Prayer Book: Daily Meditations, Inspirations, Rituals, and Incantations*. New York: Citadel Press, 2000.

West, Katie, and Jasmine Elliott, eds. *Becoming Dangerous: Witchy Femmes, Queer Conjurers, and Magical Rebels*. Newburyport, MA: Weiser Books, 2019.

Witch Bree. *Witch's Brew: Good Spells for Creativity*. San Francisco: Chronicle Books, 2002.

———. *Witch's Brew: Good Spells for Love*. San Francisco: Chronicle Books, 2001.

———. *Witch's Brew: Good Spells for Prosperity*. San Francisco: Chronicle Books, 2001.

BIBLIOGRAPHY

Amos, Jonathan. "Ancient Phallus Unearthed in Cave." *BBC News*, last updated July 25, 2005. http://news.bbc.co.uk/2/hi/science /nature/4713323.stm.

Artress, Lauren. *Walking a Sacred Path: Rediscovering the Labyrinth as a Spiritual Practice*. New York: Penguin Books, 1995.

Baker, Jean-Claude, and Chris Chase. *Josephine: The Hungry Heart*. New York: Cooper Square Press, 2001. Kindle.

Belloni, Alessandra. *Healing Journeys with the Black Madonna: Chants, Music, and Sacred Practices of the Great Goddess*. Rochester, VT: Bear & Company, 2019. Kindle.

Berg, Wendy, and Mike Harris. *Polarity Magic: The Secret History of Western Religion*. St. Paul, MN: Llewellyn Publications, 2003.

Bowers, Ellen. *The Everything Guide to Cognitive Behavioral Therapy: Learn Positive and Mindful Techniques to Change Negative Behaviors*. Avon, MA: Adams Media, 2013. Kindle.

Bret, David. *Greta Garbo: Divine Star*. London: The Robson Press, 2012.

Buckland, Raymond. *Buckland's Book of Spirit Communications*. St. Paul, MN: Llewellyn Publications, 2004.

Chinn, Peggy L. *Peace and Power: New Directions for Building Community*. Burlington, MA: Jones & Bartlett Learning, 2013.

Cortambert, Louise. *The Language of Flowers*. Philadelphia: Carey, Lea & Blanchard, 1835.

Cunningham, Scott. *Magical Herbalism: The Secret Craft of the Wise*. St. Paul, MN: Llewellyn Publications, 1993.

Daly, Mary. *Beyond God the Father: Toward a Philosophy of Women's Liberation*. Boston: Beacon Press, 1995.

———. *Gyn/Ecology: The Metaethics of Radical Feminism*. Boston: Beacon Press, 1978.

Daniel, Marilyn F. *Kitchen Witchery: A Compendium of Oils, Unguents, Incense, Tinctures, and Comestibles*. York Beach, ME: Weiser Books, 2002.

Dean, Alexandra, dir. *Bombshell: The Hedy Lamarr Story*. 2017; New York: Zeitgeist Films, 2017. Blu-ray Disc, 1080p HD.

d'Este, Sorita, and David Rankine. *Hekate Liminal Rites: A Study of the Rituals, Magic, and Symbols of the Torch-Bearing Triple Goddess of the Crossroads*. London: Avalonia, 2009. Kindle.

Diaz, Grace. *How to Use the Yoni Egg for Sensual Healing*. Self-published, Xlibris, 2018. Kindle.

Dugan, Ellen. *Practical Prosperity Magick: Crafting Success & Abundance*. Woodbury, MN: Llewellyn Publications, 2014.

Eisler, Riane. *Sacred Pleasure: Sex, Myth, and the Politics of the Body—New Paths to Power and Love*. San Francisco: HarperCollins, 1996.

———. *The Chalice and the Blade: Our History, Our Future*. San Francisco: HarperCollins, 1987.

Elbe, Lili. *Man into Woman: The First Sex Change*. Edited by Niels Hoyer. London: Blue Boat Books, 2004.

Elks, Sonia. "Factbox: Murders of Transgender People Rising Worldwide." Reuters, November 20, 2018. https://www.reuters.com/article/us-global-lgbt-murder-factbox-idUSKCN1NP0WJ.

Food and Agriculture Organization of the United Nations. *Livestock's Long Shadow: Environmental Issues and Opinions*. Rome: Food and Agriculture Organization, 2006. http://www.fao.org/3/a0701e/a0701e00.htm.

Freeman, Mara. *Grail Alchemy: Initiation in the Celtic Mystery Tradition.* Rochester, VT: Destiny Books, 2014.

Gardner, Kay. *Sounding the Inner Landscape: Music As Medicine.* Gainesville, FL: Caduceus Publications, 1990.

Glynn, Sarah Jane. "Breadwinning Mothers Continue to Be the US Norm." Center for American Progress, May 10, 2019. https://www.american progress.org/issues/women/reports/2019/05/10/469739/breadwinning -mothers-continue-u-s-norm/.

Goddard, Amy Jo. *Woman on Fire: 9 Elements to Wake Up Your Erotic Energy, Personal Power, and Sexual Intelligence.* New York: Avery, 2015.

Goldsmith, Barbara. *Other Powers: The Age of Suffrage, Spiritualism, and the Scandalous Victoria Woodhull.* New York: Knopf, 2011.

Guiley, Rosemary Ellen. *The Encyclopedia of Witches and Witchcraft.* New York: Checkmark Books, 1999.

Hanh, Thich Nhat. *No Mud, No Lotus: The Art of Transforming Suffering.* Berkeley, CA: Parallax Press, 2014.

Higginbotham, River, and Joyce Higginbotham. *Paganism: An Introduction to Earth-Centered Religions.* St. Paul, MN: Llewellyn Publications, 2002.

Horne, Fiona. *Witch: A Magickal Journey: A Hip Guide to Modern Witchcraft.* London: Thorsons Publishing Group, 2001.

Leon, Vicki. *Uppity Women of Medieval Times.* New York: MJF Books, 1997.

Lister, Lisa. *Love Your Lady Landscape: Trust Your Gut, Care for 'Down There,' and Reclaim Your Fierce and Feminine SHE Power.* Carlsbad, CA: Hay House, 2015.

Matthews, Caitlin, and John Matthews. *The Element Encyclopedia of Magical Creatures: The Ultimate A–Z of Fantastic Beings from Myth and Magic.* New York: Sterling, 2005. Kindle.

———. *The Encyclopaedia of Celtic Wisdom: The Celtic Shaman's Sourcebook.* Boston: Element Books, 1994.

McKennett, Hannah. "The Bizarre History of Sex Toys, from Ancient Butt Plugs to Steam-Powered Vibrators." All That's Interesting, last updated October 6, 2020. https://allthatsinteresting.com/history-of-sex-toys.

Monaghan, Patricia. *Encyclopedia of Goddesses and Heroines.* Novato, CA: New World Library, 2014. Kindle.

Mountainwater, Shekhinah. *Ariadne's Thread: A Workbook of Goddess Magic.* Brattleboro, VT: Echo Point Books, 1991.

Moura, Ann. *Grimoire for the Green Witch: A Complete Book of Shadows.* Woodbury, MN: Llewellyn Publications, 2010.

Penczak, Christopher. *Gay Witchcraft: Empowering the Tribe.* San Francisco: Red Wheel/Weiser, 2003.

Pesznecker, Susan. *Crafting Magick with Pen and Ink: Learn to Write Stories, Spells, and Other Magickal Works.* Woodbury, MN: Llewellyn Publications, 2009.

Pew Research Center. "Religion and Living Arrangements Around the World." Pew Research Center, December 12, 2019. https://www.pew forum.org/2019/12/12/religion-and-living-arrangements-around -the-world/.

Ranganathan, Janet, and Richard Waite. "Sustainable Diets: What You Need to Know in 12 Charts." World Resources Institute, April 20, 2016. https:// www.wri.org/blog/2016/04/sustainable-diets-what-you-need-know-12 -charts.

RavenWolf, Silver. *Solitary Witch: The Ultimate Book of Shadows for the New Generation.* St. Paul, MN: Llewellyn Publications, 2003.

Ridoutt, Bradley G., Peerasak Sanguansri, Michelle Nolan, and Nicki Marks. "Meat Consumption and Water Scarcity: Beware of Generalizations." *Journal of Cleaner Production* 28 (June 2012): 127–33. https://doi.org /10.1016/j.jclepro.2011.10.027.

Riggenbach, Jeff. *The CBT Toolbox: A Workbook for Clients and Clinicians.* Eau Claire, WI: PESI Publishing & Media, 2012. Kindle.

Rosean, Lexa. *The Encyclopedia of Magickal Ingredients: A Wiccan Guide to Spellcasting.* New York: Simon & Schuster, 2006.

Saltzman, Stephanie, and Jenna Rosenstein. "How to Take a Good Selfie: 12 Selfie Tips to Consider." *Allure,* July 13, 2017. www.allure.com/story /how-to-take-good-selfies.

SARK. *Eat Mangoes Naked: Finding Pleasure Everywhere and Dancing with the Pits!* New York: Atria Books, 2001.

Scull, Andrew. *Hysteria: The Disturbing History.* Oxford: Oxford University Press, 2012.

Sethares, William A. *Tuning, Timbre, Spectrum, Scale.* 2nd ed. New York: Springer, 2005.

Sprinkle, Annie. *Dr. Sprinkle's Spectacular Sex: Make Over Your Love Life with One of the World's Great Sex Experts.* New York: Jeremy P. Tarcher/Penguin, 2005.

Stachel-Williamson, Maree. *Stop Painful Sex: Healing from Vaginismus.* Self-published, Createspace, 2013. Kindle.

Starbird, Margaret. *The Woman with the Alabaster Jar: Mary Magdalen and the Holy Grail.* Rochester, VT: Bear & Company, 2006.

Starhawk. *Dreaming the Dark: Magic, Sex, and Politics.* Boston: Beacon Press, 1997.

———. *The Spiral Dance: A Rebirth of the Ancient Religion of the Great Goddess.* New York: HarperCollins, 1999.

Starr, Nicole Phoenix, and Sally Jayne Lemmon. *How to Use Jade Eggs: Menstruation to Menopause and Beyond; A Guide for All Ages.* Self-published, Nikstarr Publications, 2016. Kindle.

Sylvan, Dianne. *The Body Sacred.* Woodbury, MN: Llewellyn Publications, 2005.

Troy, Eric. "What Is Cambric Tea?" CulinaryLore, September 23, 2015. culinarylore.com/drinks:what-is-cambric-tea/.

Webster, Richard. *Candle Magic for Beginners: The Simplest Magic You Can Do.* Woodbury, MN: Llewellyn Publications, 2004.

Wheeler, Marjorie Spruill, ed. *One Woman, One Vote: Rediscovering the Woman Suffrage Movement.* Troutdale, OR: NewSage Press, 1995.

Winks, Cathy, and Anne Semans. *The Good Vibrations Guide to Sex: The Most Complete Sex Manual Ever Written.* San Francisco: Cleis Press, 2002.

Witch Bree. *Witch's Brew: Good Spells for Creativity*. San Francisco: Chronicle Books, 2002.

———. *Witch's Brew: Good Spells for Love*. San Francisco: Chronicle Books, 2001.

———. *Witch's Brew: Good Spells for Peace of Mind*. San Francisco: Chronicle Books, 2001.

———. *Witch's Brew: Good Spells for Prosperity*. San Francisco: Chronicle Books, 2001.

Woodfield, Stephanie. *Celtic Lore & Spellcraft of the Dark Goddess: Invoking the Morrigan*. Woodbury, MN: Llewellyn Publications, 2011.

Workman, Miranda K., and Christy L. Hoffman. "An Evaluation of the Role the Internet Site Petfinder Plays in Cat Adoptions." *Journal of Applied Animal Welfare Science* 18, no. 4 (2015): 388–97. https://doi.org/10.1080/10888705.2015.1043366.

Worth, Valerie. *The Crone's Book of Wisdom*. St. Paul, MN: Llewellyn Publications, 1993.

Zell-Ravenheart, Oberon. *Companion for the Apprentice Wizard*. Franklin Lakes, NJ: Career Press, 2006.

———. *Grimoire for the Apprentice Wizard*. Franklin Lakes, NJ: Career Press, 2004.